SUNLIGHT
through
DUSTY WINDOWS

SUNLIGHT
through
DUSTY WINDOWS

The Dorcas Smucker Reader

DORCAS SMUCKER

Good Books

New York, New York

Contents

Contents

Acknowledgments

Thank you to the *Register-Guard* for your support and for carrying my column for 17 years.

Special thanks to my family for all the love, laughs, and patience, and for letting me write our stories.

Ordinary Days

Table of Contents

Introduction

*M*y relatives were wonderful storytellers. *Fertsayluh* they called it in Pennsylvania German—the art of spinning tales and of seeing the quirky and unusual in the most ordinary events.

At family reunions, my Aunt Vina would mesmerize us with stories of how Grandma cured warts or the time the cat ate the dishrag. Even if we had heard the story a dozen times before, we always savored that same delicious waiting as the story progressed and anticipated that expertly timed ending when the room exploded in laughter.

I don't *fertsayle* much at family gatherings, but I like to think that I learned from my relatives to see the profound and the humorous in simple things. I have many opportunities to do so, living with a husband and six children in a 95-year-old farmhouse in Oregon's Willamette Valley.

This book is a collection of stories about our lives, telling of simple blessings and ordinary days. Many of these stories refer to our five children. After this book was written, we welcomed a sixth child into our family: Steven, an active, imaginative, 10-year-old boy from Kenya.

These essays do not appear in chronological order, and they are meant to be sipped one at a time like a mid-morning cup of tea, rather than devoured in one sitting like Thanksgiving dinner. I hope they will echo in your own life, reminding you of family times, lessons learned, and God's loving touch on all of us.

Family

Expecting
the Unexpected

One of the first things I noticed about my friend's house, when I stopped in last Christmas, was that her Nativity set looked like it hadn't moved an inch from where she first set it weeks before. This friend, I should add, doesn't have children.

I have five children and, at my house, I never knew what my Nativity set would be doing when I walked into the living room. Sometimes I found Joseph and the shepherds lying on their backs because 1-year-old Jenny thought they needed to go night-night. At other times, I've found my 10-year-old using the figures to act out the Christmas story, with Mary pinch-hitting as a wise man and riding off on the camel.

I can't help but compare my friend's life, with its order and routine, to mine, with its constant unpredictability.

When our first child was born, I didn't know what to expect in my new role as a mom. Fifteen years and four more children later, I still don't. This was a journey into the unknown, with unexpected curves in the road and surprises around each corner. Motherhood keeps me guessing, always a bit off balance, braced for a twist in the plot when things appear most predictable.

For one thing, I am often amazed at how much it hurts to be a mom, from the pain of childbirth to the sick, bottomless ache when a child is lost. Even more, I am stunned by the joy—when I hold each child for the first time, when the lost ones are found, when I get a hug from a difficult child when I least expect it.

Another unexpected twist is the questions. I always knew that young children ask a lot of questions. What I didn't expect was when, where, and on what subjects. The most startling ones were hissed in my ear when I was absorbed in the sermon at church.

"Mom! Do you have a baby in your tummy or are you just fat?"

"Did you know the Blackbird airplane flies so high that the pilots have to wear space suits?"

In addition, there are what I call Clear Blue Sky questions, which pop out with no preliminaries.

"Did we go opposite of the other people?"

"How does Becky hold carrots?"

"What's that stuff beside the other stuff?"

Appearing out of nowhere, these questions make me dizzy, and I end up asking 10 or 15 questions myself before I figure out what they're talking about.

As a mom, my plans seldom work out like I think they will. My fear of snakes and crawly things is, I believe, a learned phobia, and I was determined not to pass it on to my children. So I let them read *National Geographic* books with explicit photographs of snakes and even took them through the reptile house at the zoo. "Oh, look at the pretty snakes," I gushed, and tried not to let them see me shudder.

I was successful: none of my children is afraid of snakes. But I was much more successful than I planned to be. Matt wants a snake for a pet, and Emily sits in the garden and drapes earthworms over her hands. One day, when the baby was fussy, Amy gave her a rubber snake to chew on. I turned around and there she was, blissfully gnawing. I gasped, horrified, and thought, *This wasn't what I had in mind at all. All I wanted was for them not to be afraid to walk through tall grass.*

My family, I found, doesn't fit into the experts' easy models. Discipline, according to the books, is supposed to fit a formula: clear instruction plus logical consequences would equal disciplined kids and satisfied parents. One spring I bought an expensive rainbow-colored stamp pad for making greeting cards. I knew my daughters would want to use it, so I gave them clear instructions.

"You can use this, but when you're finished you always slide this little knob over here so the colors don't run together, and you always put the cover back on so it doesn't dry out. Do you understand?"

They understood.

A few days later, I stopped by my rubber-stamp desk and there was my new stamp pad, cover off, colors bleeding together. Nine-year-old Emily was the culprit, I soon found out.

"Do you realize how much I paid for this thing?" I ranted. "And I told you to take care of it, and you didn't, so you won't be allowed to use it anymore."

Emily looked at me with big, blue, tear-filled eyes. "I'm sorry, Mom." Then she added softly, "I used it to make a Mother's Day card for you."

Then there was the day when I had four children under nine years old and we were all having a bad day. Everyone was grouchy and uncooperative. Nothing I did seemed to change things, so, even though I knew better, I tried to fall back on guilt.

"I feel like quitting!" I announced dramatically. "Nobody likes me. Nobody listens to me. Maybe I should just quit and let someone else be your mom."

There was a brief silence and then my 4-year-old chirped, "Okay! I want Aunt Bonnie to be my mom!"

Someone certainly went on a guilt trip, but it wasn't any of the children.

On another bad day a few years later, I wasn't happy with how I handled things. That evening I sank into a chair in the living room and moaned to my husband, "Please tell me I'm a good mom."

Paul can be expected to indulge me even if he has to stretch the truth. He managed to sound sincere as he assured me that yes, I'm a good mom. What I didn't expect was the sudden chorus of little voices agreeing with him.

"Yeah, Mom, you're a good mom."

"You are, really."

"I think you're a good mom."

Things don't stay put at my house, my plans seldom work out, and I never know what to expect from one minute to the next. But, all things considered, I wouldn't trade this job for anything.

Matt Learns to Drive

My son Matt seems 4 years old again, walking from my parents' house to his cousin Leonard's next door. He grows smaller and smaller on that long, dusty lane as I watch from the porch.

He is 7, calmly posing for a photograph while he waits for his ride on his first day of school, then asking sweetly, "Now would you like me to take a picture of you crying?"

And he's 11, calling, "Mom, look at me!" from 70 feet up a Douglas fir at Alsea Falls. And I, forcing myself to stay calm, am shouting back, "If you fall out of there and break both legs, don't come running to me!"

And now he's 15, counting the days until he gets his driver's license.

Matt has always had a tall-tree-and-lightning relationship with disaster. He imitated Calvin and Hobbes, washed a disposable diaper with a load of black jeans, and almost set the house on fire with his scientific experiments. He needed ipecac, tetanus boosters, and emergency surgery.

When he learned to drive, I only imagined more disasters. I pictured him on dark streets coming up on grandmas at crosswalks, and on I-5 making split-second decisions among wolf-packs of cars and semi trucks roaring behind him like charging bulls.

After he got his permit, the first time Matt drove the car was to church one evening, where he sailed down the driveway and kept going so fast that he almost hit the brick planter at the end of the parking lot. Even his mild-tempered dad raised his voice.

The next morning Matt drove the van to school, again with Paul supervising. He turned into the driveway, I was told later, and didn't straighten out the wheels but drove onto the grass, where he bounced along for 50 feet and then turned back onto the driveway while the other students at school and the sewing-circle women in a nearby church-fellowship hall watched in astonishment.

"Why did you do that?" everyone asked him later.

He had no idea.

I found that I couldn't chew gum while Matt drove, for fear I'd inhale it while sucking in air through my teeth. I also found myself leaning to the left, not politically, but literally, as though it would keep us from lurching off the edge as he hugged the white line on shoulderless country roads.

Paul let him drive on the freeway when we went on vacation. To me, it was sheer, terrifying lunacy to fly along at freeway speeds with the fate of our van, family, and vacation in Matt's uncertain hands. I finally convinced my husband of this—or so I thought. Then I heard him having a little man-to-man talk with Matt in the front seat, and it sounded suspiciously like, "Well, we both know you can drive perfectly well, but Mom is kind of scared, so let's humor her, shall we?"

"It's a guy thing," my sister told me later. "They love freeways and think they're the best place to train new drivers. My-father-in-law takes the freeways all over Seattle," she went on, "and my mother-in-law hates them and takes all these complicated back roads."

Drivers'-education classes started in October at Linn-Benton

Community College in Albany. The teacher was a brisk, no-nonsense woman who seemed capable and intimidating— just right for teaching this roomful of 15-year-olds to drive.

A parent was required to attend the first class, so I got to watch a gut-wrenching film about accidents involving newly-licensed drivers. The parents in the audience wiped their eyes. The teens didn't seem affected.

Every Monday night for six weeks, we made the half-hour drive to Albany, where I shopped or read for three hours until the class ended.

"A policeman showed us slides of accident scenes," Matt told me after one class. "One picture showed half a body over here and the other half 10 feet away."

I said, "Eeewww, how awful." I thought, *Yes! Bring it on. Whatever it takes.*

On the night of the final exam, Matt came to the car with a dejected look on his face. "How did you do?" I asked anxiously.

His shoulders slumped. "Flunked," he mumbled.

I admit, I screamed—thinking of all those hours and all that money wasted. Matt let me rant for about 30 seconds then sat up straight and grinned. "Just kidding, Mom. I actually did fine."

Then came the behind-the-wheel sessions, where I again dropped him off at the parking lot and hung around town for three hours, certain that every siren I heard involved my son.

Rain blasted down like a Minnesota thunderstorm the night of Matt's last lesson. I half expected his teacher to tell us that the session was postponed. But no, there she was, waiting in her car, smiling, even. I pictured myself riding with two 15-year-olds in the pouring rain, gathering darkness, and glaring streetlights. Never.

Afterward, Matt casually informed me that his instructor told him he was driving too fast and if he goes over the speed limit once—once!—he fails the course. He passed. I drove home in the storm and Matt—Matt?—kept asking me nervously to slow down.

After Christmas we took a trip to the Middle East to visit my sister. Matt loved to stand at her upstairs window and watch the traffic below. Battered white Toyotas wove in and out of traffic in a constant game of "chicken" and the only requirement for drivers, it seemed, was knowing how to honk the horn.

"Man, I wish my drivers'-ed teacher could see this," he kept saying. "She'd think I wasn't so bad after all."

Matt no longer sighs when I hand him newspaper clippings of accidents involving teenage drivers. He stays in the center of his lane and glances over his shoulder before changing lanes. Paul lets him drive in Eugene and tells me he does very well.

Sometimes my daughter wants to go to the library and I don't have time to take her. Or I'm making supper and discover I'm out of cheddar cheese. Then I think, with sudden, satisfying anticipation, *You know, Matt gets his license in only 26 days!*

Just Like Mom

I came home from a dentist appointment one Monday in March and found six lambs in my kitchen. Only a day old, baaing hungrily in cardboard boxes, these were "bummer" lambs whose mothers were unable to care for them.

As my husband mixed the milk and fed them, he explained that a call came unexpectedly that morning from the Oregon State University sheep barn. The lambs were available, but the little shed he was building for them in the orchard was only half finished.

Until the shed was finished the next day, the lambs stayed indoors. My 2-year-old daughter Jenny fell in love with them. She'd reach out hesitantly to pat their backs, then squeal wildly when they touched their cold noses to her arm.

I was cleaning up the kitchen after lunch when I heard a little voice behind me commanding, "Hold still! Now, blow your nose. Blow your nose!"

I turned around. There was Jenny, leaning over the side of a box, trying to hold a tissue to a lamb's nose. The lamb was shaking his head from side to side, and Jenny, getting more and more frustrated, was determinedly trying to wipe a bit of moisture off that small black nose.

The scene was adorable, of course—a pert little girl with red-gold curls trying to control a woolly, long-legged lamb that had no intention of cooperating. But the reason I stared, dumbfounded, was because in that moment I saw my mother in my earnest little daughter.

It was over 30 years ago, the spring that Dad traveled so much. We had a flock of sheep in a pasture across the creek, and whenever Dad left, the sheep immediately began giving birth. One evening we spent several hours penning up the new mothers in a shed and making sure the lambs were nursing.

I still remember the icy cold in the air that evening as we finished up and Mom, my sister Becky, and I left the shed to return to the house. We hadn't gone far when a sad-faced old ewe came wandering over to us, looking like she was begging for help. She obviously had a cold, with a terribly runny nose, which Becky and I thought was disgusting.

Mom, however, took one look at the ewe and pulled an old handkerchief out of her coat pocket. With a quick swipe, she reached out and wiped that awful slime off the sheep's nose. That was even more disgusting, I thought, but we all laughed anyway. The ewe looked grateful, and we walked on to the house.

Whatever quirky little gene inspired my mother to wipe a sheep's nose apparently lay hidden for a generation and then suddenly showed up on this Monday afternoon in my feisty 2-year-old.

I find it fascinating, these mysteries of mothers and daughters, of genes and generations. What is it that makes me repeat my mother's habits and patterns, or that makes bits of my mom show up, at the most unexpected moments, in myself and my daughters?

Shopping for comfortable shoes, I try on a pair, look down, and there I see an exact replica of my mother's ankles and feet. I glance in the mirror while braiding my daughter's hair, and there are my mother's hands, braiding my sister's long brown hair with the same firm strokes.

Even the circumstances around the lambs held an uncanny resemblance to Mom's experiences. Just a few days after we got the lambs, Paul had to leave for a 12-day trip to Mexico to visit several churches he oversees. I was left with the responsibility of mixing milk for the lambs and feeding them four times a day. Paul felt badly about adding to my duties, as he had hoped the lambs wouldn't arrive until after his trip.

When Dad left to do his research on Amish schools that spring in the 1960s, Mom no doubt felt some of the same resentment I did when her husband's project turned into another responsibility added to her enormous load. But I remember the rapturous smile on her face whenever she saw a new baby animal on the farm. I have a feeling that, like me, she found the newborn lambs irresistible as they braced their skinny legs and drank hungrily, their tails fluttering like a flag in a stiff wind.

On Sunday afternoons, my mother was always making scrapbooks to give away to elderly people or invalids. These were not the photo-album variety that are so popular now, but her own unique blend of pictures and Bible verses. She would scan magazines and junk mail for appropriate illustrations. Then she'd glue a picture on a scrapbook page and find a coordinating Bible verse to write underneath it. To this day, whenever I see a picture of mountain goats I immediately think, *"The high hills are a refuge for the wild goats"—Psalm 104:18.*

Our 11-year-old daughter Emily decided to make a book for Jenny's third birthday in April. She nosed through catalogs and magazines, then sat snipping and gluing at her desk, utterly absorbed and contented, a replica of Mom at the dining-room table on a Sunday afternoon. The result was a revision of "Little Miss Muffet" in which Little Miss Jenny sat on a penny and a bug gave her a hug.

"She's just like your mom," my husband told me, amazed, leafing through the book and looking at the cut-out, glued-in magazine pictures of a little girl, a bug, and the shoes Jenny wore to chase the bug away.

Mom is almost 82 years old, and the gradual loss of her sight is curbing her boundless creativity. Much as I hate to admit it, I know she won't always be with us. But I am comforted knowing that, years from now, I will turn around at unexpected moments and, in the mirror or in my daughters, I will catch a vivid glimpse of Mom.

Wallpaper Gifts

I believe we were on the third strip of wallpaper when I quit wondering what was wrong with our marriage.

Every year, with the flood of holiday advertisements, I find a nagging little question deep inside me: If our marriage is as solid as I think it is, why do Paul and I have such a hard time buying Christmas gifts for each other?

Surely, among all this excess of things, he should be able to direct me toward something he wants. Just one gift—we try to keep it simple. And not too specific—I like to surprise him. Hobby supplies? He likes birdwatching. What do you buy a birdwatcher who already has a bird book and binoculars? Should I get him a sweater? No, he can't reach the pens in his shirt pocket. He's not into gadgets, electronic toys, or music. He likes sports, but he doesn't need any equipment. Tools and computer programs are too specific. If I pick out something, it'll be the wrong thing. If he tells me what to get, there's no surprise.

"Which is it?" I ask him. "Are you so un-materialistic that nothing appeals to you, or do you buy everything you need?"

Probably both, he says calmly.

He is all science and logic. I am all impulse and emotion. And we don't know what to give each other.

I could think of a hundred things he could buy for me; he can't think of one. He wants a specific assignment, and I want to be surprised. Craft supplies? He is as ignorant of rubber stamps and needlework as I am of car repairs and carpentry. Clothes, I suggest, like a sweater or a new dress, and he gets a nervous look in his eyes. Last summer, he repaired a roof 90 feet off the ground. Last week, he killed a mouse that was caught, alive and clattering, in a trap in the kitchen cupboard. He would rather do both of those than navigate the ladies' clothing department at JCPenney.

"Why don't you buy me fabric for a dress?" I suggest. "Four yards. Then you don't have to worry about sizes."

"What if you don't like it?" he asks.

"I'll like it because you picked it out for me," I say, knowing that he doesn't understand this and probably never will.

And I worry about our marriage.

This year, the annual worries cropped up on Thanksgiving Day, when the newspaper came stuffed with sale flyers from almost every store in town. It was also the day that we wallpapered the kitchen. This odd combination came about because our invited guests didn't come for Thanksgiving dinner because of illness in the family, and we were on our own.

Paul, the family organizer, wanted to make sure we all had a special day despite the change in plans. For him, this meant going ahead with the big dinner. For the children, hours of table games. And me? I wanted to start and finish a big project.

"Like what?" Paul asked.

"Like papering the kitchen," I said, since the wallpaper I ordered had just arrived, and I was eager to transform our bare kitchen walls into something more colorful.

The children and I cooked a huge turkey dinner while Paul put up new smoke alarms, fixed the screen doors, and shaved three doors that always stick.

After we ate and cleaned up the kitchen, Paul and the

children started playing Skip-Bo, while I gathered rolls of wallpaper and a container of water. I would put wallpaper on the lower 40 inches of the south half of the kitchen, I decided, then top it with a border. Then, I would put a border all the way around the top of the kitchen walls.

The work was a bit tedious, I found, but not difficult. I measured, cut, and soaked each strip, then flattened it against the wall, matched the blue flowers, and smoothed the paper with a wet rag. In the living room, Paul and the children worked through a wild game of Pit and a quieter Phase 10.

By the children's bedtime, I was ready to start on the upper border of wallpaper. I pictured myself, five-feet-three, up on the stepladder, fighting with 15 feet of slimy wallpaper, next to a nine-foot ceiling. This was a two-person job. Paul said he'd help. We put the children to bed and started in.

Things are sometimes tense when he gets involved in my projects, and this was no exception. I was ready to plunge the first roll of border into a bucket of water, but he insisted that there was a much more efficient way to do it, and began to fold the paper back and forth like a giant Christmas bow. I thought, but did not say, *Listen, is this my project or yours?*

He lowered the wallpaper bow into the water, let it soak for 10 seconds, and pulled it out. We were ready to attach it when I noticed the dry sections on the paper, every two feet. We headed back to the bucket as he admitted he was wrong, and I thought, but did not say, *I told you so.*

We tried again. He stood on the ladder and carefully fitted the paper into the corner and along the wall. I stood on a chair and played out the wet paper, not too loose, not too tight. Then he moved the ladder, I stood on it, and we both smoothed the paper with wet rags. The tension eased as, within a few minutes, we were working like a well-trained team.

I matched the flower pattern on the beginning of the second strip to the end of the first, and we moved slowly along the west wall of the kitchen. Up on the counter, down on a chair. He moved the ladder for me; I moved a chair for him. We both leaned over the refrigerator, trying to reach and smooth the last of the air bubbles out of the wallpaper.

Half done. Already the kitchen looked brighter, more cheerful. We started in one corner and I planned to keep going around the room, left to right, solving problems as I encountered them. But Paul, who sees the big picture, suggested that we backtrack and do the east wall next, from right to left, so that we would have a short end of wallpaper to fit around the chimney.

I am better with details, so before long I was standing precariously on the edge of the dishwasher, craning my neck, trying to fit the wallpaper around the chimney where Paul's great-grandpa built it crooked 90 years ago. To do this, I had to slit the wet paper with a razor blade and carefully overlap. I was sure that, as Garrison Keillor once said, I was going to fall over backwards if I had a serious thought in the back of my head. Paul didn't say, but I'm sure he thought, that my fears were completely illogical. Nevertheless, he stood on the floor behind me until I had finished, and helped me down.

By the fourth strip of wallpaper we were amazingly coordinated, inching along the kitchen counter and placing the wallpaper on the wall above the cupboards, tucking it into corners and smoothing it down. Last of all, I stood with one foot on the counter and one on the dishwasher, slicing off the extra wallpaper and matching the two ends. Then we were done. I hopped down and we high-fived in our beautifully transformed kitchen.

I was no longer worried about our marriage, or about gifts. Maybe I'd give him cashews for Christmas; maybe he'd give me socks. It didn't matter.

The best gifts are given daily, and I am daily surprised.

Emily's Song

My daughter Emily lay on our bed not long ago, propped on pillows, knitting her first tentative rows. I sat beside her, reading aloud from *James Herriot's Dog Stories*. The rest of the family was away at some activity that Emily was too sick to attend.

Staying in bed is unbearably boring for a 12-year-old, and the knitting and reading were my attempts to keep Emily occupied. But deep into the story of Tricki Woo, the Pekingese, I realized that we were actually having a good time—just the two of us, relaxing and having fun in a way that we would never have taken time for if she were well. Perhaps, after all, something good could come out of this long ordeal.

I didn't think too much of it when Emily got sick and missed more than a week of school at the end of the fifth grade. The flu and end-of-year stress, I figured.

She had frequent headaches over the summer and into the next school year. She also seemed to catch every cold and flu she was exposed to. We were soon in a frustrating cycle in which she would come home from school with piles of homework because, she said, she'd had another headache and couldn't study in school.

For a long time, I dealt with each symptom as it arose, doling out Tylenol, taking her temperature, trying to decide if she was well enough to go to school. I found her headaches and illnesses annoying. Was she making them up so she could stay home from school? Why couldn't she be more disciplined, more brave, more stoic?

Moms are sometimes the last ones to see the forest for the trees, and it was a long time before I finally stepped back, looked at Emily, and admitted that something was wrong.

While it was frightening to admit, it was also liberating. When her friends said, "Emily's sick again?" I could say, "Yes. We think something's wrong with her, and we're trying to find out what it is."

Few things are as painful as watching a child suffer, few things as trying to one's faith. For me, the most painful moment was one evening when Emily went to bed with an excruciating headache that nothing alleviated. When I went upstairs to bed, I heard her wispy voice coming out of the darkness in her room, singing "How Great Thou Art." I asked her why she was singing.

"Because there's nothing else to do," she said.

My own faith faltered sometimes, wanting an explanation that would all make sense, that would explain how a loving God could let a child suffer. But faith, finally, consists of trusting when there are no easy answers, singing in the dark because there's nothing else to do and finding it to be everything.

Emily was sick with the flu one evening, lying on the couch reading an *American Girl* magazine. She read a sad story of a girl whose parents were divorced. The girl had to spend alternate weeks with each parent.

"Maybe that's why I have to go through this," Emily said, "because God knows I'll never go through that and he wants me to sympathize with people who suffer."

While Emily was brave, grateful, and endlessly sweet when she was sick, I could always tell when she was recovering because she would tease her little sister until she screamed. My emotions were tangled enough without this added complication: As soon as she was well, Emily became a typically moody 12-year-old who tried my patience to the breaking point.

Having had two previous 12-year-olds, I knew another year or two would take care of most of the obnoxious behavior. But solutions for her physical problems were much harder to find.

Narrowing thousands of possible diagnoses and remedies down to one or two seemed impossible. While we researched all we could, most of the insights we gained were ones we stumbled across accidentally.

I was brushing Emily's hair one morning when she flinched and said, "Ouch! When you brush my hair, it makes that side of my head hurt more."

"That side of your head?" I said.

Yes, she said, her headaches were almost always on one side. So, in all likelihood, she had migraines. Not a pleasant diagnosis, but at least it narrowed our field ever so slightly.

We soon found that over-the-counter painkillers seldom worked. One day, impulsively, Emily picked up my cup of black tea and drank it. To our astonishment, her headache went away. It didn't always work, but it was a tiny step forward.

We kept a food diary and slowly, a few patterns emerged. MSG, a common flavor enhancer. Sugary things for breakfast.

But there were no long-term solutions, and Emily got worse instead of better.

I thought of dozens of possible causes. Did she have some terrible disease such as leukemia? Was it psychological, and she was being abused in secret by someone? Did I have that strange disorder where a mom subconsciously tries to make her child sick? Did she have the digestive disorders that run in my family?

We went to our family doctor, of course. The medical field, for all its efficiency with broken bones and ear infections, seems strangely helpless in the face of a chronic illness with vague symptoms.

"You'll have to experiment to see what triggers her headaches," the doctor told me. "If they persist, we might have to put her on a preventive medication all the time."

Twelve years old and dependent on a prescription medicine—that didn't appeal to me at all. So I hesitantly opened the door into the world of alternative medicine, feeling like one of the gullible acquaintances (whom we made fun of), who were always hunting down a new doctor or a new magic cure.

I didn't find chelation therapy or mineral baths, but I did find a remarkable variety of "natural" remedies.

I also found myself bombarded from every side with people who emerged from the woodwork with their own suggestions and cures.

"Acupuncture! It works wonders for migraines! But you have to get the right practitioner."

"You should get her eyes checked. My daughter had all these headaches and they quit as soon as she got glasses."

"Have you heard of essential oils? Here, listen to this tape and see what you think."

"Have you taken her to a chiropractor? I wonder if her neck is out of place."

"I really think you need Juice-Plus to build up her immune system."

"I wonder if she has allergies. I've noticed she has dark circles under her eyes."

"I have a wheat allergy and a lot of her symptoms sound like mine. There's a naturopath in Portland that I really like."

"Sugar in the morning gives her headaches? I'll bet it's her pancreas! Here, try these herbal pills."

Since most of these people gave suggestions rather than commands, we felt like there was a vast network of people who supported us, cared for us, and wanted to help.

Eventually, I found a doctor who understood my medical misgivings and my goal of finding the causes of Emily's problems. I talked to him on the phone one day when Emily had an unusually painful migraine.

"I'm wondering if we need to get a prescription painkiller," I said. "I gave her an adult dose of Excedrin Migraine and it's not doing a thing."

"Before we do that," the doctor said, "try this: Put her feet in hot water and put ice on her head."

I felt like the biblical Naaman dipping in the Jordan for his leprosy, but I hoisted Emily onto the bathroom counter, put her feet in a sinkful of hot water, and held a bag of frozen peas on her head.

Half an hour later, the migraine was down in the bearable range and she no longer had that agony in her eyes. It felt like a giant step forward.

As I write this, Emily has been well for a week, the longest stretch in several months. We continue to research, take blood tests, and monitor her diet. I am home schooling her, thus avoiding that tough decision every morning of whether or not she's well enough to go to school.

We savor the time we spend together and the people who show us they care.

And most of all, we never give up hope, even if it means singing in the dark, at times, because there's nothing else to do.

Two Babies

August, 1998—I'm pregnant. Paul and I are happy but realistic.

September—I lie curled up in bed and fight a terrible, constant nausea 24 hours a day. I get a phone call from Simone, who married Paul's cousin Darrell last May. "I'm pregnant," she says. "I'm happy, but I'm really sick."

I tell Simone the things I need to hear: This will pass. It will all be worth it. In the end, you'll have a baby.

October—Simone and I keep in touch. We share tips for survival—foods that stay down and how to brush our teeth without throwing up. I make the decision to take medication for the nausea. Simone chooses to tough it out with no medication.

Spring, 1999—Simone and I are back on our feet. I worry about our baby. I'm 36 years old, and I know my chances of having a baby with Down Syndrome increase with age. And the medication I took is supposed to be safe, but what if it isn't entirely? I ponder the fierce protectiveness I feel toward this child, this intense desire for everything to be normal. Is it for the baby's sake, or mine? I've heard that Downs babies have a single crease across the palm of the hand, instead of two creases going partway across, like the rest of us. I hope desperately for two creases.

April 21—I sit in a tub of water in our dining room, surrounded by Paul, my midwives, and a swirling cloud of pain. *I can't do this,* I think; *please get me out of here.* Suddenly, the agony vanishes and I'm holding my squirming, wet baby daughter.

31

There's nothing in the world like giving birth, nothing to match this relief and euphoria. Jennifer Anne is here and I love her completely. Awed, we inspect this wonderful little person. With my thumb, I pry open her little fist. Two creases. But I know now I would love her just as much with a single crease.

May, 1999—The new-baby adjustments are a hundred times easier with the fifth than with the first, I decide.

Simone's baby is due three weeks after Jenny. I wait for news—three weeks, four weeks, five. Finally, after six weeks, the phone call from Paul's mom: Darrell and Simone have a baby girl named Dawnisha. I sense in my mother-in-law's voice that this isn't the normal she's-here-and-everything's-fine phone call. I'm right. "But . . . ," she says, and I feel a fist in my stomach. Something's wrong; a few fingers missing; she's not entirely sure. They're taking the baby to a hospital in Portland.

Over the next few days, vague reports filter through the Smucker grapevine. It's not just fingers missing; there's something about her arms. And her face. How is Simone? we ask each other. And Darrell? No one seems to know, only that Simone doesn't want visitors. *What should we do?* we wonder. *What should we say?* Mostly we leave them alone with what must be a confusing mixture of joy and pain, and each of us grieves as well. I sit in my rocking chair and feed Jenny, stroking her perfect little hands and weeping.

Finally, someone has been to see them. We all want news. Darrell is as proud as a dad could be; strong; okay. Simone is more fragile. Dawnisha has a strawberry birthmark on her forehead and a purple splash over her nose. Her left arm is three-fourths the normal length, with three fingers. Her right arm is only a small hand with three fingers at the shoulder.

But—a hopeful "but" this time—everything else seems to be okay. The doctor predicted she'll do everything but throw a ball.

July—A Smucker gathering; Darrell and Simone are coming. We are all eager to see the baby. Eager, and apprehensive.

My first impulse, when I see Dawnisha, is to gasp. My second is to hold her and love her. She looks somehow long and narrow; she feels like she will slip out of my hands. I never realized before how a baby's arms make it look balanced, and how one naturally grasps a baby under the arms. Dawnisha opens her eyes and looks at me. I have never seen such eyes on a baby—calm, wise, aware. This baby will be fine, her eyes tell me.

The cousins take turns holding Jenny and Dawnisha. I can't help but compare these two babies, and I feel guilty for having a "perfect" baby, like I should take her out of the room so no one can compare the two.

Simone has so much piled on her at one time. The adjustments to a dependent new baby are difficult in the best of times. On top of that, nursing isn't going well; Dawnisha isn't gaining weight and doesn't sleep well. Simone had hoped to have her baby on a schedule; it's not working. Simone has a bad case of post-partum depression. And, of course, the baby is handicapped.

Why her and not me? I wonder, over and over. I was the one who took medication for the nausea. I, at least, had already been through the enormous adjustments to motherhood itself. Was I incapable of loving a handicapped child, so she was given to Simone and not to me? Or had I already learned the lessons Simone was supposed to learn through this?

Pondering this tangle of questions leads me nowhere, of course. With time, I am able to accept that this is how things are, how they were somehow meant to be. I have Jenny; she has Dawnisha—both miracles, both gifts, both loved.

August—Simone switches to formula and gives up on breastfeeding. She abandons her schedule. Dawnisha begins to gain weight. Everyone is happier.

Fall—Jenny can smile, babble, reach, grab. She learns to sit up, then crawl. Dawnisha is also acquiring skills, with her own unique twist. She reaches with the longer of her arms and pinches things with her fingers. She learns to sit up, kick her legs, and swivel in circles on the floor. When she's happy, her grin radiates from her entire face.

At church one Sunday, Jenny is too noisy to remain in the service. I take her to the foyer and set her on the floor to play. Darrell soon joins me with Dawnisha and sets her beside Jenny. Dawnisha drops her pacifier. I see her looking at it, lying on the floor in front of her. She swivels one way, then the other, and can't reach it. *Please get it,* I think. *Please find a way.* Dawnisha leans forward and scoops up the pacifier with her mouth. I'm ecstatic. Behind the pacifier, I see Dawnisha's delighted grin.

I compare Dawnisha's progress with Jenny's, and am troubled when Dawnisha lags behind. When I examine my attitudes, I don't like what I see. Why do I place so much value on accomplishment and beauty? Why can't I celebrate each child's uniqueness?

July—Simone and I sit in my front yard under the oak tree. I'm having a yard sale; she's helping me out. We watch Jenny and Dawnisha play, rescue them occasionally, scoop them up to hug them. Simone talks about mothering a handicapped child. "I'm no longer uncomfortable when I meet a person in a wheelchair," she says. "I go up to them and talk. Having a child like Dawnisha opens up a whole new world. I've met the most wonderful people."

We sit in the shade and wait for customers.

"What's been the hardest thing?" I ask her.

"It's the people who pity me!" Simone says emphatically. "They come by, pat my shoulder, 'Oh, bless you, bless you.' I want to ask them, 'Why do you feel sorry for me? *Why?*'"

We leave her question hanging in midair, unanswered. I think of a conversation I had recently with a woman whose son has cerebral palsy.

"I've decided," she said, "that my son isn't the one with the problem. He is fine. It's the rest of us who have the problem."

A car pulls in the driveway and a young woman jumps out and asks how to get to Monroe. I give her directions and she hops back in the car. Simone looks at me, stunned. "Did you see that? She had only two fingers on her hand! I'm going to talk to her!"

Simone sprints off after the car. Two minutes later, she is back. She has exchanged phone numbers with the young woman and is having her over for dinner soon.

Twenty feet away, Jenny and Dawnisha sit in a patch of sunshine and help each other pull apart a stack of books, carefully, one by one. Taking turns, it seems.

Dealing With Matt

Things haven't been easy lately with a teenager in the house—conflicts flare up at odd moments over the oddest of issues. Also, we keep running out of food, which is why Matt, age 14, and I are in the van, headed to WinCo on a Saturday night.

Not long ago, Matt found an article in *Reader's Digest* that he thought I should read. It was titled "What Moms Need To Know About Sons" and encouraged mothers to make deals with their boys. I've been trying, but with Matt's quick logic, I usually find myself caught in a fog of reasoning that ends us up far away from my intended goal. When he was a toddler, I used to go to bed and cry because I was sure he was going to end up in prison. Now I go to bed and worry that he'll be a slick lawyer, keeping criminals out of prison on technicalities.

But tonight I've struck a deal that works: "You eat so much, you help me get groceries. Deal?" Deal.

At a garage sale recently I found a book that I thought might help us. It's called *But You Don't Understand*. Before I had a chance to read it, Matt started reading it and thought it was just what his parents needed. My husband, in a moment of dubious generosity, told Matt to indicate which passages he wanted his parents to note especially. So as we head down the long straight stretch of Highway 99, Matt is beside me frowning over the book, enormous left shoe hooked over bony right knee, highlighting in yellow the passages meant for his dad and underlining in black the things I need to hear. The page he's on now is evidently meant for both of us; it looks like the back of some giant mutant bumblebee.

I ask him bravely what it is right there that I need to hear.

"This talks about listening to your teenager," he says off-handedly, and keeps on underlining.

I am stunned. He thinks I don't listen to him? I think back over the years, all the times I put down a book to listen to a mind-numbing play-by-play of his soccer game at school. And what about the thousands of questions I've answered? Doesn't that count for anything? When he was 3, I decided to count, and in one day he asked—and I answered—115 "why" questions.

"So you think I don't listen to you?" I whimper.

He is matter-of-fact: "You don't listen to me when I try to tell you something you should change."

So that's it—how dare he? I flare up in self-defense, then realize just as quickly that that's exactly what he's talking about. So I shrivel up, chastened, and say, "Oh."

We pull into the WinCo parking lot, get out, and find a cart. He loved to ride in the cart when he was little. Later he liked to grab the handle when I wasn't looking, set his feet on the bar at the bottom, and ride off down the cereal aisle like Blackfinger Wolf in *The Great Supermarket Mystery*. I consider asking if he wants to ride in the cart, just as a joke, but decide not to. I tell him this, so he knows I'm catching on.

He says, "It's a good thing you didn't. That book says that you shouldn't treat your teen like a baby."

While I compare prices on diapers, he takes off for the

bulk foods and weighs out bags of jawbreakers and bubble gum. A bundle of paradoxes, he wastes his money on junk food but economizes by buying it in bulk. And he is endlessly patient with his baby sister but got revenge on the little cousin that pelted him with a green walnut. He takes meticulous care of his pets' cages but lets his bedroom look disastrous. Part little boy, part grown-up, he keeps me guessing.

We stroll down the laundry aisle, and suddenly I spot it: "Zout!" I exclaim. "Yes! I've been looking everywhere for Zout! This is absolutely the *best* stain remover. I'm getting two!"

Matt taps me gently on the shoulder. "Uh, Mom? That book I'm reading says you shouldn't embarrass your teenager by making a scene in public."

He calls this making a scene in public? I wish he could remember the time he begged for a pack of gum and screamed so loudly that we got dirty looks from all over the store. Or the time we got on a plane and he wailed, "But I don't wanna go on the big airplane" over and over. We had to deal not only with him but with the advice of a dozen well-meaning strangers who were as desperate as we were to turn off this flood of noise.

In the cereal aisle, I bypass the boxes and head for the big cart-filling gunny sacks of Toasty-O's and Marshmallow Mateys. I had heard that teenage boys eat a lot, but I still wasn't prepared when Matt hit a growth spurt at 13. His favorite breakfast consists of a huge bowl of cereal followed by four pieces of toast slathered with peanut butter and jam. Speaking of peanut butter, we pick up a four-pound barrel of it at the end of the aisle. If we're lucky, it will last for two weeks.

On the way home, Matt is quiet and the book stays,

unopened, on the dashboard. I treasure these moments with him, undistracted by younger siblings, just the two of us. I ask him what animals he'd like to get.

"Well, of course, I always want a milk snake, but I don't suppose you'd let me."

"That's right."

"But you've kind of gotten to where you think my lizards are cute, right?"

I nod.

"Well, I have this plan. I figure if you've gotten used to anoles, then next I can get long-tailed lizards until you get used to those, then I'll get legless lizards, and then I'll get a snake and you won't mind."

I snort. "You'll have to do better at keeping your animals contained if you ever want a snake. I don't appreciate getting woken up at 5 in the morning by a hamster tapping on my head."

He chuckles. "Oh, *Mom*, hamsters are different. I wouldn't let a snake get out of my room, okay?"

We slow down to drive through Junction City.

"Would you mind if I got a centipede?" he asks.

I picture a harmless three-inch worm and am about to tell him it would be fine. However, I haven't lived with him for 14 years for nothing. "What kind of a centipede are we talking, here?"

When the subject is animals, he always sounds like he's reading out of a book. "It's called a Giant Peruvian Centipede and on average it's about 17 inches long." (I picture a 17-inch centipede on my pillow at 5 a.m.) "But it has a bite that's mildly poisonous, and we do have a baby in the house, so I would settle for a millipede that's 7 inches long."

I sigh. I'm happy to see this concern for his sister, but still, he would "settle for a millipede"? Who said we were making a deal here?

The house is dark when we get home. Matt helps me carry in groceries and says he's going to bed. I remind him to brush his teeth. (We have a deal—he'll take better care of his teeth and I'll consider Madagascar hissing cockroaches.)

"Good night," I say. "Thanks for your help. I love you."

"Uh-huh," he says, his mouth full of Kit Kats. He heads upstairs, placing his enormous tennis shoes cautiously on each step—his baby sister and the lizards are sleeping, you know. He'd hate to wake them up.

Later, I pick up *But You Don't Understand,* flip to an underlined page, and begin to read. "Mutual Respect" is underlined and highlighted. Sounds like a deal to me.

Seasons

Harvest

When I first came to Oregon, I thought I knew a lot about farming.

After all, I had driven pickup loads of pigs to the sale barn and skipped school to drive a Farmall M tractor all day. And I could drive by a farm and tell with one sniff if they raised pigs, cows, or chickens there.

I knew quite a bit about Minnesota farming, I guess, but I didn't know anything about Oregon farming.

In the Willamette Valley, I found myself surrounded by the grass fields between Halsey and Harrisburg. I was fascinated by them—"Once a farmer, always a farmer"—but I found the local farming a strange, new world.

I had always thought that all respectable fields sprouted in the spring, grew all summer, and turned brown after the first frost in the fall. Then, of course, they remained frozen all winter. Oregon fields were harvested in midsummer and turned green again in the fall, then they stayed green all winter. Rain and green grass in January—it was like seeing the sun rise in the west.

Oregon farmers also had a vocabulary all their own—ryegrass, fescue, orchardgrass. (I imagined a newspaper headline—"Rescue in the Fescue.") Instead of taking their seed to an elevator in town, it seemed that every other farmer had a "warehouse" of his own. This was not only a storage building, I found out; it was also a place to clean and bag the grass seed.

In Oregon, teenage girls drove enormous John Deere combines during harvest. Where I came from, combines were driven by beefy men in Pioneer seed-corn caps. Then, after harvest, the Oregon farmers deliberately set their fields on fire. Amazing.

"You need to stay around for harvest," people kept telling me that first winter. They said the word like it was special, weighted—*"Harvest."* So, after my teaching job was finished, I found short-term work and followed their advice. That summer I was an observer. In recent years I have become a participant, as my husband Paul first managed and then bought his dad's warehouse.

Harvest, I've learned, is much more than bringing in the crop. For the farming community, it's the focal point of the year. Harvest implies the ambiance of warm summer days, of family history, of the land. Harvest is a hurricane, predicted and anticipated, that blows in and sweeps an entire community into the storm.

For farmers, the seasonal cycle converges at the end of June. Their entire livelihood depends on this narrow window of just a few days, when the seed is ripe for cutting. Cut too soon, the seeds are not filled out well. Too late, and they shatter easily and fall to the ground. In the months leading up to June, as the grass grows taller and forms heads, cousin Trish's husband, Richard, starts having nightmares: his neighbor is already out cutting. Richard panics and then wakes up, startled, relieved to know it's only a dream.

The combines start whining into the fields about a week after the grass is cut. From mid-morning, when the dew dries, until the dew forms again after dark, they circle the fields, eating up the neat windrows and spitting a stream of seed into the tank behind the driver. When the tank is full, a truck pulls alongside the combine. A long arm, like the head and neck of a dinosaur, swivels out from the combine and coughs the seed into the bed of the truck. From there the seed is taken to a warehouse.

Our warehouse was built by Paul's grandfather, Orval Smucker, who was one of the many farmers after World War II who grew grass seed and built a warehouse to process it themselves. He built it several hundred yards away from his house, across Muddy Creek, which meanders by in a U shape.

The end of June, with its warm, sunny days after months of rain, matures the crop to perfection. It also lures children to the creek. Generations of Smucker children have spent their summer afternoons playing in the water. Little children play in the ford, skittering out of the way when a combine comes by to cross where the creek is shallowest. While their dads sweat in the heat and dust of the warehouse or the fields, the medium-sized cousins float on inner tubes near the bridge, and the biggest kids swim down by the "deep hole."

This summer, our 14-year-old son Matthew has graduated from swimming in the creek to working in the warehouse for four hours a day. Before his first shift, I look at Matthew's skinny, freckled arms and try to imagine them lifting 50-pound sacks.

"Paul, are you sure he's ready for this?" I ask.

Paul is sure. He knows, better than I do, this rite of passage. He and dozens of others in the family and the neighborhood were once skinny, freckled teenagers who went from playing in the creek to that first real job—sacking seed in the warehouse or working in the fields.

At the warehouse, Matthew works on the bottom floor of a tall building that vibrates and rumbles as the seed passes through the cleaners—a series of fans and screens. This removes the weed seeds and chaff, and the pure seed falls into a hopper. Matthew slips a bag onto a weighing machine at the end of the hopper, and the bag fills with 50 pounds of seed. Some types of bags close by themselves. Other bags are sewn shut with a portable sewing device dangling from the ceiling. He then stacks the bag onto a pallet and repeats this process up to 80 times an hour. The pallets of seed are stacked in another part of the warehouse until they are sold and shipped.

Amy is 12. She hopes in a couple of years to get a job driving a combine. Again, I can hardly imagine it—this petite, feminine child handling such a behemoth of a machine. Her aunts will no doubt assure me that she will do fine. I vividly remember Paul's sisters Rosie and Barb stumbling in the door at 10 on summer evenings after a day on the combine. Invariably they were exhausted and covered with dust. Despite the dust, I saw a sense of pride. They had handled the behemoth all day, done a good job, earned some money. And when the time comes, I won't deny Amy the same sense of accomplishment.

Everyone approaches harvest a bit differently, but they share a commitment to getting the job done. No one takes a vacation now, and anything optional is postponed. Paul has the cleaners running 24 hours a day during July and August. He leaves the house early in the morning and works at the warehouse for up to 14 hours a day. Sometimes he gets up in the middle of the night to repair a cleaner that breaks down.

One farmer we know works at night to cut the grass—the seed doesn't shatter as much at night, he says. Another one is up at 6 a.m. to haul screenings—warehouse byproducts—before he starts combining at 10. Some people work seven days a week, like Roy, who drives seed to our warehouse. He works all day, every day, for two months. Paul, on the other hand, takes Sundays off, and we all go to church, where sunburned farmers nod off during the sermon.

Harvest always disrupts our family's routine, and it falls on me to keep everything running smoothly behind the scenes. I fit meals around warehouse schedules, put the children to bed at night by myself, and wash piles of dirty laundry, first emptying handfuls of grass seed from Paul's and Matthew's pockets.

Most of my friends are in the same situation. Margaret's husband hires a crew of up to 10, most of them teenagers, every summer. Margaret goes from cooking for two to driving out to the fields every evening to feed 10 or 15 people a hot meal from the back of her pickup truck. In addition, she becomes a mom to the five teenagers who stay at their house—cooking for them, doing their laundry, and reminding them to use deodorant. Trish leaves her toddler with her mother-in-law and drives a combine for two weeks. Other women drive trucks from the field to the warehouse, or spend hours on the road, driving to town for parts for machinery that breaks down.

This, too, is how it has always been. I remember how, when we were first married, I watched my mother-in-law with a sense of awe. It wasn't possible to get any busier than this, I was sure, as I watched her flying in a dozen directions to take care of her family during harvest. She'd prepare a huge, hot meal at noon for anyone who happened to be in the house. Then she'd fill plates and deliver them to anyone who wasn't at home—Rosie on her combine, Barb on hers, a husband and son at the warehouse.

After lunch, the "night guy," who worked the night shift

at the warehouse and boarded with my in-laws, would wake up and stumble downstairs. Anne would scurry around the kitchen to fix him bacon and eggs. I suggested once that she save herself some work and let the night guy eat whatever she had made for lunch. Anne wouldn't hear of it. Everyone deserves a proper breakfast when they wake up, she said. This was Harvest, after all, and this was her calling—to keep everyone fed and cared for.

Harvest is an exciting time, busy, suspenseful. But underneath is an awareness of danger. A spark from a combine can quickly ignite a dry field, bringing fire trucks wailing down the back roads. Paul's cousin Don lost both of his feet when they were caught in a combine header almost 30 years ago. Field burning, once popular but now done less often, has its own dangers. Paul's sister burned her legs one summer when she was igniting the straw from the back of a pickup truck. A brother-in-law was caught in a field fire when the wind shifted. He survived, but with scars.

Many farmers mourn the demise of field burning. They now have to find new ways to get rid of the straw and deal with insects and disease. While the cycle of the seasons remains the same year after year, change is inevitable.

"In my opinion, farming has changed more in the last five or 10 years than it did in the previous 25," says Richard Baker, a local farmer. "The way the seed is marketed, the way we treat disease, everything. And I think it will keep changing just as fast."

Farming may change, but a farmer once is a farmer always. Paul's grandpa Orval is now 94 years old. His awareness is gradually dimming, but even in the last few years it is obvious that he is a farmer at heart.

"That ryegrass is about ready for cuttin,'" he'd shout at

me in his raspy voice as I drove him to my house.

Every time he saw me sewing he would tell me about an accident at the warehouse one harvest.

"You ever get'cher finger in that sewing machine?" he'd shout. "I had a guy at the warehouse one time was sacking seed, and when he sewed up the sack he sewed right through his thumb! When I got there, there was a whole bunch of guys around him tryin' to pick this string out of his thumb real careful. Well, I just went up to 'im and took hold of that string and gave it a good yank and out it come! No need to be so careful with it!"

He always chuckled, and I always shuddered in sympathy for that poor warehouse worker. Grandpa repeated and embellished this story a number of times—one version even had the guy sewing his lower lip to the sack. Later I learned that, in reality, the worker had been taken to the doctor to have the string removed from his thumb.

Orval is in a nursing home in Eugene, and his grandson now owns the warehouse. A new young man is sacking seed, and new ways of farming are blowing into the Valley. But, once again, it's July and farmers anxiously watch the weather, children play in the creek, and the grass lies piled in neat windrows, waiting to be harvested.

As one of my favorite Bible verses promises—"As long as the earth endures, seedtime and harvest, cold and heat, summer and winter, day and night will never cease."

Daffodils in Spring

Someone asked me not long ago if I prefer the climate here in Oregon or in Minnesota, where I grew up.

"I like both," I said. And then, growing nostalgic, I added, "But I really miss the snow."

In Minnesota, the weather was dramatic. Terrible thunderstorms in summer were followed by crisp fall mornings that turned everything brown. The first real snowfall changed the landscape, overnight, from a dull brown to a gleaming white. Fierce blizzards blew in, shut everything down, and then sculpted a dazzling landscape of sharp-edged, curving drifts. And in spring, the landscape changed again, from white, to a muddy brown, to a sudden green.

When I first came to Oregon, I researched the climate by looking on a map. It looked like I would be living just as far north as I was in Minnesota, so I concluded that the climate would be pretty much the same. That fall, in Oregon, I kept waiting for the cold weather, for snow, for winter. Instead, each chilly, rainy day was followed by another. I asked my roommate when the fields would start turning brown. She replied that they stayed green all winter, and I thought she must be crazy. I asked her where I should plug in my car at night when it got cold, and she thought I was crazy.

Christmas came—still no snow. Surely it was illegal to have Christmas with rain and green grass outside. The weeks and the weather dragged on, with none of the drama of a good thunderstorm or blizzard, only this constant, dripping, disgusting, sloppy, wet rain. I thought it was awful.

I admit, there were also a few disadvantages to a Minnesota winter: slippery roads, shoveling snow, and February. We called it the February blues, this malaise that settled in when Christmas was long gone, the cold was unrelenting, and it seemed that spring would never come. The snow, piled beside streets and sidewalks, was gray and dirty. We were all tired of starting cars on cold mornings and wearing parkas and boots. With this fatigue came a dullness, a lack of motivation. Who could get inspired to try something new when the world was locked in by cold and we were focused on surviving, on waiting for spring?

I had a touch of the February blues my first winter in Oregon—I was sick and tired of dull gray skies and unrelenting rain. Then, one afternoon when the rain let up for a little while, a friend from next door asked me to go on a bike ride with her. I was hunkered down by the electric heater, as I recall, trying to solve my Rubik's cube, but I agreed to leave my comfortable spot and go with her. We headed down the country roads, past wet, mossy trees, wet grass in the ditches, wet fields, and wet blackberry bushes.

Suddenly, I spotted something astonishing: daffodils. Right there, growing in a field beside the road, were dozens of green clumps, bursting with hundreds of daffodils.

"What are they doing there?" I asked my friend. "Who planted them?"

She shrugged. "I don't know. They just grow there."

I couldn't believe it—daffodils. Not coaxed carefully out of a flower bed in May, but popping, all on their own, out of a mint field in February. Such lavish extravagance. It was like finding pearls in a sack of potatoes. I was still waiting for winter, and here in front of me were hundreds of daffodils like pert little girls in ruffly sunbonnets.

I had a new perspective after that. Winter in Oregon might be dripping and dull, but, before it was over, long before spring, it treated me to an abundance of flowers.

The February blues crept up on me again this year, even though there was less rain than usual. I had too many pounds left over from Christmas. The children ignored too many of my requests, and I was letting too many people take advantage of me. Things needed to change, and I needed motivation to change them.

My mother-in-law's daffodils were always the first ones in the neighborhood to bloom. When she and her husband moved out of their house, and we moved in, I wondered if the daffodils would bloom for me like they did for her. By the end of January, a row of bushy green clumps of leaves grew under the grape arbor. Soon, buds formed.

I bought a jump rope and began using it, stumbling over the rope and gasping for breath. One weekend, I went to a church women's retreat at the coast, finding new strength in walks on the beach, talks with other women, and ideas from the guest speaker.

"Don't yell or nag at your children," she told us. "Say the child's name, wait until he looks at you, and then give a command in a quiet voice."

When I came home, the house was clean and a bouquet of daffodils stood on the kitchen table. "I picked them," my daughter beamed. "Did you know they're blooming?"

No, I hadn't known, and found a childish delight in knowing that I, like my mother-in-law, could grow the first daffodils in the neighborhood.

In the next weeks, as more and more daffodils bloomed and bouquets dotted the house, I worked my way up from a hundred rope-jumps a day, to two hundred, to three. I tried the retreat speaker's advice with my children and found that such a simple thing made an amazing difference. I found the courage to say "No" to unreasonable expectations—once, then again.

While I still get nostalgic for winter in Minnesota, with glittering snowdrifts under a blue sky, I've decided that I love February in Oregon, where daffodils bloom staunchly in the rain, and change seems possible—not in dramatic leaps, but one, small, confident step at a time.

Summer Vacation

I paid 10 cents to see the performance, and it is easily worth the money.

Three days into summer vacation, my 11-year-old daughter Emily and her cousin Stephanie have formed Ladybug Enterprises. This is their first business venture, a play called "Let Sisterly Love Continue" which, since three of us came to watch, will net them exactly 30 cents.

Having handed over my red ticket, I perch on a tiny folding chair in my children's playhouse and watch as the girls pretend to be two sisters, "Sara" and "Jo," who can't get along.

The play involves an awful lot of costume changes and exaggerated arguing, along with occasional suffocating squirts of garage-sale perfume and hissed reminders—"No, Stephie! You don't say that now! Remember?"

Proceeding with dreamlike slowness, the plot moves from planning a party, to shopping for the party, to—finally—the party.

"Did you remember to invite Jason Fife?" "Sara" asks "Jo."

Jason Fife? Ah, yes, the Ducks' quarterback. I must be dreaming. "Sara" rushes to the door to let him in, and there is 8-year-old Ben, his dad's old suit coat hanging to his knees, an ominous lump bulging under his T-shirt, high on his chest.

"Jason" swaggers into the room and immediately eats an enormous amount of hors d'oeuvres, to the girls' dismay. He also keeps hitching up the lump, which wants to slide to his stomach. I see through the neck of his T-shirt that it's his sisters' old rag doll.

Ben's role is obviously a generous attempt by the girls to involve him in the action. The only thing he does to advance the plot is increase the sisters' rivalry when he pays more attention to "Jo" than "Sara."

The performance eventually ends with the "sisters" apologizing and mending their relationship, wild applause from the audience, and Ben shedding his costume with a sigh of relief.

"Why the doll?" I ask Ben. He shrugs. "To look, you know, buff."

Emily adds, "We thought it would look more realistic on his shoulders, but we couldn't get it to stay there."

This is why I like summer vacation.

Math and science are good things, of course, and I'm grateful that my children can get an education in a school that reinforces our religious beliefs—with their dad, no less, as the principal. But I am convinced that while subjects and schedules nourish a child's mind and self-discipline, something in his spirit goes hungry.

This year, as always, the last weeks of school were a flurry of finishing—tests, the yearbook, and preparations for the end-of-year program. In contrast, the sun shone warm on the basketball court, and the poppies beside Highway 228 waved serenely as we drove home from school.

On that last Friday, folders and battered pencil cases were hauled home in grocery sacks, and the program proceeded without a ripple.

And then, officially, it was summer, a block of time so vast that, to a child, it might as well be forever. September is a dim shore on the other side of the ocean as they launch out from May, a vague ending to a vast sea of opportunity.

For children, the best thing about summer is that, at last, there's time. No rush to be out the door by 8 a.m. No precious evenings swallowed by homework. There's time to not only imagine, but to test their ideas, modify them, and try something new. There's enough time to plan a treehouse for the walnut tree or a raft for the creek, and enough time to build it, play in it with the cousins, remodel it, and have it turn into a fort, a ship, or a dozen other things by the end of the summer.

Ladybug Enterprises has already considered a dozen money-making schemes, usually over the phone. The play, of course, was a success. Other ideas were rejected.

"Hello, Stephie? I don't think I can get Dad to build us a little craft shop after all."

And others are still being tested. "Stephie? I have an idea. Maybe we can bake cookies and put them at the warehouse to sell after harvest starts. And I planted a bunch of mari-golds in my garden. Maybe we can make bouquets and sell them."

Summer gives children a chance to work with their hands—to plant corn in freshly-tilled dirt, to hoe the weeds, eventually to harvest and eat the corn. Or to hang heavy, wet towels on the clothesline and bring them in hours later, warm with sunshine and smelling of summer. For 16-year-old Matt, sacking 50-pound bags of grass seed all summer provides an entirely different sense of satisfaction than fin-ishing a research paper.

For me, summer has always been a time of transition, a time to look back and evaluate, and to look ahead and plan. The change from the old year to the new on January 1 has always seemed much too abrupt. Thanks to a teacher dad, my own school years, a teacher husband, and my children, I have been able to work with the rhythms of the school year for most of my life, easing out of the old year and into the new with a complete change of schedule and activities in between.

Eventually, of course, I'll receive a back-to-school flyer and I'll look at the calendar and count, shocked to realize that only a few weeks of summer remain. I will suddenly grow tired of sticky orange Kool-Aid spots on the kitchen floor, and Ben will flop on the couch and moan, "I'm bored!"

Soon, crisp new school uniforms will hang in the closets, the house will seem full of restless children, and a strict schedule will sound strangely appealing.

Then, tanned, refreshed, and nostalgic, my children will rush out the door on a September morning. Savoring the peace and quiet, I will untangle the last wet, wadded swimsuit in the laundry room and reflect gratefully on summer vacation, when anything is possible, and for a dime I can see my son turned into a quarterback, buff and hungry.

"Hunting" Season

The children are easy to rouse on this Friday morning, bouncing out of bed with a sense of anticipation. "I wanna go to the godge sale," my 2-year-old Jenny squeaks from her crib. I've trained her well.

Garage saling involves many things: family bonding, adventure, and thrift. But primarily, like a New Guinean tribal ritual, this is all about "The Hunt." Equipment, strategy, and prey. Success or disappointment.

While the children eat breakfast in the early-morning chill, I gather my supplies. My hunting equipment comes not from Cabela's but from garage sales: wallet, tote bag, toys, and snack containers.

I scan the garage-sale page in the classifieds and choose the terrain: the Ferry Street Bridge section. Smugly, I pull out my cleverest hunting tool, designed to give me an edge over all the amateurs out there. It's a map I cut from the phone book and then laminated. I call out the name of a street—"Brewer!" and my daughter Amy finds it in the index from the phone book—"F-11!" I mark the street with a washable marker, and soon the map is dotted with little red lines.

Then, with a sense of urgency, we grab the bags and water bottles and pile into the car. Buckle the baby, check the supplies, and, as always, take a few seconds to pray. "Dear God, please watch over us today, and help us find a few bargains."

It's 8:15 already. Someone else is there ahead of me, I'm sure, loading up the toddler bed I want, picking through the fabric, taking the white Corelle dishes. As my Aunt Vina used to say, rushing toward Iowa City, "We need to hurry before all the hoarders get there!"

Our first stop is at Harry's Berries, south of Coburg, only now the fruit stand is full of crocheted doilies and home-school books instead of strawberries. Amy tugs on my sleeve and says she wants to show me something. It's a piece of luggage, on wheels, just what we've been looking for. A Samsonite, and only a dollar! There must be a catch. Wheels are good, handles attached. There it is—the zipper is torn at one corner.

This is the great garage-sale gamble. If I can fix it, it'll be the best bargain of the day. If I can't, it'll be a dollar wasted and a big piece of junk on my hands. I examine it further.

"You know, if I'd stitch it up right there, the zipper couldn't go past that bad spot, but I could still use it without that little bit of zipper at the end." Verdict: I'll take it.

Mrs. Garage Sale, a delightful elderly woman, is eager to talk. She recently got married, she tells me, and her husband makes the most wonderful things out of wood, including this lovely bench. I agree, it really is a beautiful bench, and just what I want to put along one side of our kitchen table. But for $25? New things, however fairly they may be priced, seem absurdly expensive at garage sales. Plus, I'm not sure the bench is long enough. Verdict: No.

Most of us garage salers have severe Someone-Could-Use-This syndrome. We give our moms copies of cookbooks they already own and buy our nieces clothes that are the wrong size and don't match anything in their closets. Cell phones, thankfully, are changing all that. I whip out mine and call my friend Simone.

"You know that book you told me I should check out of the Harrisburg library? *Lord Foulgrin's Letters?* I'm at a garage sale and they have a copy of it here. Three dollars." Yes, she'd love to have it, but I'm supposed to read it first. Deal.

South on Coburg Road, right on Crescent. Garage sale signs pop out of the trees, luring us down side streets. There are two kinds of garage sales, my husband says: the kind where people are trying to get rid of stuff, announced by hand-lettered Magic Marker on cardboard. And the kind where people are trying to make money, indicated by carefully stenciled letters on wood. Not that there's anything wrong with making money, but we brake for cardboard.

Sandals, wedding decorations, Yosemite souvenirs. The thing about being poor in America, my brother says, is that you can live so well off wealthier people's cast-offs. I find a children's book for Jenny—hardcover, like new, beautiful watercolor pictures of farm animals. New price: $15.99. I pay 25 cents.

We work our way southwest: Brewer, Lemming, Goodpasture Island. High chairs, 8-track tapes, paperback romances. A rack of blouses, just my style and colors, but double my size. Jenny finds chairs to sit on, the older girls rummage in "free" boxes, and 8-year-old Ben, already bored, stays in the car and reads.

Amy and Emily discover a dress and beg me to buy it. "Wouldn't this be adorable on Jenny?" It's worth a dollar to find something the three of us agree on. I buy it.

Fishing poles, orange stuffed chairs, coffee pots. I briefly consider an electric knife, still in the box, as a potential gift. Yes, I confess: I've given garage-sale items as gifts, although I've never experienced what a friend of mine did. She bought a slightly-used Crock Pot, along with the box, at a garage sale, then polished it up and gave it as a wedding gift. Later the bride told her, "We got quite a few Crock Pots at our wedding, so I took yours to Kmart and exchanged it for something else. I hope you don't mind."

Amy wants me to buy her a flower-shaped key chain that costs 50 cents. Too much, I think.

"But, Mom, it's all sparkly, and see, it's a little picture frame, too."

Should I offer less? Dickering at garage sales is allowed, even encouraged. My husband almost always offers less than the posted price, just to see what happens. I dicker only if I feel the marked price is too high. Just as I am ready to do so, the owner offers to reduce the price to 20 cents. I take it.

By 10, we're all hungry, the children are ready to call it a day, and Jenny is whining in her car seat. Reluctantly, I agree, as I still need to get groceries and want to be home by 11. Ben hands out snacks as we head for WinCo.

Garage sale signs flutter from stop signs, beckoning me.

"HUGE SALE."

"MULTI-FAMILY."

All right, just one more.

This one turns out to be an estate sale, full of expensive old things I don't want, which serves me right. We leave, and the signs continue.

Look! Right here! Please? It'll only take a minute! Just one more!

Resolutely, I set my face toward WinCo and pass them by.

At home, we unload the car and eat lunch, weary hunters home from the hill, sailors home from the sea. I hold Jenny on my lap and we read her new book, where the cow, the pigs, and the chickens all go to sleep. Soon, she joins them.

"Hunting" season will be over when the rains begin. In a few weeks, while the weather holds, I'll catch a whiff of bargains in the wind, and we'll set out again on a chilly Saturday morning. Just once more.

Autumn Harvest

*A*fter years of hit-or-miss breakfasts, my husband Paul and I decided three years ago to start getting everyone up for a sit-down family breakfast every morning. We drew up a chart, and each of us was responsible for setting the table and making breakfast one morning of the week.

For a long time, Paul and I were the only ones who put any effort into our breakfasts, his specialty being pancakes, and mine, breakfast burritos. The children, on their mornings, all served the same easy cold cereal and toast. We decided not to push the issue, hoping that eventually maturity and initiative would blossom and the children would try something more complicated. But the cereal and toast continued, week after week, month after month.

Last week, however, I was awakened at six one morning by clattering in the kitchen. I found Amy, age 13, dressed and alert, stirring up a batch of muffins for our breakfast. She found a recipe in an American Girl cookbook and decided to try it, she said. A few days later, as 11-year-old Emily headed upstairs to bed one evening, I heard her asking Paul to get her up early so he could teach her how to make blueberry pancakes.

For me, these two incidents were like finding the first ripe tomato hidden in the vines—a rich reward for a summer of waiting and work.

At this time of year, signs of fall are all around. When I park under the oak tree, I often am startled by a loud bang on top of the car, the sound far larger than the acorn that caused it. Across the driveway, walnuts lie scattered on the grass like Lego blocks on a bedroom carpet. The maples arching across Powerline Road drip wet, yellow leaves on my windshield as I drive underneath.

It's the season of ripening, harvesting, and gathering in.

The grapevines south of the house were stripped weeks ago. The apples from our trees are stored in grass-seed sacks in the back porch or turned to applesauce. In the garden, the beans are tilled under and the cornstalks chopped down and hauled away. Fat jars of green beans sit placidly on my shelves, and the corn is tucked away in the freezer, stiff and yellow in Ziploc bags. I canned the last of the tomatoes not long ago, listening for that satisfying little "ping!" as the last jar sealed.

Summer is the season of diligence: weeding, watering, and watching for bugs. Now, I'm leaving the garden to marinate in mud until next May. All summer, I hovered over the potted plants, pinching here, coaxing there. In the fall, I compost the leftover petunias and stack the flowerpots in the back porch. The walnuts are drying in old pillowcases by the furnace. At our grass-seed warehouse, the summer's crop is cleaned and bagged, and Paul is planning projects around the house—insulating under the floor and installing the new range hood in the kitchen. It's time to unpack my wool sweaters, plan sewing projects, and watch the leaves on the snowball bush turn red.

Nature and the calendar tell me it's fall, but in the timeline of our lives, our family is only in mid-summer.

Our five children range in age from 2 to 15, and this is our season of hard work, constant activity, and endless vigilance. The laundry hampers always seem to be full, triple batches of cookies disappear magically, and the kitchen floor seldom stays clean for more than half an hour. Our schedules are full of school and church activities, doctor and dentist appointments, piano lessons and drivers'-ed classes. I am constantly vigilant: alert, monitoring, averting disaster. Does Jenny have an earache? Is Amy extra quiet, or is it just my imagination? Ben needs new jeans for school, Amy needs new contact lenses, and Emily needs a birthday gift for her friend's party. I never know when I'll find 2-year-old Jenny snipping my grocery coupons into little pieces, or when Matt's latest scientific experiment will dim all the lights in the house.

"Enjoy these years," older women tell me, and I do. I'm past the teenage agonies of wondering what to do with my life, and I treasure this time of knowing exactly what I'm supposed to be doing. Raising my family is, I believe, the most important work I'll ever do. At this stage I am never bored, constantly entertained, and seldom alone or lonely.

Yet, in this summer of my life, I watch for signs of fall. For our family, it's still a long way off.

"Do you realize," my son asked me last year, "that you're going to have at least one teenager in the house for the next 18 years?"

My husband's aunt, I'm told, can stitch a quilt in a week. "She likes to finish!" her sister tells me emphatically. "It's not that she enjoys the actual quilting that much. She just likes to finish!"

I, too, like to finish. I admit, I get such a thrill out of checking an item off my to-do list that I'll even write down something I already completed, just for the joy of checking it off.

As much as I enjoy this season of my life, I find that the most difficult thing about it is that it's so hard to finish anything—from sentences to grocery lists to painting a bedroom. My day's planned activities give way to a series of interruptions. My Saturday cleaning frenzies are never quite completed before it's time for supper and baths.

Of course, the biggest project of all takes the longest to finish—this enormous task of turning children into adults, responsible for their own decisions, capable of taking care of themselves.

I look forward to autumn. I anticipate a day when my children will apologize without being prompted and I'll hear one of them say, "Sure, you can sit in the front seat if you like." I look forward to seeing them consider our advice and then launch out on their own. Someday, I hope to complete this work, to feel finished, and to see the results of all these years of working and waiting.

This Thanksgiving, I am thankful for fall, this annual ritual of reaping and resting. I am thankful for my family and this season of our lives. And I give thanks for muffins and blueberry pancakes for breakfast, the taste of a fruitful autumn yet to come.

Christmas Memories

My mother always celebrated the holidays with huge Thanksgiving and Christmas dinners, homemade gifts, and cinnamon rolls for the mailman.

Best of all, she made candy and cookies: cut-out sugar cookies from the *Mennonite Community Cookbook*, fudge, "Divinity," and date pinwheels. We children helped with cutting out the sugar cookies and dipping peanut-butter balls in chocolate to make buckeyes.

Mom's Divinity was, as the name implies, almost divine. She would whip a bowl of egg whites, then stand at the stove and cook a sugary mixture to just the right temperature. She didn't have a candy thermometer, so she'd drop a dollop into a cup of cold water and expertly judge the temperature. Then the hot sugar syrup was folded into the egg whites and spread into a cake pan, where it cooled into a white, airy, irresistible treat.

For years, every November, I was struck by an urge to recreate these same memories for my children. It was this compulsion that made me say "yes" the time my friend Earl Baker offered us a turkey for Thanksgiving.

"You'll have to dress it yourself," he said. "Are you sure you know how?"

I had visions of chicken-butchering days on the farm—frosty mornings with steam rising from buckets of boiling water, Mom in her kerchief and old coat, and my sisters and me plucking the feathers. So I told Earl, "Sure, I know how to butcher a turkey."

66

That year on Thanksgiving, I kept glancing anxiously into the oven as the turkey turned a golden brown, and an ominous bulge by the neck grew larger and larger. Just before the guests arrived, I took the turkey out of the oven and inspected the bulge. It was the crop that I had forgotten to remove, and if I didn't cut carefully, I was going to have roasted grain all over the meat.

It may have been the same year that the children helped me make Christmas cookies. We began enthusiastically, but as the afternoon wore on, interest waned and tempers got shorter. By evening, every surface in the kitchen was sticky with icing and sprinkles, and stars and lopsided gingerbread men covered the counters.

My husband worked late that day so I had to clean up by myself, plus get all the children bathed and to bed. I kept turning up the thermostat and getting colder and colder.

Finally, I took my temperature and discovered I was coming down with the flu.

Then, 9-year-old Matt came slinking out of the bathroom. "Mom, I want to confess this before you discover it yourself: I made a tidal wave in the bathtub."

We mopped up the water and just as I collapsed into bed, Matt stuck his head in the door and told me that 2-year-old Ben wasn't sleeping, but was up and playing on the floor of their bedroom.

I survived that episode, of course, but I wondered if my children were going to remember only bumbling disasters at holidays. I had always assumed that my own warm memories of holiday traditions were a result of careful planning on Mom's part, a determination to make sure we grew up with a generous stash of traditions and memories.

But I began to change my mind with a phone call from

my sister a few years ago.

"Did you know that Mom doesn't remember making Divinity?" she demanded, consternation in her voice.

"What?" I asked.

"I'm serious. I called her for the recipe and she said, 'Divinity? Did I used to make Divinity?'"

There was silence on both ends of the line. *What did it mean? Alzheimer's? Dementia? Divinity was such a big part of Christmas,* we thought. *How could Mom possibly forget?* Yet her mind was still as sharp as ever in other areas, her letters interesting and articulate. It didn't make sense.

The next year, half afraid, I called Mom and asked for her buckeyes recipe.

"Buckeyes?" she said. "Hmmm . . . are those the ones Ervin Lyddie used to make?" (That would be my Uncle Ervin's wife, Lyddie, identified by her husband's name first in the Amish custom.)

"Ervin Lyddie?" I yelped. "No, Mom. *You* used to make them! Don't you remember?"

She didn't, at first, but then as I described them further she remembered that yes, maybe she had made them a time or two and had the recipe somewhere.

I made the buckeyes, dipping them in chocolate and wondering what to make of Mom's strange memory lapses.

Now, a year later, I've concluded that Mom forgot simply because it wasn't that important to her. Christmas candy was only one of a thousand details of her life that gradually changed as her children left home, and it wasn't important enough to remember 25 years later.

My sister once gave me a book called *Let's Make a Memory*. A collection of ideas for family activities, it encourages a goal of sending children into adulthood with a stockpile of good childhood memories.

This concept, I've decided, is born of the same era as self-esteem, quality time, and endlessly sharing one's feelings.

Mom had no use for such nebulous parenting. She believed in hard work, good food, fearing God, and having fun. In the process, our memories would take care of themselves.

Like the time I made Divinity—or tried to. I was probably 15, more into books than cooking, but Mom decided it was time I learned to make Divinity. She got out the recipe, gave me a few pointers, and went off to do something else. I separated the eggs, beat the whites, and cooked the sugary syrup.

Mom wasn't in the kitchen when I faced the next step, and the bare-bones recipe didn't tell me either. Was it syrup into egg whites or whites into syrup? Whites into syrup, I decided rashly, and when Mom came back into the kitchen I was staring, aghast, at the sick, crumbly mess I had just created, so different from Mom's fluffy Divinity.

She didn't get upset—that's what I remember best. She hated wasting food, and I often tried her patience. Yet, this time, when I did both, she was calm and reassuring.

"Hmmm," she said, poking dubiously at the gray mass, "Maybe Dad will eat it."

At our house, this was a polite way of saying, "I don't think the goats would touch it."

She was sure I'd remember next time. And I have never forgotten; it's syrup into egg whites. Even more, I haven't forgotten her response—warm and forgiving.

This year we want to make candy, give gifts, and eat a big Christmas dinner—with no memorable disasters, I hope.

Ultimately, though, Christmas is about love and redemption. If I focus on those gifts, the warm holiday memories are inevitable.

I think Mom knew all along that memories creep in when you're busy doing something else and when you least expect them, like a cat that slips in the front door when you open it to let your dinner guests come in.

And, like a contented cat, good memories curl up in a quiet corner and purr.

Relatives

An "Irrelevant" Generation

The paper dolls always remind me of the afternoon last fall when I took Dad to the museum in Harrisburg. I find the dolls when I clean my daughters' room: chains of little girls, holding hands, all their braids connected to each other.

Mom had stayed with the children that afternoon, and when we came home, she was sitting on the couch with a narrow piece of folded paper in her hand. She cut a snip here, a careful curve there. As the children watched, fascinated, she slowly unfolded the paper and there was a row of little girls. She repeated the process and out came a chain of little boys in straw hats and bare feet. Before long, the children were folding and snipping under their grandma's direction. To me, it was confirmation that my parents' wisdom and skills were still relevant for my children, even though their lives are so different from Mom's and Dad's childhoods.

My parents had come from Minnesota by Amtrak to spend a week at our house. Mom is 80 years old; Dad is 84. Both grew up Amish, children of the Depression. In their younger years, they were ambitious, influential, and adventurous, pursuing travel and an education, unusual choices for the Amish. They married when Mom was 33 and Dad was 37, and had six children.

But now that my parents are older, it sometimes seems that the world has no use for people of their generation. They

73

are vast reservoirs of knowledge that no one is interested in.
And modern society is a foreign country to my parents. It
moves much too fast for them, and they are strangers in it,
mystified by the customs, baffled by the language. They
make brief forays away from home, then retreat gratefully
back to their farm, where the phone still has a rotary dial,
no one owns a credit card, and the chickens scratch and
peck out by the barn. My parents are shocked and bewildered by modern lifestyles—all the wealth, the computers,
the waste, the fast food, and the fractured families.

Mom and Dad's only source of world news is a weekly
magazine. Mom reads about all the people making money
on the stock market or the Internet. She sees them as vastly sophisticated but ignorant of the most basic skills.

"What if there was another Depression?" Mom often
says, shaking her head. "How would people make it?"

She told me about the neighbor girl who came over to
see if Mom and Dad wanted any kittens. "She had this
skimpy little top on," Mom said, "with a ring in her belly
button." Imagine.

Young people like that might drive their own cars and be
experts with computers, but do they have any idea how to
grow their own food, bake bread, butcher a chicken, or mend
clothing? Mom doesn't think so. She worries about them.

I suggested one day that we all write an e-mail to my sister in Yemen. I got the computer ready and Mom sat down
in front of it. Cautiously poking the right keys, she typed,
"Dear Rebecca."

"Now what do I do?" she asked. "I want to go down to
the next line."

Obviously, this wouldn't work. Instead, Mom and Dad
wrote letters in longhand, and I typed them into the com-

puter and announced that their letters would be at Becky's house within hours. Mom and Dad acted impressed, but their enthusiasm seemed a bit forced. *After all,* they probably thought, *a letter was a letter.* With one method, it would get there sooner and show up on a computer screen. With the other, it would take longer, but Becky could hold it in her hands and see Mom's firm handwriting with the spiky M's and Dad's perfect Palmer Method cursive. And who was to judge which was better?

We were shopping for a van during Mom and Dad's visit. On the way to Portland one day, Mom mended a pair of my son's jeans. Without measuring or marking, she cut a new patch, exactly the right size, out of a scrap piece of denim. Then she put her left hand up inside the pant leg and with her right hand sewed the patch with firm, even stitches. She loves to help me out in this way. But when it came to advice about vans, she and Dad felt like they had nothing to offer. Both of them were in their fifties when they first learned to drive a car, and motor vehicles are still a mystery to them. So they watched, listened, and kept their opinions to themselves. If we had been shopping for a horse, they would have had volumes of excellent advice.

Knowing his love of history, I took Dad to the Harrisburg Museum one afternoon. Headed by Al and Iris Strutz, the museum is a testimony to their dedication and to the work of many volunteers. Al served as our tour guide. Dad and I stepped into the restored kitchen at the museum, and suddenly our roles reversed. I was tentative and unsure of myself, wondering, "What *is* this stuff?"

Dad acted like he had just come home. "My mother had one like this," he told me, touching the iron fondly. "And like this—it's a slaw-maker, you know, a cabbage cutter."

I recognized the cream separator for what it was, but Dad and Al went on to discuss the relative merits of the DeLaval separators versus the McCormick-Deering.

Upstairs in the museum bedroom, we found a little book with all the dates of the year printed inside, and people's names written in old-fashioned script. "A birthday book," Dad explained. "My sisters used to have these to keep track of their friends' birthdays." He flipped a few pages, then stopped. "Noah Mast from Thomas, Oklahoma, 1889. I knew the man."

I couldn't believe it. History at the Harrisburg Museum had reached out and touched my father.

We went on to the farm-equipment building. Dad pointed out one item after another and told me what it was, what it was for, or how much it held. Dad, the wheat farmer from Oklahoma, and Al, the wheat farmer from North Dakota, soon discovered how much they had in common. They walked around the enormous steam engine, affectionately patting it, and reminisced about wheat harvest in the old days. They inspected the threshing machine and Dad guessed, "This probably had a 28-inch cylinder and a 46-inch separator." Sure enough, there, stencilled in faint letters on the side, were the words, "28-inch cyl.—46-inch sep." I kept thinking, *I never knew my dad knew all this stuff.*

It was time to go, but Al wanted to start the motor on a huge, lime-green, cast-iron contraption.

"This was the original irrigation pump out at OSU in the 1890s," Al said proudly. "It still works." He poured in a bit of fuel and positioned a rod. Then he stepped on one spoke of a wheel that was almost as big as he was, grabbed onto another spoke, and slowly turned. We heard a wheezing sound from the motor, then a small pop, then nothing.

"It's okay," I said. "You don't need to start it for us."

But Al, determined, kept turning. "It always starts on the second try," he insisted, puffing slightly. But by the fourth turn nothing had happened.

What should I do? Mom was home with the children and I was sure they were getting hungry. Al gave the wheel another turn. There was another puff, then nothing. Suddenly, this motor seemed symbolic of my parents and their generation—a relic of another era, something wonderful in its heyday but irrelevant, almost pitiful, now.

"We really need to go," I told Dad, and, to Al's disappointment, we edged out the door and climbed into the van.

Dad had barely closed his door when we heard a tremendous BOOM! behind us. Another followed a few seconds later, then more in rapid succession. I looked around, frightened, and saw Al running out of the building, grinning triumphantly, waving his arms.

"It's going!" he yelled. We returned to the green monster, now chuffing and turning in perfect coordination. The wheel turned, the piston pushed, the gears meshed at the right moment. Perfect.

Dad and Al couldn't stop smiling, watching this dead machine come back to life. Did they sense, as I did, that there was something of themselves in this lime-green pump? "Don't give up on us. Give us the right spark, ask us the right questions, listen to us—you'll be amazed at what we have to offer."

Then we came home and there was Mom, bringing to my children's childhood a piece of her own: a paper chain of dancing little girls, holding hands, all their braids connected to each other.

Orval

I was almost finished gathering the walnuts from under the tree when a sudden gust of wind sent dozens more thumping to the ground all around me. I was struck, not by a walnut, but by the sudden realization that Orval would never shell my walnuts again.

He used to lower himself stiffly down into a kitchen chair and demand, in the heightened decibels he used for all converation, "You got any nuds to crag?" I'd bring him a small bucketful and he'd start in, first demonstrating his special pocket-knife technique that split the shell neatly in two without damaging the kernel inside. He'd stop for a bit of lunch, then work steadily until mid-afternoon, when I would insist on his nap.

"You got any more nuds to crag?"

"Why don't you go take a nap?"

"It ain't nap-time! I'm here to shell walnuts! Didn't you know what I'm here for?"

"You're supposed to lie down and put your feet up, aren't you?"

"My feet are right on the ground where they belong. Me sittin' here, this is worthless!"

"What am I going to do if you come next time and I don't have any nuts left?"

"I'll have to sit home, I guess!"

Often I gave up at this point and brought him some more walnuts.

"Oh, thank you, thank you!" Then, in German, cracking contentedly: "One is barefooted and one has no shoes. Now which would you rather be?"

"Barefooted," I'd answer for the twentieth time.

"How come?"

"Because he might have shoes at home."

"Hrah! Hrah! Hrah! Well! Little and smart is worth something, too!"

That was his favorite German expression. I never did figure out what he meant by it.

Orval Smucker was my husband's grandfather, and he died at the age of 94. Paul's sister took care of Orval for four years, and every so often Paul and I would take him for the day to give her a break. Sometimes I'd take him out for coffee at the Hungry Farmer, out by the Harrisburg exit.

There was no sneaking into a booth with Orval. He would shuffle determinedly to the counter, sit on a stool, and holler in his raspy voice for a cup of coffee. Then he'd talk to me.

"This is a Japanese family that owns this, you know," he shouted at me one day between slurps of coffee.

"They all work together. That girl over there is one of theirs. Hey, Sis! You work here, huh? With your family? No, no more coffee. I take it a cup at a time. You know those fellows that bombed that building in Oklahoma City? They're probably gonna electrocute them."

Orval died on a Saturday, and on Tuesday evening, after the viewing, we all went out to Abby's Pizza to celebrate Uncle Milford's birthday. I thought, *Pizza? With Grandpa lying in the funeral home just a few blocks away?* But I went along, not wanting to miss the party. I watched the noisy mixture of Smucker personalities (Family motto: "What's the use of an opinion if you don't state it emphatically?"), and I sensed that Orval would have approved. It was only natural that his descendants would meet at a restaurant to celebrate a birthday, discuss the world, and have a good time. Pizza after a viewing? "Why sure!"

When he got too tottery to go to restaurants, I'd set him at the kitchen table and offer him a cup of coffee.

"Why sure! I alwiz tell'em a cup at a time."

"Do you want sugar?" I'd ask.

"Naw, I quit sugar a long time ago. I had diabeades so I had to quit sugar."

"Do you still have diabetes?"

"Naw, not that I know of. I went to George Kanagy and he cured me of it."

"How did he do that?"

"He gave me food capsules. He tested me. He said, 'You got diabeades, the worst kind.' Well, George said my pancreas gland had quit working. He said, 'You should get a food capsule to strengthen your pancreas gland so it don't pull this trick again.' He got me these food capsules and as far as I know I never had diabeades again. Now you tell me what a food capsule is! I've asked every doctor I've seen and I'm gonna keep asking people—see if I can find somebody that knows. I've never been able to get anyone to tell me, and George is dead and gone."

Today, two of Orval's granddaughters are in medical school. I like to think that a touch of their grandpa's curiosity and persistence inspires them. Maybe someday they will finally discover what was in those mysterious food capsules. Perhaps they will even make sure we can buy Orval's favorite ointment at the pharmacy—something he called DMSO Oil.

Grandpa would follow me around the house, overalls loose on his bony frame, shouting about this wonderful potion.

"Now you cain't buy it in the drugstore, you know. I alwiz get mine from the vet. And every time I get a cut on my hand, I just rub that stuff on and it heals right up. Why sure! And that oil isn't just for the outside of you! That stuff goes through your skin right into your bloodstream. I have no intention of dying of canzer like my neighbor lady did. They say those canzer cells get in your blood. Well! If any would try it on me, that DMSO Oil would kill them right off. Why, one time I found a lump and I was afraid it was canzer so I rubbed DMSO Oil on it and, wouldn't you know, it went away!"

Will Paul be like this in 50 years? I used to worry. Already, I could see similarities sifting through the generations: the bristly eyebrows, the strong nose, the lanky frame. What if Paul ended up this raw, this unrefined, with a whiskery, wobbling chin? On the other hand, what if he ended up this colorful, this full of personality, this undefeated by old age?

It was Orval's sheer orneriness that won me over, almost in spite of himself. That, and the odd honor of my being the only one in the clan who was fluent in his native German dialect of Pennsylvania Dutch. He never did remember my name, but always referred to me as That One That Talks Dutch. Orval would confront me anywhere, especially at quiet places like church, with a wild, *"Vell! Vee geht's?"* (Well! How's it going?) followed by his famous laugh— Hrah! Hrah! Hrah!

As Orval lay dying in a nursing home in Eugene, he turned his head and followed me with his eyes as I entered the room. The nurse was astonished, as he had been unresponsive all morning. Perhaps, she said, it was because he knew I was That One That Talks Dutch. I leaned over his bed and told him good-bye, telling him, in German, to go when it's time to go, not to hang on. But Orval, being Orval, hung on for hours and days longer than anyone thought possible.

At the burial, the grandsons took shovels and, in our faith tradition, helped to fill the grave. I saw in them all, bent to their solemn task, a touch of their hardworking farmer grandpa, always determined to get the job done.

And now, at last, he had finished.

But every October, when walnuts shower from the tree in a gust of wind, I remember him. Little and smart may be worth something, as Orval always said, but old and full of life is worth much more.

Aunts

When my son Matt answered the phone on his 18th birthday a few weeks ago, we heard a staticky but beautiful "Happy birthday to yooooou" warbling from the receiver. The other kids glanced at each other.

"It's Aunt Barb," they said, knowingly.

For years, my husband's sister Barb has called her nieces and nephews on their birthdays. Despite her siblings' growing number of offspring (27 and counting), plus her years of work, college, medical school, and now her residency, Barb has faithfully kept up this tradition.

"Well, see, I'm kind of stuck in my math class," Matt confided, halfway through their conversation. "Did you ever study limits in calculus? It has to do with, like, derivatives."

Barb couldn't help him, but it turned out that she had had the same math teacher at "LB" (Linn-Benton Community College) and, discussing college and calculus, she helped Matt feel like the adult he now officially is.

Barb's conversation with Jenny, whose fifth birthday was two days before, was vastly different from the calculus discussion.

Jenny yelled into the phone, "We had *tea* for my party and we dressed up like *fancy ladies!*" Barb, being the flexible aunt that she is, seemed just as interested in tea and cupcakes as she was in limits and derivatives.

We honor our mothers in May and dads in June, but I think the aunts in our lives deserve recognition as well. Theirs is a pleasant role that, unlike parenting, is as simple or complicated as they choose to make it. Their influence can vary from the simple stability of being there to the profound impact of active involvement.

Aunts experience the love and pride of parenting without the pain or responsibility. I discovered this when I first became an aunt at age 17, when my mother woke me up in the middle of the night and told me my brother and his wife had just had a baby, a girl named Annette.

I am astonished, now, at how many square, Instamatic pictures we took of Annette as a small child—holding a kitten, opening gifts, on our laps. Everything she did was cute and amazing and wonderful. But when she had a messy diaper or was hungry or upset, I plopped her back in her mother's lap.

Today, when I see the funny yet level-headed person Annette has become, I know it's because of her parents' choices, and her own. But, as her aunt, I feel entitled to share in her parents' pride.

With small gestures, aunts make a big imprint on a child's memory. This is why my sister bought a bag of orange marshmallow circus peanuts one summer when she came to visit, and we sat down after supper and ate them slowly and ceremonially.

"Ewww, what's so special about those weird candies?" my daughter wanted to know.

"Aunt Edna used to babysit us when Mom went grocery shopping," we explained, "and she always had this jar of circus peanuts up on the shelf. We thought it was the most wonderful treat in the world."

My daughter didn't understand, of course. But, reverently chewing, we relived that feeling of being indulged and cared for at Aunt Edna's.

Often, in adolescence, we feel trapped in our family's patterns and wonder if we will ever be able to escape. Aunts give us a glimpse of a different way of life, a vivid object lesson that while our genes determine that we might be skinny like the Yoders or stout like the Millers, our choices make the biggest difference, and we are not destined by fate to follow in our parents' footsteps.

Aunt Vina seemed vast and expansive in all the areas where my mother was tight and restrained. She breezed in from Iowa a couple of times a year and greeted us with enveloping hugs; in our family, we didn't hug.

She freely spent money at the grocery store and introduced us to such modern wonders as Hidden Valley Ranch dressing. Who knew something so delicious existed, so unlike Mom's Miracle Whip and vinegar mixtures?

Vina's house was Interior Decorated, a sophisticated term that meant thick carpets, complementary colors, and something very different from the cozy farm-sale-furniture hodgepodge at our house.

That she shared my mother's genes was obvious from looking at her, but Vina showed me that I could be as different from my mother as I chose to be.

The aunts who make the biggest difference are the truly dedicated ones such as Barb and her sister Rosie. They arrange annual activities for all the nieces and nephews— camp-outs, trips to the beach, and jaunts to the hills to play in the snow. Each trip to the coast means elaborate sand castles on the beach, and every ride home brings a long, made-up-as-we-go story from Rosie that my kids remember in vivid detail, even years later.

Most importantly, Barb and Rosie care for the kids on a personal level, aware and concerned. While I appreciate this, I felt a confusing mixture of gratitude and resentment the time Rosie got into a long discussion with the teenage girls during a walk on the beach. They weren't sure they liked being Mennonite, the girls told her, among other dismaying facts that they had never divulged to their mothers. While I was glad my daughter had shared her feelings, I was troubled that she hadn't shared them with me.

When we were in Kenya, the orphan boys we were teaching had been capably cared for by an all-male staff for some time. The atmosphere changed when a young woman named Nancy was hired to be an all-purpose secretary, nurse, and organizer. Suddenly, the boys seemed drawn to her desk, confiding in her, telling her things they had never told the houseparents or anyone else.

We mentioned this to our Kenyan friend Vincent. "She's being their auntie," he said, as though it was perfectly logical. "Traditionally, Mom is the cook and nurse and disciplinarian in an African family, but not the friend and companion. This role is reserved for the auntie."

I don't know how the parents choose the particular auntie, but she takes a personal interest in the child and guides him or her through childhood and adolescence.

I know plenty of mothers who, as I did, suffered from guilt and a sense of inadequacy when their kids confided in another woman. I also have been in the opposite role, when teenage girls told me things they couldn't bring themselves to tell their mothers, and I listened with a sense of guilty betrayal.

Perhaps the Africans are on to something wise, frankly recognizing that Mom cannot always be all things to all people, and that sometimes it's hard to confide in her, and then wisely assigning a specific role to a parent's sibling to meet this need in a child's life.

It didn't take me long to recover when my daughter confided in Rosie, since Rosie was wise and level-headed and would tell me if there was anything I really needed to know. And I had to admit I find it hard to listen to my daughter without lecturing.

Looking back, I now realize that Rosie was truly being an auntie in the African sense.

Mom and Dad deserve the honor they receive in May and June, but I propose we send applause and flowers to the aunts in our lives as well—the ones who give us circus peanuts, the ones who teach us to hug and, most of all, the aunties who listen and care and who remember, 27 times a year, to pick up the phone and sing "Happy Birthday."

Becky

I love this. My sister Becky is 39 years old and I'm only 37.

For most of the year she is only a year older than me, but from June 8 to June 29 she appears to be two years older. She used to remind me of this, in her maddeningly superior way, by spending those three weeks chanting in Pennsylvania German, *"Ich bin 9 un du bisht usht 7!"* (I am 9 and you are only 7.) Or whatever the numbers happened to be.

Of course, Becky was maddeningly superior in many ways. Cool and controlled where I was feisty. Socially adept when I was awkward. And she was pretty. When we were in elementary school, our next-oldest brother Fred would tell Becky that all his friends liked her.

Becky, in turn, would haul me in front of the mirror. "I want to show you how I'm pretty and you're not. See, my face is longer and yours is more round, and Freddy says I'm prettier. And my nose is more straight (Freddy says) and yours points up at the end."

I believed everything she said.

To the rest of the family, we were *de maet,* "the girls," born between three older brothers and another sister six years younger than me.

When we were teenagers, it was Becky's job to reform me. She was constantly adjusting my clothes, telling me to stand up straight, and scolding me for talking too much when her friends were over. We looked a lot alike, enough so that people took us for twins. But mostly I was aware of our differences. She had Dad's thin frame. I had Mom's thick ankles. At school, she spent the lunch hour standing by the heater in the hall, talking with friends. I stayed in the library and read.

Recently I read a T-shirt slogan, "God made us sisters; Prozac made us friends." In our case, it was a wealth of shared experiences that eventually dispelled the rivalry and forged a powerful bond between us.

Like the night of the dripping water tower when we were about 16 and 17. Dad had gone by bus to visit his mother. For some reason Becky and I were chosen to go pick him up in St. Cloud, 40 miles away, at 2 a.m. And, Dad told us on the phone, the bus station was closed so a friendly police-man had taken him to the police station.

We set out, almost alone on the country roads, carefully following the directions Dad gave us. Into town, then a right turn onto a deserted street. This didn't look quite right, but eventually we found a little brick police station, and beside it was the water tower that was supposed to be there, but everything was dark.

We parked the car and cautiously got out. The night was warm and quiet, with a light breeze. We crept to the door and knocked, but no one answered. The water tower loomed high above us, a ghostly silver in the moonlight. Stray drips of water dropped down from high above and swept toward us in the breeze. It was utterly creepy.

We drove the deserted streets, mystified, coming back several times to knock on the door and shiver under the shadow of the hulking water tower. Finally, a young police-man showed up and told us that this was actually Waite Park, a small town at the edge of St. Cloud. He directed us to the right police station, and we found Dad and drove home. But for years we shivered at the memory of the dripping water tower in the night.

We went to high school together and were the first in the family to graduate. We worked on the farm together, stacking hay bales, picking rocks, and weeding the garden. We found more and more odd similarities between us, like the fact that we prayed the same fervent silent prayers whenever we worked on the farm: that we would be kept from seeing any garter snakes.

Becky worked at a nursing home during my last year of high school. It was our first experience of being separated, and it was worse when she worked the afternoon shift. When our schedules coordinated again, we'd sit at the kitchen table and talk well into the night. Dad would shuffle by in his pajamas and exclaim, *"Ach, maet,* go to bed!" But he would grin a little bit—glad, I imagine, to see us enjoying each other's company.

Becky left for college the next year. On weekends she'd catch a ride partway home with friends, and I'd go pick her up and bring her home. One afternoon we drove home in a blizzard, with gusts of windblown snow obliterating our view. It took us an hour-and-a-half to drive 25 miles. Another day we were making a left turn and were hit by a car that had suddenly decided to pass us. Becky and I had glanced at each other just as the car hit. Our heads knocked together and we got matching bumps on our foreheads.

I went to live in Oregon while Becky was still in college. I missed her terribly. One year she decided to spend her spring break in Oregon and we arranged to go to the coast for four days. Such a wonderful opportunity—we wanted to make the most of it. First of all, we decided, we wouldn't eat junk food, and we stocked up on veggies and peanut butter. But our motel in Florence happened to be next door to a Dairy Queen.

Such an opportunity—we couldn't pass it up. So we limited ourselves to one DQ treat a day.

We grew up without television, so watching TV in a motel was always a big temptation. This time we decided we shouldn't watch—such a waste of time. But, being young and reckless, we checked the *TV Guide*, just in case, and discovered that *Gone With The Wind* was going to be on the exact three nights we were there. Such an opportunity— we couldn't pass that up either. So each evening we sat on the bed with a pile of celery sticks and a jar of peanut butter between us, and watched *Gone With The Wind* for an hour.

Whenever the movie was scary, we ate faster. When Scarlett and Melanie hid under the bridge, we frantically stabbed celery sticks into the peanut butter and crunched faster and faster. When the crazy Yankee soldier came to the house, we were almost too terrified to eat. I hopped off the bed and tested the doorknob to make sure it was locked. The next morning, we discovered that we had left the keys in the other side of the door all night.

Our twenties brought changes for both of us—jobs, marriage, children, moves. In many ways our lives diverged, but the bond between us was strong enough to survive these changes. Our thirties brought more changes, as Becky, her engineer husband, and their son moved to the Middle East. Communication was frustrating—letters were slow and phone calls were expensive. Then came e-mail. Suddenly there was once again an immediacy to our communication, a sharing of casual trivia, like talking over the supper dishes.

As we get older, we keep finding more similarities between us. We both have asthma, we like navy-blue and pink sweaters, and we love to read. In other areas, our roles slowly change. She now envies my nose, as it's smaller than hers. I find myself giving her advice when we go shopping.

I have a "Stone Soup" comic strip that I plan to send to Becky next year when she turns 40. Joan tells her sister Val, "You always lorded it over me. You dated first, drove first, left home first. . . ," then she grins and adds, "but now. . . you're going to hit 40 first."

I'll let myself gloat for a while. But, really, it wouldn't be fair to let Becky experience her forties all alone. So, a year and three weeks later, I'll join her.

Oregon Fruit

*M*y children and I and various in-laws are at Oxbow Orchards, picking blueberries. My second bucket is half full and I still gasp at the size of these berries—they hang there like clusters of grapes and slide almost effortlessly into my bucket. My 10-year-old son is down the row, steadily picking. The younger three are gradually picking less and eating more. I can't see them; the bushes are taller than I am. But I hear them calling up and down the rows.

I marvel at my bush and its infinite supply and think of my blueberry-picking attempts six years ago when we lived in Canada. Scruffy little bushes and pea-sized berries, a howling baby in the stroller, and always a wary eye for black bears. Matthew, age 4, who liked to pick but not eat, would hand all his berries to Amy, age 2, who liked to eat but not pick. If I went home with a quart of berries, I was happy indeed.

It's no wonder Grandma used to talk about Oregon like it was the Garden of Eden, I think, popping an enormous berry into my mouth. Grandma and her family had lived in Oregon when she was a teenager. Then they moved back to the Midwest and none of her children or grandchildren had ever come back here to live until I married an Oregonian and eventually we ended up in Oregon. Now I was an awed participant in my in-laws' summer ritual of harvesting and preserving an astonishing parade of fruit.

As I pick, I remember sitting around the kitchen table in Minnesota, making applesauce with the few precious apples available to us. Grandma was across the table spinning tales about a wonderful land out West that was the most beautiful place she had ever seen. Oh, the mountains! (Mountains? I imagined a series of up-ended cones, all snow-capped.) And the fruit. There was no way to describe the wonderful fruit in Oregon. Berries, peaches, pears—almost every kind of fruit you could want. There was so much of it, she couldn't begin to tell us. And it was all lovely, not like these little crabapples we were cutting up.

I jerk to the present and ease out of my bush to check on the children. Matthew has picked almost a gallon, amazing child. Amy has picked half a gallon and gone off to play with her cousin Jessica. The two youngest have given up all pretense of picking and are wandering down the rows, happily eating.

Grandma was the third oldest of 15 children and felt much of the responsibility of providing for them all. She loved to tell of the summer she and her sister Katie picked cherries off their tree and sold them door-to-door in Portland to help support the family. But the cherries wouldn't sell, since all the housewives wanted to know what kind they were and Grandma and Katie didn't know. Finally the sisters had a little conference beside the road and decided to call them Black Pippins. After that they sold them all.

Then Grandma would always tell the story of when they still lived in Minnesota and the only food they had put up for winter was a quart jar of rhubarb. A quart of rhubarb and all those children—I couldn't imagine. How did they survive? Grandma couldn't remember, but somehow God had provided and there she was, still with us. It was no wonder Oregon had seemed like the land of plenty.

I've picked far more blueberries than I ever intended to.

We gather the buckets and discarded sweatshirts and reluctantly leave the patch. *Is it possible to appreciate enough the
lush bounty of all these berries,* I wonder, *all this food, these
well-fed children climbing into the van?*

I pay for the berries and drive away, thinking about my
life and Grandma's. My life is so much easier than hers
ever was, and it's a lot easier now than when my children
were smaller. I worry that I could get so used to all these
blessings that I'd start to take them for granted.

Later, running the berries through my hands and into
the sink, I somehow feel sure I never will. I see a different
kind of fruit, values that Grandma unknowingly handed to
me and that I can pass to my children and beyond. I see the
value of family, resourcefulness, hard work, and—most of
all—a joyful appreciation of all God's gifts.

$\mathcal{T}raditions$

On the first Thanksgiving after Paul and I were married, we gathered at Paul's grandparents' house and everyone slipped into familiar roles.

Paul's mom and the aunts bustled around the kitchen preparing a huge dinner. The young moms chased after toddlers, the teenagers played basketball, and the uncles sat around the living room and talked about farming. I felt nervous and a bit overwhelmed, unsure of my place in this noisy bunch of people.

Sixteen years later, I take my role in the family with the same ease that everyone else did on that long-ago Thanksgiving. I treasure the patterns and rhythms of family, the mix of personalities, the familiarity.

My husband and his six brothers and sisters all happened to be in Oregon at the same time last August, so we gathered at the coast. Anne, my mother-in-law, left the organizing to her daughter, Lois, who hoped to find a house at the coast but felt fortunate, on such short notice, to find a few motel rooms near the beach. All 37 of us came, from Wilton and Anne—now Grandpa and Grandma of the clan—down to the three babies, all born last year.

At the motel, we filled the small living room and overflowed onto the deck. Again, we slipped comfortably into the familiar rituals of family. We moms cooked, walked on the beach, chased toddlers, and put children down for naps. The dads hauled in tents and suitcases, made emergency runs to Safeway, and organized a crabbing trip.

Barb and Rosie, Paul's two single sisters, took all the

middle-sized nieces and nephews down to the beach to build elaborate sand castles, a yearly tradition. Enthusiastic kids dug in the sand or scampered for buckets of water. The castles were finished in late afternoon, just as the tide was coming in and, as always, the children hated the thought of all their efforts getting washed away.

"Let's pray!" suggested 10-year-old Emily, so all the children gathered around their castle and prayed that, just this once, God wouldn't let the waves wash it away.

In the evening, we crowded into the living room, ate homemade snacks, and talked. Waves of boisterous little boys rushed through the room as Anne cuddled her grandbabies; Rosie updated us on her frustrating love life; and Wilton and his sons talked about grass seed.

Like waves rolling up on the beach, the familiar rhythms of family surrounded me. But underneath I sensed a troubling current of change. I had thought of it first when Anne relinquished her spot as the family organizer and, instead, Lois coordinated the motel and meals. But I saw other indications as well.

One evening, we cooked up a huge pot of clam chowder. Before every family dinner there is a moment when, almost by instinct, the conversations hush, the children stop playing and join their parents, and Wilton, or whoever is hosting the meal, asks the blessing on the food or chooses someone else to do it. This time, however, we were at a motel, and no one was host. There was a pause—who was in charge? Then Paul said quietly, "Dad, would you ask the blessing?"

It was a simple question, but to me it symbolized another change—Wilton, like his wife, was stepping back and letting someone else take over.

We bowed our heads as Wilton led in prayer, but my

thoughts were interrupted by my 7-year-old son, who turned to me and whispered, "Mom! Did you ever notice that Grandpa always starts his prayers, 'We thank thee, Lord'?"

I smiled and nodded. Like the sand castle that washed away despite the children's prayers, changes had come to this family in the last 16 years. But like the sand and the sea, their faith and love—and Grandpa's prayers—hadn't changed a bit.

Angels on Interstate 5

I grew up on a farm beside a gravel road in Minnesota, where I learned to wave at every passing car when I was working outside, and at every vehicle I met when I was driving. Not to wave was to be stuck-up, unfriendly, unneighborly.

Now, in Oregon, a narrow cow pasture separates our home from I-5. We are close enough to hear every car that goes by and read brand names on motorhomes, but too far away to distinguish faces. We are close enough to wave, but we don't.

When we first moved to this house, the constant stream of traffic made me vaguely apprehensive. It never stopped. The roar of passing vehicles was always there, and when I went to bed at night I could still see a long line of headlights coming from the south. I wanted to go out on the overpass and hang up a sign: GO HOME AND GO TO BED.

For the first weeks I didn't like to be home alone with the children after dark. I felt vulnerable, this close to all those passing people. One of them might be waiting for a chance to harm us. My logical husband finally convinced me that this was unlikely. If someone wanted to hurt us, they would not bother to climb a fence, find their way through a pasture, and stumble over an electric fence in the dark to do so.

So my fears and apprehensions eased and the freeway traffic became part of the scenery. Now I seldom notice vehicles, and the noise fades into the background. Although thousands of people drive by every day, they seem like faceless forms, insulated from my life even though they pass nearby. I suppose we are only part of the scenery to them, a farmhouse between Eugene and Albany.

But, to my delight, every now and then someone emerges from the background to become a real person whose life connects with ours.

Our children's pastime of "honking trucks" was our first way of communicating with individual drivers. Of course, the children think of it only as a fun diversion on walks. We stop on the overpass above the northbound lanes, and they pump their fists in the air and wait anxiously to see how many trucks honk their horns. Many of them oblige. From the smiles on their faces, I can tell the moment makes my children and the truck drivers equally happy.

Apparently some of these truck drivers have decided to keep honking at us, because every day I hear a honk or two from passing trucks. It makes me feel like I'm back in Minnesota, with friendly neighbors waving as they drive by. Mentally I wave back—Hello to you, too, whoever you are.

Sometimes a freeway misfortune brings drivers to our door—a car breakdown, running out of gas. We hand them the phone or a container of lawn mower gasoline. Without exception they are grateful and generous, insisting on paying $5 for a gallon of gas. Are these people the angry drivers that crowd my back bumper on I-5? If they are, they turn into likable people when they are out of their vehicles and we meet on our front porch.

We try to be as helpful as possible, not only to be neighborly, but also because the Bible reminds us that the strangers we help may be angels in disguise. So after someone leaves, our family starts guessing—were they or weren't they? The young couple who landed in the ditch. . .hmmm . . .do angels have blue hair and rings in their noses? Who knows? Or maybe it was the well-dressed businessman who ran out of gas. Or the desperate fellow who was late for a job interview.

One evening my husband worked late and the children and I were eating outside at the picnic table. Two young men walked in from the freeway. They had been pulling a car on a trailer and it slid off, so could they have some boards to make a ramp to load the car again? I found a few of my husband's 2x6s for them, then offered them some of the tacos I had made for supper.

"No thanks," they said, "but we'd take some ice water." I gave it to them, and as they turned to leave they offered to pay for the boards. This time I said "no thanks" but said my husband would appreciate if they returned the boards or placed them where we could easily get them.

As soon as they left, the speculating began. Weren't they nice? Mom, do angels eat? Surely it was a sign of angel-ness to forgo the tacos but drink the water. Now, the crucial test—would they return the boards or not? (Why would they need 2x6s in heaven?) The children waited anxiously, but the young men never returned and the boards disappeared. Too bad. Maybe next time.

As I said, most of the time I-5 fades into the background of our lives. But we never know when someone will emerge from the freeway to become a real person with a face and personality. So we listen for the honk, we answer the knock on the door, and we watch for angels.

1000-Story House

*M*y husband and I sat in an office in Albany and signed a bewildering array of papers for 45 minutes. When we finished, the house was ours.

I remember when I'd first drive by this house, nearly 20 years ago. It always came looming at me on one of the sharp curves on Powerline Road, near Harrisburg—a plain, boxy, white farmhouse, with only a few small trees beside it to soften the sharp edges. It looked like a child's block, tossed onto the corner of a kitchen table.

What I didn't realize was that the house belonged to Wilton and Anne Smucker, whose son I'd marry three years later.

Paul and I have lived in nine houses in the last 15 years, from an apartment in Woodburn, Oregon, to a cabin in the Canadian bush, to a farmhouse whose dining room was once a chicken house. We enjoy travel, new experiences, other cultures.

In the last few years, however, we find ourselves wanting to home in, settle down, and find a place we can make our own. Too soon, our children will be off on adventures of their own. We want them to leave with a sense of place, of roots, of their role in the family history.

So we are buying Paul's parents' house, that plain, square house on Powerline Road. It is, I have discovered, a two-story house with a thousand stories.

According to my father-in-law, the house was built in 1911 by a man named Daniel Kropf. It has been in the family ever since. Now, Daniel's great-great-grandchildren will be moving into it.

I hope someday one of my kids will find the bullet hole. Back in the height of World War I, the story goes, Daniel was bishop of the Harrisburg Mennonite Church down the road. Not only did he preach in German, but he discouraged his flock from joining the Army. His views didn't make him popular in the community, of course, and one morning Daniel found a yellow stripe painted around the church and the doors padlocked shut. Not long after that, someone came by and shot at Daniel's house. The hole is still there, somewhere, the family says.

Daniel's granddaughter Elsie was next to live in the house, with her husband Vernon and their six little Knox sons, who turned out to be the Knox Brothers, well-known Southern-Gospel singers.

I'm sure my children will wonder about the funny-looking fiberboard rectangles all over the walls and ceilings of two of the bedrooms upstairs. I'll tell them that Elsie's son Wayne and his family were the next ones to live there, and those rooms were the Knox Brothers' sound studio. If my kids think the fiberboard looks funny, I suppose they should have seen the walls when they were also covered with egg cartons to further improve the acoustics.

The house was transferred to a different branch of the family tree in 1979. Daniel Kropf, the original builder, had a son, Frank, who married a widow named Annie Smucker. Annie had two young sons named Orval and Herman from her first marriage. Orval turned out to be my husband's grandfather, but first he and Herman gave the family tree a violent twist when they married their step-father Frank's younger sisters.

I've had this explained to me a dozen times by the great-aunts, but I still have to draw diagrams on the back of an envelope when my 6-year-old asks me how he is related to his little friend Spencer. (Let's see, Spencer would be a grandson of Frank and Annie's son Lloyd, so *this* way you would be third cousins, and *that* way you're half second cousins once removed.)

So in 1979, Orval's son Wilton and his wife Anne bought the house, relocated it a mile up the road, and moved in with their seven children. They turned the house 180 degrees in the process, forever confusing the relatives who stopped in, who would gesture toward the bay window that they needed to run in to Harrisburg, when actually Harrisburg was toward the kitchen. Wilton's family also removed the egg cartons (filling a tin can with tacks, recalls Anne) and turned the sound studio into two bedrooms.

I entered the picture at this point, some months after I saw the house for the first time, when I got to know Wilton and Anne's daughter Barb. We'd sit crosslegged on the beds in the bedroom at the top of the stairs and talk for hours with the sun shining through the leaves of the walnut tree and into the tall windows. Barb did her best that summer to match me up with her handsome brother Paul, who had just finished his first year of teaching and was working nights in Wilton's grass-seed warehouse. Unfortunately, I seldom saw him because he spent his days sleeping in the southeast bedroom with the shades drawn tight.

My children love the story of the first time I ate a meal at "Grandma's house." We were sitting around the oval kitchen table one evening, just as we would so many times in the future. The china cabinet was behind me and the two potted philodendrons twined up to the ceiling and then on around the room. Anne was hopping out of her chair every minute or two to make sure everyone was properly served. Paul was there that night, and after the meal he impressed me enormously when he politely thanked his mother for the dinner. (So you see, children, it always pays to mind your manners!)

That was my first meal with the family, I tell the kids, and thankfully the only one where I dropped my ice cream into my lap when dessert was served. I managed to keep cool and Paul never noticed. But eventually Barb's efforts paid off and he noticed me. And now here we are, 18 years later, getting ready to move into that same house. It still looks just like it always has, except now it looks like home.

And the house is ready, too, waiting for our children to come and create a thousand stories of their own.

Road Trip

We pulled into our driveway at 7 on a Friday evening. I sang the "Hallelujah Chorus," and the kids burst from the van in a jubilant explosion. First we wandered through the house and around the yard, getting reacquainted with our home. Then we carried our luggage into the house and put everything away—shoes into closets, dirty sweatshirts into hampers, and the mayo into the fridge.

I also pulled out the memories and looked at them, one by one, then tucked them away where I could easily find them again: bubbles on Bear Tooth Pass, a penny in pickle juice, heads of styrofoam and heads of stone, a waterless day in Wisconsin, and my daughter's "Grandma's House Gazette." Good memories, and also some not-so-pleasant memories, that I hoped, with time, would turn into something positive.

Taking our family on a four-week road trip, after school and before harvest, seemed like a good idea last winter. By the middle of May, however, I wasn't so sure. The preparations seemed endless, and my list grew to five pages: "Ask Kropfs to mow the lawn. Find someone to keep Matt's hamster. Pack: sleeping bags, contact-lens solutions, atlas, flashlight, sandwich supplies, diapers." I weighed all this preparation against what I hoped to accomplish: Seeing people and places, making memories, getting away, reflecting.

My sister-in-law warned me that driving to the Midwest from Oregon is like putting your whole family in the bathroom and staying there for three days.

Actually, all the hours in the van were less stressful than we expected. Except for the times Emily and Ben played Trouble and disagreed every 28 seconds about which way the dice lay, most of us got along. As the hours and miles stretched on, we often settled into a sort of hypnosis, lost in our own thoughts, focusing on tiny details. Like Emily's penny, which I think of now sometimes when I put dill pickles on sandwiches. We found the penny, battered and tarnished, at a rest area in Iowa on our way home. Emily wanted to polish it.

"I need vinegar and salt, right, Mom?"

"Right," I told her, "and we don't have either one, so you'll have to wait until we get home."

But Emily persisted, holding the penny in her hand and thinking of creative alternatives. "Hey, the pickles!" she exclaimed, miles later. "Isn't there vinegar in the dill pickle juice?"

There was. We dropped the penny into a cup and poured the green liquid over it. Now: salt. We pondered for more hypnotic miles, then found an answer: the crumbs at the bottom of the pretzel bag. The penny soaked in this mess, and slowly Lincoln's head became visible.

Lincoln's head was much more obvious at Mt. Rushmore. Of course we had seen their pictures many times, but it was nothing like actually seeing those massive stone faces gazing out of the mountain. Sadly, the visitor's center, with its detailed displays on how this incredible project was completed, was almost deserted. In contrast, the gift shop, with its T-shirts and toothpick holders, was so full of people that I wouldn't let the children leave my side for fear I'd lose them in the crowd.

I admit, our skulls weren't exactly made of inch-thick styrofoam for the first half of our trip, but some of us felt like they were as we endured the pressure changes in the mountains while battling sore throats and earaches. Getting sick on vacation is an experience that, we hope, will eventually redeem itself as having drawn the family closer together, built our characters, or something equally valuable. During our week in Canada, as we visited, canoed, and fished in the area where we used to live, we discovered that the doctor shortage there is now so acute that even the doctors that delivered my babies refused to see us. So we altered our plans and headed for the best hospital in the world—Mom's house.

My parents' place in Minnesota is like the stereotypical "Grandfather's Farm" (red barn, white house, one cow, five chickens) featured in many of the storybooks I used to read to the children. It is also a restful retreat for adults, a place of endless discovery for kids, and a gold mine of memories. The young cousins explored Grandpa's haymow, hunted for kittens, and built a fort with straw bales. Amy discovered an old Royal typewriter in the basement and pounded out copies of a little newspaper she named the "Grandma's House Gazette."

"Sara Yoder (Grandma) made cinnamon rolls today," she wrote. "They smelled and tasted delicious. They are not available for sale, but if you ask for one, Grandma will probably give you one." She also noted, "Today there were several interesting games played in Grandma's basement. The noisiest ones were Rubber Band Fights and Mouse Trap. The rubber band fights were terminated because one player was harmfully injured."

The "harmfully injured" child was typical of the health crises we faced in Minnesota—momentarily frightening but turning out fine in the end. One of Dad's lambs was bottle-feeding so enthusiastically one day that it pulled the nipple off the bottle and swallowed it. A nephew ate a bad hot dog at my brother's house and threw up 40 or 50 times that night. Thankfully the rubber band fighter, the lamb, the nephew, and our family all recovered, and we left for Wisconsin refreshed and rested.

Paul's brother Phil and his family live in the middle of Wisconsin's dairy country. The electricity went off one morning while the last piece of toast was in the toaster. With 10 children, lots of mud and puddles, and no water in the faucets, we found it almost impossible to keep clean. Seven-year-old Ben, hunting for earthworms in the pasture, stepped in a fresh cow pie. Without electricity, he couldn't hose off his feet. I held the reeking shoe at arm's length and reminded myself that making memories was one of my goals for this trip.

I have a feeling that in summers to come, when I drink a glass of lemonade, I will also remember the children's business venture in Wisconsin. Ben and his cousin Caleb wanted to set up a lemonade stand and wouldn't give up, despite the obvious limitation of not having running water in the house.

"Mom, can we have a lemonade stand now?" they persisted. "Huh? Please? Can we mix up some lemonade now? Huh? Can we?"

At one point Caleb flew into the kitchen and grabbed a small bucket and funnel-type filter that they use for milking goats, then dashed off. Later, Ben informed me that they got the bright idea to take water from a puddle in the driveway, put it through the milk filter, and use it for making lemonade. They tasted the water and, hey, it wasn't bad. I was sure they'd get diarrhea or worse. Eventually, we got water from the neighbors, the lemonade was mixed, and the boys earned $1.20. And they didn't get sick.

We had taken along jump ropes, Frisbees, and a scooter to occupy the children at rest stops. We also took a spill-proof bottle of bubble soap for 2-year-old Jenny. Over and over, at rest areas all over the West, the older kids tried to teach her to hold the wand to her mouth, "No, Jenny, not *on* your mouth. Right in front, like this. And blow out, not in!" But Jenny couldn't seem to understand.

Years ago, my parents drove over Bear Tooth Pass, near the northeast entrance to Yellowstone Park, and Mom tried to describe it to me.

"You just go up and up and *up!*" she said. "I never saw anything like it. Oh, it's just . . . ." and she shook her head, unable to find the words.

Intrigued, we decided to try that route into Yellowstone. First, we found ourselves in a deep valley, with towering mountains on all sides. Looking around, we realized that the mountain to our left, impossibly steep and high, had a road on it. We caught glimpses of switchbacks—there . . . and up there . . . and oh, look, way up there! Was it actually our route, and would we actually end up way up there on top? Incredible.

We began ascending, grinding slowly up and up, stopping often to look way down below where we'd come from, and gasping at how far we still had to go. Then we'd move on, gradually upward. As we rounded one particularly awesome curve, with all of us gazing, open-mouthed, out the windows, we suddenly became aware of bubbles, a gentle whoosh of soap bubbles that drifted, sparkling, inside the front half of the van. We had been focused on the scenery outside, but now our attention was jerked back inside. Where did these bubbles come from?

Jenny, of course.

She sat in her car seat, grinning triumphantly. In the middle of Bear Tooth Pass, with everyone's attention elsewhere, Jenny had somehow reached the bubble soap and learned, all on her own, to blow bubbles. When we reached the top of the mountain, we felt like we were on top of the world. Jenny, proudly clutching the bubble wand, was without a doubt on the very top of hers.

In all, we traveled almost 7,000 miles and spent nine nights in motels, with all seven of us in one room.

Emily yelled, "Oh, no, I can't find my other sandal!" before approximately 18 rest stops. We saw 13 moose, and we ate at least 50 cheeseburgers.

Was it worth it? I ask myself now, looking over my five-page list one last time before I toss it. *Did I meet my goals?*

Yes, but maybe what really matters is that in the end we still loved each other, all of us were utterly happy to come back home, and we have a new file of memories, safely tucked away where we can easily find them again.

Winds of Change

A cold wind sweeps under the Burnside Bridge as my daughter Amy and I wander from booth to booth at Portland's Saturday Market. It's early— not yet 9—and people are still setting up: wind chimes, pottery, velvet hats. I buy a blue spoon rest to put on the kitchen stove at home—something to remind me of today. Then we walk on, shoulders hunched in the cold.

I remember that a warm wind was blowing the night Amy was born, almost 13 years ago. It was close to midnight when we left for the hospital. As I shuffled to the car, leaning on my husband's arm, the wind blew in over the meadow by our house, soothing and refreshing me.

In the pool of our lives, our first child was a rock that landed in the middle with a huge splash. Amy, two years later, was a leaf that fluttered down and floated gently on top. Those first few years she was tiny for her age, with a cloud of red-gold curls on her head—a quiet, calming presence in our lives.

Amy was never as talkative as her siblings. Instead, she stood back and watched the action, then came to me and carefully summed it up in a concise sentence or two, astonishing me with her vocabulary.

"Matthew turned on the faucet and my dress got all wet," she told me one day when she was barely 2. She wrote me her first note before she was 4 years old—I love U Mom— the word "love" represented by a fat, uncertain heart.

Until she was about 11, I thought Amy would always be this way—quiet, observant, affectionate. Then, like a sudden, chilling gust of wind, she began to change. I first noticed the physical changes, as she grew taller and sturdier. Next came a disquieting stage where she compared me with her friends' moms.

"Phebe's mom makes really good tetrazzini, Mom. Maybe you should get her recipe. Yours is okay but it tastes, well, kind of weird.

"Oh, Mom, can't you do something about those open shelves in the bathroom, with all our towels and stuff?

"When I grow up I want to be like Rita becasue she has lots of little children but she still has a clean house."

That stage soon passed, but the changes continue. She tries on personalities like outfits, switching moods and interests from day to day. I look at her and wonder what happened to the child I knew, how I should respond, who she will become. I seek for ways to reach her, for things we have in common.

This trip to Portland was my husband's idea. A few years ago, he suggested that I take each of our children on an expedition of some sort when they are 12 years old, and then he'll take them on a trip when they're 13. Bonding and memories, you know, and time spent one-on-one.

So, here we are, wandering the Saturday Market because the Lloyd Center doesn't open until 10. We caught the 6:30 Amtrak out of Albany, sipping tea and orange juice from the bistro car as the train swished past Woodburn. The Lloyd Center is our main destination for the day because Amy is "into" shopping. I seldom enjoy shopping, but this is her day; we'll shop.

We are two country girls in the big city, bent on adventure, finding our way together. Our map is our lifeline and we consult it often, our heads bent close together, our fingers touching on the bus routes.

We find the MAX stop near the Saturday Market and together we figure out how to get our tickets from the machine. Amy pushes the buttons; I insert a $10 bill. To our delight, the machine blesses us with a shower of Sacajawea coins in change, our first ones. We inspect them together, oblivious to the cold wind and the people around us.

I notice one of Portland's famous rose gardens on the map, not far from where we're going, and wonder if Amy would like to see it. "I mean, the roses wouldn't be blooming yet but I'm sure it would still be pretty."

"Mom, the Rose Garden is where the Blazers play basketball," Amy says quietly, like you would explain something to your grandma. She's right—and there it is, a big arena.

I need a map for this relationship, I think, *with all the routes marked.* When do I give in and when do I stand firm? Should I hug her if she says she doesn't want to be hugged? I want signs to indicate the landmarks: what will matter 20 years from now? What won't? Most of all, I wonder how to connect with this person she is becoming—confident, outgoing, with friends and interests (like Blazers basketball) apart from mine.

At the Lloyd Center, we wander from store to store, looking at clothes. She has Eddie Bauer tastes; I prefer Goodwill. At Sears, we buy her an outfit that's a nice compromise between her tastes, my tastes, and our budget. She hugs the package and thanks me, her eyes shining.

We take the MAX back to downtown and pore over the map at our table at Baskin-Robbins. We have an hour left—where should we go? Amy discovers a Daisy Kingdom logo on the map and wonders if I'd like to go there. Daisy Kingdom is the home of some of the prettiest fabrics in the country—of course I'd like to go. I used to dream of the day when Amy and I would plan projects together and shop for patterns and fabrics. We set out, standing on street corners to get our bearings, the map flapping in the wind.

Before long I am rummaging through stacks of fabrics in the discount room at Daisy Kingdom, lavishly promising Amy that she can have any she wants. Just as I discover a table of angelic pastels, I take a good look at Amy and realize that she is . . . bored.

"It's just that this fabric is kind of babyish," she explains.

She's right, of course. Most of Daisy Kingdom is designed for the preschool crowd. Her comment forces me to face the truth and my own disappointment: she is no longer a little girl, and despite all my hopes, she doesn't share my passion for sewing.

We walk the remaining blocks to the train station, Amy leading the way. The ride home is quiet; both of us are tired. Long after dark, we pull into our driveway, safe at home. She sits on the couch and shows everyone her purchases, telling about our day, flicking her long, red-gold braid over her shoulder.

I watch her, thinking about who she is and who she is becoming. All in all, this has been a beautiful journey, being her mom. She will go places I will never go, but I believe she will always find her way back home, a warm and gentle wind blowing into my life, soothing and refreshing.

Muddy Creek

I'm looking at ordinary things in a new way these days, making a conscious effort to be like my son and not—God bless her anyhow—like my aunt.

In 1983, after I had lived in Oregon for two years, I went back home to Minnesota for a year. One weekend my mother and I drove down to Kalona, Iowa, to spend a few days with relatives—Mom's, mostly, but we also made a dutiful trek to Dad's sister Erma's house.

Erma was Amish, and one of the most talkative people I have ever known. She would lean forward with her chin in one hand and with two fingers pushing into her cheek, talking steadily and batting her eyelashes.

When we arrived, we seated ourselves in her dining room and I took the hickory rocker she offered me. After one attempt at conversation—that was instantly interrupted by Erma—I gave up on talking and decided to keep track of how often she interrupted my mother. In the next hour, Mom made exactly five attempts to speak but never got to finish a sentence. Each time, Erma cut her off mid-sentence and went rattling on.

Somewhere in this amazing monologue, Erma told us about her Western Trip, which is a sort of pilgrimage that many Midwesterners make at least once in their lifetimes. The Amish, who don't have cars or cameras, hire a driver and come home with souvenirs of Yellowstone Park, the coast, and the redwoods. Mennonites come home with slides that they show at family gatherings, and everyone is awed by this incredible geography, so different from the cornfields of Iowa.

Erma batted her eyelashes at me. "Oh, you were in Oregon, weren't you? We were in Oregon on our Western Trip, and we went to see a nice pond."

I thought, *Pond? A pond is where cows come to drink. Why on earth would she have gone to see a pond in Oregon?*

I didn't ask her, of course; I didn't have a chance. Erma must have noticed my puzzled expression because she said, "I have a picture of that place in Oregon," and gestured at a calendar on the wall. And there was a photograph of Crater Lake.

"Be gentle with your judgments of Erma," my dad always said. "She never had the opportunities you've had."

Erma died a few years later. As it turned out, she had the opportunity to see Crater Lake long before I did, and I thought of her recently when we took a quick family vacation and I looked out over Crater Lake for the very first time. Words were inadequate, so I drew in a deep breath of the cold air and exhaled in a long, enchanted "Ahhhhhhh." We drove around the lake and looked at it from a dozen different angles, amazed and awed.

I saw another body of water for the first time not long ago. Not that I hadn't looked at Muddy Creek a thousand times, but that day I really saw it. Our 7-year-old son Benjamin had begged me for weeks to walk along the creek with him so he could show me all his favorite places to play. Finally, one hot afternoon, I took the time to go with him.

Crossing the road, I was in charge, making sure we looked both ways. But as soon as we crossed, he became the guide and I followed.

Gingerly, I followed him through the gap under the fence. He led me across the pasture, hot and dry in the sun, to the welcome coolness of the shade along the creek.

Muddy Creek was wide, dark, and slow, with clumps of soft green moss growing at the edges and bits of sunlight sprinkled on top of the water.

Ben found the cow path and bounced along in his black sandals, stopping abruptly to show me his favorite spots. "Here's where I skip rocks. And one time I skipped a rock that was not round and not square! It was a triangle!

"Here are our forts. There's Emily's and here's mine."

Forts? I looked closer. Pieces of wood were stacked up beside one tree, an old coffee can stuck in the roots by another. All the hours he and his sister spent playing at their forts, and this is what they were?

Ben bounced on, running ahead, then coming back to tell me more. I could tell he felt at home here, that he was in love with this world of quiet creek and tall trees and flickering sunlight.

"I want to build a raft and go floating down the creek," he said. "I'll build it like a pallet and put jugs inside to make it float.

"Pretty soon we'll get to the bridge Dad made," Ben announced. And there it was, an old telephone pole laid across the water. I inched across, wanting to look at my feet but getting dizzy from the dark water flowing underneath. Ben reassured, "The water isn't very deep here, so if you fall in, it's okay."

Across the creek, the grass was taller and tangled bushes grew along the water. "Here's where I pick blackberries," Ben told me, "and there's our warehouse—sometimes I stop in to see Dad."

He led me past the warehouse, down to the ford, where the little cousins go swimming. For the next half hour, he showed me how to float with the current and hunt water skippers, long-legged spidery bugs that prance on the surface of the water. Then it was time to go home, with seeds from the dry grass clinging to our wet feet, past the warehouse, along the creek, over the bridge, among the trees, under the fence, across the road, and home.

I thought a lot about Ben and the creek over the next few days. I had never known that he found so many things to do along Muddy Creek, that he loved it so much, that when he looked at it he saw not an ordinary little creek but a magical river of possibilities.

To me, Muddy Creek had always been, well, just Muddy Creek. Maybe I wasn't so different, after all, from Aunt Erma, who looked at Crater Lake and saw a nice pond.

Oregon Coast

I always know when we need a trip to the coast. Whenever the daily details of dishes and bills and overdue library books close in like a cloud of mosquitoes, or when the irritations in our marriage become larger than the things we appreciate, I know it's time.

I found myself at that point in mid-January. Paul, who is practical and efficient, picked up his phone and calendar, and three days later, we were headed west, the tightly coiled wires in my head slowly unwinding as we drove through the hills.

Somehow, I finished the complicated logistics of leaving five children for two days and I could relax at last, leaning my seat back for a nap as Paul drove and the sun broke through the clouds like a heavenly blessing.

I knew I'd feel even better when I got rid of the two pillows in the black garbage bag in the back seat.

My husband stole them last August.

We had spent the night at the LaurenSea Motel south of Newport, a homey place where the owners happily accommodate large families and the children can walk to the beach without crossing the road. We were all packed up to leave when Paul and I made a last sweep through our suite.

While I looked under beds for socks, he snatched the two pillows off the hide-a-bed, thinking they were ours, and stuffed them in the back of the van. I found them that evening when we unpacked. Horrified, I immediately called the motel to explain.

"Yes, my husband noticed they were gone," Mrs. Motel said, a bit coldly, not that I blamed her. "But you don't need to pay for them," she added. "Just return them the next time you come to the coast."

In a special jar in my mind, I accumulate our times at the ocean, much like the jar of seashells in our pantry that collects another precious shell or two every time we return from the beach. I knew the story of Paul and the pillows would eventually be funny, a story I could pull out and chuckle over for years, at Paul's expense.

One of the most vivid memories in my collection is the first time I saw the Pacific Ocean, when I was 19 years old. Coming from the Midwest, I pictured it as a glorified lake.

Nothing could have prepared me for that overwhelming moment of walking across the beach and seeing the ocean: a vast, churning, gray expanse that went on and on until it melted into the horizon.

Enormous waves surged inland, one after another, bulging out of the water and rising up and up until suddenly, the top edge folded over and the whole thing collapsed, roaring to shore with an angry, terrifying power. Then, each wave dissolved into a thin sheet of water on the sand that kept coming and coming, right at me, like it was determined to sweep me into an infinite restlessness. And all around me, I heard a deep, solemn, unending roar that seemed to fill the universe.

It was stunning, overpowering, beautiful.

Everything about the coast had a rugged and frightening beauty—the enormous logs lying placidly on the beach, far out of reach of the waves, but a reminder of the power of the winter storms that tossed them there. Cliffs that reared up harshly at the edge of the beach. Cape Perpetua Lookout, looming hundreds of feet above us, and the Devil's Churn down below, where the force of the waves was constricted into a narrow, rocky channel and the water rolled and boiled with a living fury.

Nothing had the peaceful, manageable beauty of sheep grazing in the Willamette Valley's grass fields, or the well-behaved lakes back in Minnesota, where trees on the opposite shore gave perspective, and small waves lapped delicately at the edges.

The ocean seemed too fierce and uncontrollable for affection, that first day. But since then, I have come to love it, not like I enjoy lilacs and country roads, but more like I love God, with a healthy dose of fear and respect.

Now, we go to the coast for many reasons—for fun, for refreshment, for perspective, or simply for tradition. Each trip is the same and each is different; each is a shell to drop into my jar and cherish, afterward.

I go to a church ladies' retreat every February, in a house overlooking the ocean. There, two dozen women relax and rediscover themselves, laughing hysterically, eating and baring their souls in quiet conversations.

Some summers, we drive to a house on the coast with a vanload of adolescents, children from church who memorized 50 Bible verses to earn three days of camp.

We try to keep up with them, and at 2 a.m., we massage our muscles, sore from hiking, and try to fall asleep while the girls giggle upstairs and the boys in the living room make dreadful noises and muffle their laughter with sleeping bags and pillows.

The coast is one place where it's perfectly acceptable to do something for no other reason than because we've always done it this way.

The annual aunts-and-cousins' day at the beach always,

always, includes sand castles, a shivering dip in the ocean, taffy at Aunt Belinda's in Newport, ice cream at the Dairy Queen in Philomath, and made-up stories from Aunt Rosie all the way home—for anyone who can stay awake to hear them.

I save a certain jacket for the beach, a hooded gray sweatshirt perfect for walks in the wind and rain. A garage sale find, it reads Santa Clara Women's Basketball on the front, a logo that always amuses the teenage nephews when the whole Smucker clan assembles at the beach.

"How's your team doing?" one of them asks me.

Another one adds, "Did you make a touchdown at your practice last night?"

"Touchdown?" I ask. "Isn't that football?" They laugh, surprised. Aunt Dorcas is sharper than they realized.

We go to the coast for perspective. The petty details are left behind, and, in the vast scope of the ocean, we rediscover what's truly important. The moist wind whips the dust and cobwebs out of my mind and leaves behind only what's strong and solid.

Often, I take along things to do—a book to read, a letter to write, a cross-stitch project. I never get them done. These things belong to my life in the valley, where keeping busy and getting things done seem desperately important. At the coast, they diminish in size and the things that matter—friendships, marriage, God, and family—regain their true significance.

Most of all, I enjoy the times that Paul and I get away by ourselves.

A marriage can get tired over time, frayed with silent anger and bruised with small irritations. Away from the daily patterns of behavior, we talk things out and find ways to change and heal.

We went to nearby Florence in January, where we

walked on the beach and stayed at Driftwood Shores, keeping the balcony door ajar all night so we could listen to the waves.

The next day, we wandered around Old Town Florence, and Paul waited with unusual patience while I explored the little art galleries.

Then we headed up the coast toward Newport, each curve in the road bringing another scene of damp green mountainsides or waves draping themselves over rocks and sand.

At the LaurenSea Motel, I hauled the black garbage bag to the front door.

"Ah, yes, the pillow thieves," said Mrs. Motel.

I apologized. She smiled. We left.

Normally, I would have felt irritated at Paul for wanting me to return the pillows to the office. After all, he stole them. But this was at the coast, so it didn't seem important. Hadn't he indulged me at the art galleries?

What really mattered was having the pillows off my conscience and going home, refreshed and rested, to drop another seashell in my jar.

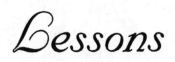

Lessons

The Cat Who Came to Stay

O n my morning walks, earlier this summer, I often saw a cat slip into the tall grass beside Substation Drive. Figuring she belonged to Aunt Susie down the road, I didn't give the cat much thought except to notice that she looked like a registered Holstein cow with that pure white fur with distinct black patches.

Our children had been asking for a cat off and on ever since we moved into this house. I always said no, knowing that cats on this corner never lived long because of all the traffic. I didn't need the guilt of seeing the children get attached to a cat and then having it hit by a seed truck. Furthermore, I didn't want a cat using the sandbox for a litter box.

But one day, out of the blue, the black-and-white cat decided to invade our lives. I saw her sitting on the front porch one morning, looking mournfully at the front door. She meowed piteously when she saw me, "Mwarrr . . . Please help me. Pleeeeease."

"What do you want, *Katz*?" I asked in Pennsylvania German, since cats understand it better than English. But the cat didn't answer.

Where did this animal come from, and why did she pick us? I checked for a collar. None. I called Aunt Susie. No, it wasn't hers. The cat looked healthy, and showed no signs

129

of pregnancy or of kittens. And she couldn't be hungry, as the children fed her bread, milk, and tuna—Bumble Bee, not store-brand. If she was looking for a husband, why did she pick our catless house? She wasn't dumped here, I reasoned, because I had seen her in the neighborhood for weeks.

"Go home, *Katz*," I told her. "We don't need a cat, or want one either. Why are you hanging around here?"

But the cat refused to go, and every day she sat on the porch and meowed at me reproachfully. She reminded me of *Gokum*, the way she marched into my life uninvited and wouldn't leave.

I first saw Bertha—"*Gokum*"—11 years ago when we moved onto a First Nations reservation in Canada to teach school. Her husband was the village chief, and they owned the little cabin we moved into, next door to their house. We called her *Gokum*, Cree for Grandma.

I came to the village with lofty ideals and high expectations, full of wisdom that I was eager to share with the local people. *Gokum's* stern face and piercing black eyes soon let me know that she thought I was the ignorant one, a silly white lady who didn't know how to take care of her own children. Since *Gokum's* English was as limited as my Cree, she used her grandchildren as go-betweens.

We lived on the shore of a lake, and the children were delighted to find that our house was surrounded by sand. On our second day there, the children sat beside the front steps digging in it.

"Our *gokum* says your children shouldn't play in the sand," the grandchildren told me. "They might get sand in their eyes."

"Don't let her intimidate you," my husband Paul said. "Of

130

course they can play in the sand."

So, trembling, I let them. Soon I heard a swishing on the front steps. *Gokum* was sweeping the sand off the steps, muttering angrily.

A few days later a stiff wind blew in. Walking down to the lake for water, Paul noticed a string tied across the path, a foot or so above the ground.

"Our *gokum* did that," the grandchildren explained. "Your children aren't supposed to go farther than that when it's windy and the waves are high."

I was humiliated and furious. Did she actually think I didn't know enough to keep my children away from the lake on a stormy day? Why was she picking on us, and why wouldn't she leave us alone?

When I did laundry in my wringer washer one day in mid-winter, *Gokum* came in the front door, without knocking, and plunged her hand into the rinse water. Talking rapidly in Cree, she grabbed a pail of hot water and dumped it into the rinse tub.

"But *Gokum*," I protested feebly, "I *like* to rinse my clothes in cold water." She didn't understand, or pretended not to.

After I hung my laundry on the clothesline and went back inside, I'd often see her adjusting a prop here and rehanging a towel over there.

"My *gokum* moved your sheets on the clothesline," the granddaughter said. "She didn't want them blowing against the tree."

I fumed about *Gokum* for the first few months, irritated at her for invading my life, wishing she would leave me alone. But by the time we left the reservation, three years later, I actually liked her. I knew then what she knew all along—I really had been ignorant about the First Nations culture and surviving in the North. She helped me in the way her people help each other, by seeing a need and meeting it without a lot of formalities.

Recently, I finally realized that the cat had done the same thing.

My sister and her husband and three boys came to visit us about a week after the cat first came to stay. Sleeping on the trampoline is a summer tradition at our house, and my two oldest nephews looked forward to it for months. At 10:30, before I went to bed, I took a flashlight out to the trampoline to check on them one last time. In the dim light I noticed an odd lump at the end of Jason's sleeping bag.

"It's that cat," he whispered, grinning. "It curled up by my feet."

Over their cereal the next morning the boys informed me that the cat ended up between their pillows, and every night the scene was repeated. No sooner would they settle down for the night than the cat would leap up on the trampoline and curl up, utterly contented at last, on their pillows.

"She slept by my head again, just like always," Keith said one morning. "This will be my best memory of this summer."

My sister and her family have left, but the cat is still here. She dozes under the car, catches mice in the fescue field, and meows only when she's hungry. She lets our 2-year-old color her back with blue sidewalk chalk. We are discussing names—Paul likes Holstein, Amy likes *Katz*, and Matt likes Daisy Mae. I went to Safeway and bought a bag of cat food, a big one.

Will she live long on this notorious corner? I wonder, anticipating the guilt. The cat twines around my ankles, reminding me that she came of her own free will, our children have a new pet to love, and two little nephews have warm memories of a furry Holstein cat hopping on the trampoline to keep them company in the dark.

Maybe what she was telling me so plaintively, when she first came, is that we needed a cat, and we didn't know it. But she did, and here she was, ready to meet that need in the only way she knew how.

Often, the things we don't know we need come into our lives without knocking.

Turning Forty

I'm going to be 40 on Saturday.

My mother told me the story of my birth every year when I was a child, how she knew I'd soon be here and Aunt Vina was rushing her to the hospital. The car kept getting hot, Mom would recall, and they had to stop three or four times to put water in the radiator.

They pulled in at one farm where a slow, talkative man wanted to discuss the crops and the weather. Vina grabbed the bucket from his hand, dashed to the pump, filled the bucket, dumped it in the radiator, and roared off, leaving the bewildered farmer behind.

And I was born just minutes after they reached the hospital. Another daughter, Mom would say. She couldn't believe how fortunate she was.

Now, approaching my birthday, it seems that turning 40 is something to dread, dismal and inevitable, somewhere between a disease and a curse.

"I'm 39 and holding," women tell me, grimacing. Party decorations for 40-year-olds are heavy on somber colors, gravestones, and banners shouting, "Over the hill!" My daughters giggle over the birthday cards at WinCo, all of which imply that next week my teeth will fall out. A bumper sticker announces, "I'd rather be 40 . . . than pregnant."

Most of all, I hear that mysterious phrase, "Life begins at 40."

It showed up recently at my sister-in-law's party, in blue icing on top of her cake. "What was it before then?" she wondered.

That saying also appeared, ironically, at my grandmother's funeral almost 14 years ago. Even if she knew what an identity crisis was, Grandma would never have bothered to have one, especially about turning 40. Her position in the family grew more powerful with each year, and she was as proud of her age as an Amish woman lets herself get about anything. When she was in her 90s we'd get postcards from her in her spidery handwriting. "I went to the John T. Yoder reunion in Buchanan County. There were 128 people there, and I was the oldest one."

Amish sermons—long, German, and preached without notes—often wander down unexpected rabbit trails. "Our deceased sister lived to be almost 104," the first preacher said at Grandma's funeral. "Now the *Englishers* have a saying, 'Life begins at 40,' because they don't like to grow older and they try to convince themselves it's not so bad. But we know that age doesn't really matter when it comes to serving God, and Sister Barbara served God for many years both before and after she was 40."

"Life begins at 40" was the only English phrase in that entire 45-minute sermon, and the only thing that my husband, bored and uncomfortable on the backless benches, understood.

It was also the only thing the second preacher had understood. A Dunkard from a neighboring church, he looked Amish but didn't speak German, and was asked to preach for the benefit of the *Englishers*, like my husband in the audience.

"I noticed that our brother thinks that life begins at 40," he said, halfway through his half-hour sermon. "But I believe I disagree with him. That is something that worldly people say because they don't like to grow older and they try to convince themselves it's not so bad. But we all know . . . ."

He went on to repeat what the first speaker said, thinking he was saying the opposite. Ever since, I have associated turning 40 with a vague sense of pathetic miscommunication.

Watching a stream of friends and relatives approach this milestone, I came to associate it most of all with a powerful restlessness.

"I have this longing for a baby girl," my sister e-mailed from Yemen a few years ago. "I love my three boys, I'm happy with them, this would not be a good time or place to have a baby . . . but I still have this incredible longing for a girl."

My sister-in-law, Bonnie, burst into the church nursery one Sunday and announced, "I'm going to open a bakery and go into foster care!"

We all looked at her, dumbfounded.

"I've felt so restless for the last year, and last week I decided what I'm going to do."

We all thought, *She's turning 40.*

"I want to do something *bad*," my brother's wife Geneva wailed on the phone. "I was always so good when I was a teenager," she went on, "and now I have this terrible urge to do something bad."

Thankfully, I've seen all of these women emerge intact on the other side of 40. Becky went back to work as a nurse instead of having another baby. Bonnie had another baby instead of opening a bakery. And Geneva managed to keep on being good until the urge to be bad disappeared.

So far, the restlessness hasn't reached me, but I expect it to hit when my youngest child goes to school. But I still face the realities of growing older, of no longer being young in a world that values youth above wisdom. Paradoxically, we all want to live a long time, but we don't want to grow old.

Often, I find, the noisiest voices in our culture have the most damaging messages, and the voices that I strain to hear speak the most truth.

"Gray hair is a crown of splendor," the Bible says, quietly nudging my conscience as I carefully isolate and pluck another wiry gray strand.

"You're going to celebrate, aren't you?" my friend Anita asks me.

Celebrate? No one had ever asked me that question, and it hadn't occurred to me to celebrate. Anita, it turns out, loves birthdays, loves to celebrate the years, loves to tell people how old she is.

"The older I get, the more I feel like I can be who I was meant to be," she says.

My friend Marilyn was a celebrating sort of person who laughed a lot, silently, her shoulders bobbing up and down. As I recall, she was too busy trying to stay alive to agonize about her approaching fortieth birthday. She was in remission one summer evening, her hair grown in short and curly after chemotherapy, when I saw her sitting on the front steps watching her 2-year-old daughter prancing on the sidewalk in her new summer sandals. Marilyn was laughing, oblivious to me, absorbed in this beautiful child skipping back to her, over and over, and announcing proudly, "I have new sandals, Mom!"

Four months later, Marilyn was dead, just days before she would have been 40 years old.

It may be a wild ride, and I might have to stop now and then to refill the radiator. But I've decided to listen to the quiet voices telling me to celebrate turning 40. I'll do it in honor of Marilyn, who never had the chance.

And someday, for Grandma's sake, I'll write a post card in spidery handwriting, "I went hiking in Switzerland. There were 25 of us, and I was the oldest one there."

Judgment Day

Glancing slyly around the courtroom, I compared myself to the others, wondering if I had any chance of impressing the judge.

Let's see. I'm older and more conservative than the neon-striped eyebrows, younger and skinnier than the plump polyester, better dressed than all the baggy khakis, more pious-looking than the gray ponytail.

Then, my conscience yanked me back to the truth. I was guilty. Despite my appearance, I knew I was guilty, guilty, guilty of driving 44 miles per hour in a 25 mile-per-hour zone in Philomath on June 23. And I was about to be judged.

June 23 was the last day of a family reunion in the Coast Range near Logsden. My husband Paul and our oldest son Matt had left early to get back to the warehouse and harvest, and I had a frustrating morning. The sausage-and-egg casserole burned when I made breakfast for the whole crowd. My 16-year-old daughter Amy was sick in bed and vomiting into a wastebasket. And I had to pack up with the reluctant help of two younger children who kept drifting off to play basketball.

We finally left with four of our children and two nephews. Half an hour later, I stopped along the narrow road to let Amy throw up. At noon, we reached Philomath. I bought gas while Amy moaned and the other kids complained of being hungry. Should I take time to buy lunch, I asked them, or cook something at home?

"Please, let's just go home," Amy begged, reclining in the front seat with agony in her eyes and her hand on her stomach.

"We can wait," the others said, generously.

Just before we passed Dairy Queen, I saw, at the same time, the police car and the speed-limit sign, and knew this was the final stroke of awfulness on an awful morning.

"You were going 44 in a 25 zone," the policeman said, smiling. "But if you show up in court, the judge is likely to reduce your fine if you have a good record. It's here in Philomath on the 13th of July." He handed me a yellow paper and left.

One hundred seventy-five dollars! Heavy-hearted, I drove home, put Amy to bed, cooked macaroni and cheese for the others, and burst into tears telling Paul about my morning.

Counting on the policeman's word that the judge would be lenient, I decided to appear in court rather than pay the fine by mail.

For the next few weeks, the impending court date dangled like a spider at the edge of my vision. I pondered the heavy theology of it all, of sin, guilt, and judgment to come.

What would it be like? Maybe it was a mistake not to watch TV all these years, since surely those courtroom shows would have given me some idea of what to expect.

My family tried to be helpful. "Be sure not to chew gum," 14-year-old Emily offered. "It's not respectful. At least that's what Randy said."

Randy is her Sunday-school teacher, known for letting the discussion wander down rabbit trails.

Amy instructed, "Don't forget to tell him you had a sick daughter and hungry kids. Make sure he knows you went 20 years without being stopped."

Emily said, "Maybe you shouldn't, because he'll think you're bragging."

Another day, Amy told me, "I have a verse for you, Mom. I found it this morning. 'When you are brought before . . . rulers and authorities, do not worry about how you will defend yourselves or what you will say, for the Holy Spirit will teach you at that time what you should say.'"

"But what about the little speech you told me to prepare about my sick daughter and hungry kids?"

Amy didn't know. That was between me and the Holy Spirit.

"Panty hose," said Geneva, my sister-in-law. "Don't wear denim. Something nice."

I chose a summery lavender dress I bought at St. Vincent de Paul.

"*That?*" Amy said. "Isn't that way too dressy?"

"It makes me feel confident. That's what matters."

At the Philomath town hall, I signed in at a table in the back of the courtroom, where a woman in a denim skirt—so much for Geneva's advice—handed me a form and told me I'd be third in line.

I found a seat on one of the dirty, cream-colored chairs and listened to the conversation behind me between Gray Ponytail and Baggy Khaki.

"This your first time?" the older man asked.

"No, I got a 37 in a 25 zone one time, and a 45 in a 25, a 75 in a 55, a 94 in a 65, a failure to stop, and a failure to use turn signal. Got my license suspended a couple times."

"Whoa, man. You need some liposuction on that heavy foot."

I smiled, comparing his record and mine. And then my smugness evaporated as a young clerk announced, "Judge

Larry Blake. All rise."

A large man in a sweeping black robe strode in, and I went weak with fear, awe, and sudden visions of Judgment Day. All have sinned, the Scriptures say, and I was guilty.

The judge sat behind a raised platform, whacked his gavel, and told us to sit down at the table in the order we signed in. We could plead guilty, not guilty, or no contest, and then we would have a chance to say something.

Plump Polyester was second. Honest, she didn't see the person in the crosswalk until it was too late to stop.

"Okay," the judge said briskly. "Pick up this form and come in two weeks to discuss this further."

My turn. I sat at the table. "How do you plead?"

"Guilty."

"What do you have to say?"

I plunged in. "I know I'm guilty but I would like to ask for mercy because I haven't been stopped in 20 years and I've learned my lesson and (breathlessly) I had six children with me that day and five were hungry and my daughter was sick and I had to stop and let her throw up and (cue for pitiful Bambi eyes) I just wanted to get *home*.

"Hmmm," he said. "Kid throwing up. That's about as mitigating as you can get."

He paused. "All right. I'll reduce the fine." Then, surprisingly, he reminisced a bit. "I have three kids myself, and I remember one time, two of them were screaming in the back seat and I wanted to get home so badly, I would have driven through floods to get there."

The judge smiled. Smiled! I rose and took the paper from the young clerk. In the back, with my hands still shaking, I wrote a check for $130 and handed it to the woman in denim.

Neon Eyebrows, meanwhile, was at the table pleading no

contest. The judge snapped, "I find you guilty."

I, on the other hand, was absolved, forgiven, and no longer guilty. I stepped into the sunshine, and pondered a generous theology of mercy and forgiveness.

Then, I drove to the ARC, my favorite second-hand store, where the quiet aisles soothed me for the next half hour. A vanilla cone at Dairy Queen completed my recovery and I got in the car and drove away, east on that long highway through Philomath, heading home. Slowly.

Panic and Pears

We were almost ready to leave for school that Tuesday morning when we heard the news of the terrorist attacks on the East Coast.

I will never forget that image of my family in a frozen semi-circle in the living room, listening to the radio. The older children stood motionless in their new school uniforms, lunch boxes in hand, and the only movement in the room was 2-year-old Jenny, oblivious to the horror, flitting around us.

I was in a daze the rest of the day. *Life ought to stop and wait,* I thought. *How could the sun keep shining, and how could our neighbor possibly be out there plowing the field next to our house?*

I heard my husband talking on the phone, "Your intermediate ryegrass came in at 95 percent, and then I got your last two purities and . . . ."

"Please stop," I wanted to say. "Give me time to catch up."

I have always been a worrier, seeing incurable cancer in every lump and picking out songs for my husband's funeral when he is late coming home. If the phone rings at midnight, it means my mother had a heart attack. So, when this tragedy struck, I immediately thought of the worst possible consequences.

The future, which had looked safe and promising the day before, suddenly seemed full of frightening possibilities.

War, more terrorist attacks, economic collapse. I began to worry, not for myself, but for all the loved ones that I felt responsible for—my five children, and my parents, both in their eighties. How could I protect them?

A box of pears had sat ripening in my kitchen for several days. They were given to us, and in happier days I may or may not have bothered to can them. But now it suddenly seemed that the future fate of all my loved ones rested in this silly box of pears, and, by hook or by crook, I was going to preserve them.

Canning pears is labor-intensive work, best undertaken with a group of children or friends to help. I was home alone with Jenny, but I grimly attacked the job. I gathered the jars, washed the pears, and prepared the sugar syrup, convinced I was somehow protecting my family from hunger, war, famine, disease, and pain.

I cut the pears in half, cored them, and peeled them. Pears are slippery, and peeling one is like giving a minnow a bath. My frustration mounted as they kept slipping out of my hands and splashing back into the water.

My Sunday-school teachers used to tell us that all the Bible verses we memorized would come back to encourage us in difficult times. If ever I needed encouragement, it was then. As I worked on the pears, odd verses popped from my feverish mind, like wads of stuffing coming out of holes in an old pillow.

"In those days was Hezekiah sick unto death."

"As vinegar to the teeth and smoke to the eyes, so is a sluggard to those who send him."

Those verses didn't help me a bit.

The first jar was barely half full when the phone rang. Curling brown shreds clung to my fingers as I rushed to wash my hands and get to the phone in time. Then I was back to work, warding off all the terrible unknowns that threatened my family. Cut, core, peel, drop it in the jar.

Jenny climbed on a chair beside me and tried to climb onto the table. I set her back down, but soon she was up on the chair again, sticking her fingers into the sugar syrup.

Cold water dripped from my wrists, Jenny kept getting in my way, and the phone kept ringing. Yet I felt compelled to keep on, pushing against the darkness that seemed to surround everyone I cared for.

"Read to me, Mom," Jenny begged, pushing against my legs.

"Later, Honey," I said. "Please, just go play." Why couldn't she understand that I was doing this for her good, for her future, for all of us?

Jenny left, but only for a minute, then she was back, hugging my legs, her brown eyes pleading. "Read to me, Mom. Please?"

Finally, I laid down my knife, washed my hands, and admitted defeat. It was no use. This wasn't about pears at all, but about my own helplessness. The raw truth was that I was powerless to protect my family, and all the pears in the world couldn't shield them against the terrible shadowy dangers we faced. Even the burst of national unity in the country, inspiring as it was, failed to reassure me.

I held Jenny on my lap and reached for *Old Hat, New Hat*. As I droned halfheartedly about all the different hats, suddenly the promises I needed began to march, unbidden, through my mind, one by one, orderly and appropriate.

"I am with you always."

"God will meet all your needs."

"Perfect love drives out fear."

"I sought the Lord, and he heard me, and delivered me from all my fears."

A few days later, my neighbor called and wondered if I wanted the grapes left on her vine. "I'm guessing there's enough for 10 or 15 quarts of juice," she said.

I told her I'd take all she had.

The grapes were so thick on her vine that we only picked half of them, filling two big bowls, a box, and two buckets. I took them home and processed them, jar after jar of rich purple juice crowding my kitchen counters, 44 quarts in all. I saw them not as my desperate defense against calamity, but as rich provision from God, affirmation that God was taking care of us.

Since then, the sun has been coming up every morning, our neighbor planted his field, and my husband continues to discuss seed-test results on the phone. I bought a package of tulip bulbs to plant beside the house.

And when I honestly acknowledge my own helplessness, I find that I am least afraid of the future.

Escapes

I am tempted sometimes to think that happiness can be found in recreation, freedom from responsibility, and self-indulgence. But any break from daily duties soon outlives its usefulness, and I come to realize that it is the routine itself, the work and service and sacrifice, that ultimately has the most value and satisfaction.

The first few weeks of June brought me a long, much-needed vacation. With all the end-of-school activities in May, my calendar was so full that appointments were spilling into the margins. I felt like a dispatcher at Sherman Brothers Trucking—answering the phone; delegating jobs; and making sure that the drivers had cars, the non-drivers had rides, and the under-10s had supervision.

In addition, everyone needed clean clothes to wear every morning and a hot supper to sit down to together at 6 p.m.

There are women who thrive on activity and having 50 things going on at once, but I am not one of them. I enjoy silence and staying at home and my own little rituals, things that don't normally occur with five children in the house. So when people asked me how I felt about more than half the family leaving for two weeks, I confided, "You know, I feel really guilty about this, but I'm looking forward to having them gone."

Paul and our two oldest daughters left for Mexico one morning after school was out to visit our church's missionaries, a yearly duty for Paul as the church's missions committee chairman. A few days later, Matt, our oldest son, left with his Aunt Barb, a new doctor beginning an internship in Pennsylvania. She had invited Matt and his cousin Keith to help drive her car and a U-Haul trailer to her new home.

So I was alone in an empty, echoing house with our two youngest, 9-year-old Ben and 4-year-old Jenny, both easy and amiable children with none of the angst or social lives or appetites of teenagers.

Every evening, I went through the entire bedtime routine with Jenny—jammies, snack, story, prayers, and bed. I could read *Bedtime for Frances* from start to finish with no phones ringing and no one hollering "Mom!" from the kitchen.

On hot afternoons, I sat outside and read while Jenny played in her wading pool. I discovered that Ben had never learned to play Andy-Over so I taught him, he and I on opposite sides of the lambs' shed, tossing a ball up and over, up and over. I took the children shopping and Ben took all the time he wanted comparing sweatbands at Footlocker.

No one was at home impatiently expecting supper before they were off to a meeting or basketball game. I stopped in at CG's Market in Harrisburg and bought a single gallon of milk. It lasted for days and days.

One night, we all slept outside on the trampoline. As the sun set, I turned off the lights in the house and then tucked Jenny into her little sleeping bag, my every move making the trampoline bob like a ship at sea.

I made sure Ben had his flashlight with him in his sleeping bag, then I settled down into mine. Jenny was soon sound asleep. Ben rambled on about basketball statistics for a few minutes, then he, too, fell asleep.

I curled up in my sleeping bag and felt like I was a good mom at last, breaking out of my routine and taking the time to do this. The fewer children I have, the better a mom I am, I decided. Just think of how awesome a mom I could be if I didn't have any children at all.

It was not a restful night. The temperature dipped into the low 40s and the trampoline turned out to be hard and uncomfortable. Katzie the cat kept climbing over us, pushing gently but firmly with her paws like a midwife feeling for the baby's position.

The next morning, as Jenny said, "We had cat feathers all over our sleeping bags."

But the sun shining through the trees cheered me up, and I had another blissful day ahead of me with no school or deadlines or places I had to go.

One day, my sister-in-law and I found babysitters and went out for lunch, lingering over iced tea for the most relaxed time of "girl talk" I'd had in months.

I thought wistfully, at times, that it would be nice if my life could always be this stress-free. Yet, as pleasant as those weeks were, I didn't want them to last forever, and I was happy to pick up Matt at the airport and to see Paul and the girls drive in.

My calendar rapidly filled up, with dentist appointments and birthday parties again spilling over into the margins. The house is noisy again, full of ringing phones and slamming doors. I buy three gallons of milk at once, wash two or three dishwasher loads a day, and get up at 6 a.m. if I want a cup of tea in peace and quiet.

But this, after all, is reality and substance, my work and purpose and ministry. This is where the rewards are found, the greatest challenges and the greatest satisfaction.

I might feel like a better mom with fewer children at home, but if I didn't have any I wouldn't be a mom at all—"Duh!"

as my kids would say. Good moms not only read all the way through *Bedtime for Frances*, they also tackle the unpleasant jobs such as insisting that their teenagers clean up after themselves in the kitchen and come home by curfew.

A week after everyone was home again and everything was wild and busy, I had an unexpected break, much shorter this time but just as refreshing.

One evening after Paul had spent the day cleaning out bins in preparation for harvest, he wondered if I'd like to go for a canoe ride. I hadn't canoed in years, and immediately took him up on his offer.

Muddy Creek is just across the road, so we didn't have far to go, yet it was like stepping out of my familiar universe and into another dimension as we pushed off from the creek bank, slipped into that quiet green tunnel of trees, and floated along below the level of Powerline Road and the ripening grass-seed fields.

We saw the neighborhood from an entirely new perspective—tombstones in the old cemetery pointed bravely toward the sky, and who knew that Leroy and Anita next door had solar panels on their garage roof? Noises were muffled, the slight swish of the paddles competing with a bird's sudden twitter or the splash of a nutria.

It was tempting to stay there forever, but before long it was time to turn around and go home. I had a fresh boost of energy as I cleaned up the kitchen and put children to bed.

As an escape from my routine, relaxing, shopping, and reading give me a new perspective and enable me to do my real work more effectively. Pursued for their own sakes, they become as pointless and unsatisfying as spending my life on Muddy Creek, endlessly paddling downstream.

The Gift
of an Ordinary Day

Yesterday was an ordinary day.

I brushed and braided my daughters' hair and drove the children to school, then stopped in to visit an elderly friend. After school, Amy, our 12-year-old, checked out an 18-inch stack of books from the library in Harrisburg. Second-grader Ben emptied the mousetraps and earned a quarter toward his next Lego set. Paul, my husband, figured out our taxes. Jenny, our busy toddler, unrolled six yards of toilet paper and dumped Cheerios on the floor. I helped 10-year-old Emily with her homework and wondered if she will ever quit making her A's look like O's. Matt, the tall teenager, poked me in the ribs to hear me shriek. That night, I snuggled next to my sleeping husband and listened to an owl hooting across the creek.

And I kept a promise I made seven years ago.

We lived in Canada then, near a camp for First Nations children and families, a hundred miles north of the Minnesota/Ontario border. With our four young children, we had traveled to Oregon for Christmas. On this particular night, January 16, 1994, we were on our way home and had only 25 miles to go. We were all tired of traveling and eager to get home after our 4,000-mile journey. Behind our van, we pulled the trailer that was to carry our belongings when we moved back to Oregon the following summer.

It was 10:30 at night and bitterly cold, probably 20 degrees below zero, with a light snow falling. The isolation of this hundred-mile stretch of road was unnerving enough in broad daylight, but at night it was almost hauntingly empty. We passed a gas station at the 40-mile mark; otherwise there was nothing but rocks, lakes, and trees. The last vehicle we had seen was a car we met just after we crossed the border almost two hours before.

Paul was driving, and the children slept. We felt safe and cozy, close together in the warm van, pushing a huge ball of light ahead of us through the darkness and the falling snow, mile after mile.

I saw it first, a shape appearing out of the darkness. A young bull moose trotted down the middle of the road ahead of us, hemmed in by guard rails on both sides. Paul stepped on the brakes and the van slipped and swerved on the snowy road. But we were unable to stop and we hit the moose with a gentle thump, like bumping your grocery cart into the one ahead of you at Safeway.

The van lurched and slid but stayed on the road. Paul eased the van on down the road a few hundred yards, where the guardrail ended and he could pull off the road. We checked to make sure everyone was okay, and Paul got out to inspect the van.

"It's not damaged that badly," he said when he came inside. "We hit it by the headlight, and the fan might be pushed in a little bit, but I'm going to leave the engine running to keep it warm in here. I think I'll go back and make sure that moose is off the road. Watch this gauge here, and if it starts to get hot, turn the engine off." He pulled on his fur hat and mitts, and left.

I sat in the driver's seat to watch the gauge, feeling calm and unafraid. Paul would soon be back and we would get home safely. After a while, I smelled something hot, just a whiff. I checked the gauge; it was fine. "I'm going to look at the engine," I told the children, who were now awake.

When I peered under the hood, nothing seemed abnormal. I walked on around to the passenger-side door of the van, opened it, and froze in shock and horror as I saw little flames shooting out of the dashboard. I couldn't think or move. Then, like a slide coming into focus on a screen, I was able to think one clear thought at a time.

Fire.

This van is on fire.

I've got to put it out.

I grabbed a sports bottle of milk by my feet and squeezed it at the fire. Nothing happened, but I inhaled black smoke that burned all the way down.

A new thought: *I've got to get my children out.*

Three-year-old Emily appeared in front of me, and I carried her out and waded through the snow to set her on the trailer behind the van.

Another thought, another child. I lifted out Amy, age 5, then Matthew, 7.

Another slide appeared on the screen in my mind.

My baby.

I reached through the billowing, burning smoke and unbuckled 5-month-old Benjamin's car seat. I pulled him toward me, grabbed his blankets, and waded back to set him on the trailer with the others.

As I did, I heard my children screaming: terrible, terrified screams that were swallowed up by the endless night and cold. And I realized I was alone, all alone with these helpless children in a world of malevolent horror, blackness, and flames. Paul was gone and we were the only people left in the world.

Another thought penetrated my dazed mind: *It's cold. I've got to keep my children warm.*

I yanked open the back door of the van. There on top was the big suitcase with their boots, ski pants, and extra wraps. That morning it had been heavy and bulky. Now, I pulled it out and tossed it far down into the ditch as though it was a basketball. Then, with mindless determination, I dug for the extra blankets that I knew were in there somewhere. The flames were almost to the back seat, but I hardly noticed. I had to get the blankets or my children would freeze.

A voice called me; a breathless, rasping voice.

"Dorcas, run!"

I couldn't run. I hadn't reached the blankets yet. Paul appeared close to me.

"It's going to explode! Get Benjy! *We've got to run!*"

Oh, yes—that gas tank under the back seat. I had forgotten.

I grabbed Benjamin in his carseat, Paul carried Emily, and with Matthew and Amy we started running, into the night, away from the van.

For the first time, I actually felt the cold. I looked down and saw my shoes, sweater, and skirt. *I'm going to freeze to death,* I thought calmly, and kept running.

Suddenly, out of the endless darkness around us, lights appeared. They were real. Headlights. What vast, glorious relief to see a pickup truck pull up beside us and a man jump out. He welcomed us into the truck and set the children into the wide space behind the seat.

Ahead of us, the moose struggled to lift his head from the highway. Behind us, orange flames leaped from every window of the van. And in the warmth and safety, I counted our children, over and over and over.

The next evening, while Paul answered calls from friends and relatives, I sat on the living room floor and read to the children. I could think clearly again, and felt the full horror of our experience wash over me, again and again. At the same time, I was overwhelmed with a sense of gratitude and wonder: we were all there. All of us. Together, whole, warm, safe, and alive.

It was the first time I really sensed how closely we walk to death, and I had a new awareness of the preciousness of the people I love. Too often, I realized, I had taken my family for granted and complained that my life wasn't exciting. Now I began to understand that even the most ordinary moments are treasures, priceless and fragile. So I promised myself that I would never lose that sense of wonder or complain that my life wasn't exciting enough.

And last night, lying in bed and listening to the owl, I kept my promise and thanked God for the incredible gift of an ordinary day.

Upstairs the Peasants Are Revolting

Table of Contents

Introduction

As an Amish child, I grew up as much on stories as on cornmeal mush and mashed potatoes. Shelling bushels of peas on the front porch, we listened to old family stories from Mom, scary stories from my brothers, memories, imitations, and quotes.

Today, as a somewhat more modern Mennonite minister's wife, I still, like my mother, feed my children mashed potatoes and stories. I repeat the ones I heard from Mom and turn our family escapades into tales to be repeated while washing dishes or snapping buckets of green beans on the front porch.

A story is much more than just a story, of course. It is entertainment, identity, interpretation, and lessons. This is who we are, this is why we do what we do, this is important, that is not, and don't ever whack your brother's finger with a hatchet like your dad did to Uncle Philip.

Writing essays about my life was a natural progression from storytelling. I write what I know: Oregon's Willamette Valley, growing grass-seed, our Mennonite church, my Amish past, our old farmhouse, my minister husband and six children. I have found what is true personally is also true universally. Even when the reader may be very different from me in location and lifestyle, we connect on the basics—friendship, family, laughter, grief, solving problems, faith in God.

The chapters in this book do not appear in chronological order and are meant to be read one at a time. I hope they remind you of stories in your own life, to be recalled and pondered and eventually retold.

Priorities and People

Barbells for My Brain

My three-year-old daughter and I had a typical conversation the other morning. Jenny finished her breakfast and gave a satisfied belch. "Cereal makes me burp!" she announced, grinning. "And pop," she added.

"Pop?" I said.

"Pop makes me burp."

There was a short pause, then Jenny asked, "Does wine?"

"Wine?!"

"Does wine make me burp?"

"I ... suppose it would."

"Every kind of wine?"

"Yes. Where did you hear about wine?"

"In my Bible storybook. There was a wedding party and there was wine."

Another pause, then another question.

"When I'm four years old am I gonna drink wine?"

"No."

"When I'm five can I?"

"Jenny," I said, "even Dad and I don't drink wine."

"Why not? Huh? Why don't you?"

"Because ... um ... you can get drunk if you drink wine."

"What's drunk?" she demanded.

I have been many things—dizzy, sick, pregnant, delirious—but never drunk.

"I think it's kind of like being dizzy," I finally said, feeling a bit dizzy with the pace of this conversation. To my relief, she dropped the subject, and I had a few minutes to recover before the next barrage of questions.

It was close to the same time that I started coming across suggestions for strengthening my mental abilities. "51 BRAINBOOSTING EXERCISES" an Internet link shouted at me. In *Reader's Digest*, I read, "Shake things up. When your brain is stimulated, new connections are thought to form between brain cells." It went on to encourage me to turn a book upside down and read it for three minutes, or to take a class, which would give me "more active brain cells."

The job of being a mom is sometimes perceived, among those who have never tried it, as a dull, unchallenging routine of washing dishes and wiping noses. But if being forced to think in new and different ways improves your brain, we moms may have the sharpest minds of anyone.

When adults ask me questions, their brains follow the same tracks as mine: "Are you busy on Friday?" "What news have you heard from your sister?"

Jenny, on the other hand, seldom thinks the way I do, and answering her questions is like driving a tractor across plowed furrows. She appears beside me when I'm typing an e-mail message and desperately whispers, "Mom! What's inside your lips?" When I'm studying a new lasagna recipe, she wants to know if the floors in heaven are brown. "How does rain make puddles?" she asks at the breakfast table—far too early, I think, for any conversation beyond "Pass the butter."

While three-year-olds ask the most questions, older children challenge my brain in different ways. Amy, who is 14, surveys the world around her and makes pithy observations that I would never have thought of. "This is the difference between Oregon and Minnesota," she told me, after a trip in December. "In Oregon, you say, 'My aunt has a broom.' And in Minnesota you say, 'My aahhnt has a brum.'" I couldn't have put it better myself.

Twelve-year-old Emily is an expert at what I call CBS (Clear Blue Sky) questions that force me to ask a dozen questions in return to figure out what she's talking about. "How old was that Amish lady?" for example. Or, "What was that guy's name?"

"Take a class," *Reader's Digest* instructed me. If learning new facts gives me more active brain cells, my two boys must keep my neurons snapping like a bag of Orville Redenbacher's in the microwave.

Both Matt and Ben have had a series of obsessions, where they were stuck on one subject for a year or more and that consumed all their thoughts and conversations. And they could never seem to process what they learned unless they ran every detail by me first.

Matt began with animals, and I'll never forget the morning he wandered sleepily into the kitchen and greeted me with, "Do you know what has the largest eyes of any land mammal? The horse!" Thanks to Matt, I learned about the relative size and habitat of the anaconda vs. the boa constrictor, the feeding habits of the Madagascar hissing cockroach, and the gestation period of the African elephant.

A few years ago Matt left animals behind and became fascinated with astronomy. He taught me that if I visited the planet Saturn, not only would I be unable to move around because I'd weigh so much, but I'd sink down into it because Saturn is actually a ball of compressed gas.

When NASA sent a small probe to an asteroid some time ago, I suggested to Matt that instead of trying to be the first man on Mars, he should be the first one on an asteroid. Somehow it seemed safer. "That wouldn't work, Mom," he said. "An asteroid is so small that I'd obtain escape velocity just by jumping." What a thought.

Ben has passed through the geography phase, when he read atlases by the hour and kept me informed on how much the population of Calcutta had increased in the past 10 years. Now, at nine, he is into sports. Just in the last few days I've learned that Shaq was six-feet-six when he was 13 years old, that Magic Johnson made $500 million in his career, and that "Arizona State University and the United States have one thing totally opposite—one is ASU and the other is USA!"

I wonder what I'll do to keep my mind sharp when they all grow up and leave home. Maybe then I'll have to read a book upside down through my bifocals or go back to school.

Or maybe, if I'm really fortunate, I'll have a few three-year-old grandchildren.

For Better, for Worse

I don't know if it was the laughter or the vomiting that made that night unforgettable, but I look back on it as one of the finest moments of our marriage.

We had been married for three-and-a-half years, and I was pregnant with our second child. A vicious stomach flu was going around, and Paul had spent the day curled up in bed, his face a delicate shade of green. I don't know if I had the flu or not, because, being pregnant, I was throwing up a dozen times a day, every day.

That evening, we tucked Matthew, who was almost two, into his crib, and then we went to bed. About 1 a.m., I heard Matthew retching in the next room. I rushed over to help him, but one whiff sent me flying for the bathroom, where I threw up into the toilet.

So Paul dragged himself out of bed and soon Matthew lay whimpering on our bed, Paul stood at the sink miserably rinsing sheets, and I continued to lean over the toilet, gagging.

When everything was cleaned up, we went back to bed, with Matthew in bed between us. Half an hour later, the whole depressing scene was repeated.

Soon, Matthew once again lay whimpering on our bed, Paul rinsed out more sheets, and I continued to heave into the toilet. We were almost ready to go back to bed when suddenly the whole pathetic situation struck us funny.

We stood in our cold bathroom, pale and thin and

sick, holding onto each other for support, laughing and laughing.

I am remembering this sort of thing these days for two reasons. First of all, our anniversary on August 10 always makes me nostalgic, and, secondly, Paul and I were asked to give premarital counseling to Konrad and Shannon, a newly engaged young couple we know.

We consented, of course, but wondered how to distill the hard-won experience of 19 years into a capsule of wisdom to give them at this crucial time in their lives, how to prepare them for the inevitable tough times ahead.

With marriages dissolving all around like sugar cubes in hot coffee, launching a young man and woman into matrimony is a serious undertaking. We soon realized that there was no way we could tell them everything we've learned. We could, however, draw a few basic lessons from our own experiences to give them a solid foundation.

We also evaluated, as best we could, their readiness for marriage and were happy to find that they were better prepared than we had been. Most of all, we wanted them to know what love really is, that marriage is bigger than the two people involved, and that a firm commitment can keep them together even in the hard times.

Love has many definitions but too often, we feel, it is portrayed as nothing but a capricious emotion. I went to college with a young woman whose husband was in the military. After he came back from a tour of duty overseas, she said, "I was afraid that when John came home I wouldn't love him anymore."

"You mean, don't you, that you were afraid he wouldn't love you anymore?" I asked.

"No," she said. "I was afraid I wouldn't love him anymore."

Seriously considering marriage at that time, I was horrified at the thought of having no control over whether or not I loved my husband. Thankfully, I learned that love is primarily a decision and a commitment. No matter how we feel, we can choose to love—to honor, to value highly, to be there, to sacrifice for and listen to.

And paradoxically, in this mundane soil of duty and forgiveness and unselfishness, feelings of love and romance are safe to sprout and grow.

As we talked with Konrad and Shannon, out by our picnic table, it was obvious that they were in love. (Konrad, I'm told, is especially obsessed, and has been known to pull Shannon's photo out of his pocket and show it to perfect strangers.) We asked them, "Which of you tends to be more emotional?" and they looked at each other, exploring the universe in each other's eyes for a long minute before they answered.

But it was also obvious that their love is built on more than their feelings. They were friends first, and Konrad was pretty sure that Shannon was who he wanted to marry. Yet, before he ever asked her out, he did some clearheaded and unromantic research, much like a prospective employer checking out references. He talked to Shannon's parents, her pastor, her friends, even her old high-school principal. After they began dating, he encouraged her to do the same with people who knew him well.

"I like it," Shannon said. "The more people I talk to, the safer I feel. It's like we have all these people behind us, supporting us."

This sense of belonging to a community was important to us as well. I have often felt reassured knowing that our family and friends are rooting for us, a safety net to catch us. At the same time, I know that the success or failure of our marriage will ultimately affect everyone around us.

We also were impressed with Konrad and Shannon's ability to communicate. It amazes me at times that Paul and I are still happily together, considering how much we had to learn when we got married. Our communication skills were poor, and in many areas we had little in common.

But what gave us a framework to work things out was a rock-solid commitment to this marriage. Not only was our marriage part of a bigger community, it also was a separate entity, somehow larger than the two of us put together. We learned that it was worth sacrificing our own wishes for the good of the marriage.

We also took seriously the biblical concept that God intended marriage to be for life, and even if the other partner bailed out, we would be stuck with our vows until death, which made a powerful incentive to work things out. Since marriage was God's idea, we knew he wanted it to work even more than we did, which was wonderfully reassuring when we seemed unable to find solutions on our own.

Nineteen years later, I consider my husband to be one of the best gifts I have ever received, and our marriage an environment where I can be myself and grow as a person like nowhere else.

Our feelings for each other change from day to day. Sometimes we love each other with a warm friendship, sometimes we're sky-high "in love," and sometimes we really don't like each other very much at all. But our emotions do not change the basic commitment to our marriage.

This is what I want for Konrad and Shannon—a loving and joyful marriage that brings out the best in both of them.

And, since difficult times are inevitable, I also want to see them determined to face those times together. As bizarre as it is, I wish for them the kind of experience we had that dreadful night in 1988.

Falling in love is nice, and staying there is better. But to have someone committed to being there and laughing with you when life hits bottom—it doesn't get much sweeter than this.

For Today,
All Is Forgotten

_H_oeing in the garden one afternoon last week, I found a nice-sized green apple lying in a corn row. Hmmmm, how odd, the orchard is a long way from the garden. I had inventoried my apple supply just the day before and realized what a meager crop was out there. We would be doing well to get a dozen quarts of applesauce, and we needed four times that much. So why was one of my precious apples lying in the garden?

I began investigating, and soon the reluctant truth came out. That morning, Ben and Steven, our two middle-sized boys, had finished weeding the hedge. Ben loves to play softball, so he suggested they have some batting practice. Furthermore, he got the bright idea to pick apples and see if they could hit them across the fence into the clover field.

"How many did you pick?" I gasped.

Oh dozens, maybe?

We will draw the curtain of charity over the rest of the scene, as Mark Twain once said, except to say that the boys' punishment was greatly reduced by a strategical error on my part. I called my husband Paul for support and sympathy, and he started laughing. "I understand them so well," he said, "because when I was a kid, I would spend hours hitting a rock over the clothesline with a broomstick."

The prosecution thought this was irrelevant, but the judge overruled, and the boys received a reduced sentence of digging an extra half-hour beside the carport where we're putting gravel in, plus a warning that they will pay for an equivalent amount of apples if I have to buy any to make applesauce.

I should be used to this sort of thing, as Ben is at the age when a boy seems to be all noise and awkward angles and disaster. He rattles the kitchen lights below him when he jumps out of bed or shoots baskets in his room, he drapes over chairs like a discarded bathrobe, and he seems to have forgotten how to actually sit upright. "But that's the whole point," he sighs when I tell him to stop doing things that make his sister scream.

But today, all my frustrations with him are forgiven and almost forgotten. Today, I am oozing with hugs and nostalgic affection. Today is Ben's birthday, and he's 12 years old.

I feel this same surprise with every child's birthday: How on earth can he be this old already, and where has the time gone? How did Ben change so quickly from a cuddly little guy with a phenomenal head of dark hair into this young man with his first pimple who in just the last few months has come up to my chin, my nose, and now my eyes?

On each birthday, I reminisce about the labor and delivery. "You sure took your sweet time about coming!" I tell Ben. "Your dad and I walked the halls of that little hospital for hours. I wore this pink and purple bathrobe that I made myself and it was so pretty."

"Interesting," Ben says, his catch-all word for "I am trying to be polite here but this really does not interest me in the least."

From there, I recount everything Ben has survived to reach this age. I recall the time he was the last child I pulled out of a van that had caught fire, the time he dumped camphorated oil on his head and into his mouth and had to have his stomach pumped, and the time he and his sister wandered off down the creek and got lost.

He has a 12-year collection of scars. One can still see where he fell down the steps and put his tooth through his lip, and a vivid white scar on his head shows us where his sister lost her temper and hit him with a bag of wood scraps and nails.

But somehow, by God's grace, he's made it to 12 years old.

Actually, as Ben pointed out to us last evening, standing by the piano and lecturing in his yellow-and-red pajamas, he was going to be 12 years old at 10:12 p.m. the night before we celebrated his birthday, since he was born at 12:12 a.m. in Ontario, Canada, which is two hours ahead of Oregon.

"Yes, Ben," we said. "You're absolutely right." Ben is the most technical and mathematical of a long line of technical Smuckers, and we have learned not to argue details with him.

In my estimation, Ben has been a math phenomenon ever since he came to me at age seven and said he had multiplied 128 times 128 in his head and it was 16,384. I grabbed a calculator and checked. He was right. Having such genius in the house scared me for about two days. Then when I saw he was still whining about green beans for supper and absentmindedly putting the paper towels in the refrigerator, I knew he was still the kid we knew and loved.

Ben's statistics keep us all informed and entertained. "There's this baseball player that has a 10-year, $252 million contract. That's $25.2 million a year! At one point, it was more than the salary of the entire Tampa Bay Devil Rays team put together!"

"I bet if you had a list of the world's 25 tallest mountains, most of them would be in Asia because, like, there's the

Himalayas and then in Kazakhstan there's some that are over 24,000 feet."

Dealing with a telemarketer, he spouts, "Sorry, we do not have a TV and I realize there's only two percent of American households that don't have a TV, so bye!"

We never know what Ben will do or say next, whether he will make us laugh or learn or tear out our hair. But as his mom, I do know he has a few special statistics of his own—he is my second boy, my fourth child, the one who looks the most like me and acts the most like his dad, yet there's no one else quite like him.

Tomorrow, I may tune Ben out when he quotes basketball numbers, grieve a bit for those apples, or yell upstairs in annoyance when the kitchen lights jangle like Salvation Army bells at Christmas time.

But not today. Today is Ben's birthday, and I have a long-range perspective: It's been a good 12 years.

Fresh Perspectives

There were seven of us in the boat, pulling in crab rings—Paul, me, and five boys from 10 to 12 years old. We motored under the bridge at Waldport, its enormous concrete mass arching over us and tapering away to the south like the tail of a gigantic lizard. Cormorants and seagulls rested on a crossbar, staring at us, annoyed, as though we had interrupted a family reunion.

"Wow," the boys said. "It's way different down here than seeing it from on top."

Like looking up at a bridge from down below, Bible Memory Camp let us see life from a different angle and thoroughly enjoy ourselves at the same time.

It all began many years ago when my husband Paul memorized Bible verses so he could go to White Branch Camp in the Cascades. Years later, he found himself pastoring with a fellow camper, Arlen Krabill, and they decided to give the children in their church the same opportunity they had had.

So every year, they specify 50 Bible verses, and any child between the ages of nine and 14 who memorizes them all gets to go to camp for three days. It isn't a specific church camp like the old days, but in tents at Clear Lake, in a house at the coast, or horseback riding in the Cascades.

This year, 15 of us went to a house in Waldport—Arlen and his wife Sharon, Paul and me, a teenaged counselor, and 10 campers. The house had only one bathroom, which, since this age does minimal grooming, was not a huge hardship.

The kids, I'm sure, saw an entirely new side of their pastors, who are usually dark-suited and behind the pulpit. One day, Arlen wore a T-shirt festooned with promises written in childish handwriting. "I promise not to sleep in church, especially during the sermon...I promise not to sing off key and always arrive on time... I never chew gum in church or sneak out early. Because I am the minister."

"My son gave it to me," he explained.

Sharon, normally a model of dignity, hiked up her skirts and raced one of the boys down the beach. (He won, barely.) Paul told stories around the campfire of his own camp days, how his dad was a counselor (Grandpa Smucker?), and some of the older boys picked him up and tossed him into the swimming pool (No! Grandpa?) and he calmly swam to the other side. (Grandpa can swim?)

Mostly, we just had fun. This age group, post potty-training and pre-acne, throws itself into every activity with the wild enthusiasm of running into the ocean and leaping the waves.

As a mom, it was good to see how perfectly normal my two middle children are with their love of heated debate and their crazy sense of humor.

The campers argued endlessly for the sheer joy of arguing. Is it smart or dumb to stay up all night at a sleepover? "It's dumb!" Emily said. "You're grouchy the next day."

"You're not grouchy if you sleep all the next day," Preston insisted.

"You get to see the sun rise! And you get to see Mars!" Ben added.

The girls went through all the chants they know, slapping each other's hands in perfect rhythm. "I don't WANna go to MEXico no more, more, more."

"That's dumb," Justin said.

"It takes coordination!" Amy snapped back.

"Guys are more coordinated than girls!"

"Then let's see you do that!"

"If girls are so coordinated, how come they can't dribble a basketball as well as guys?"

I saw my son's sense of humor multiplied by five. Dan set his breakfast plate on the picnic table one morning and went back for orange juice. Justin filched Dan's muffin and hid it in his lap. Dan returned, looked at his plate, and said, "Hey, I thought I had a muffin!" He shrugged his shoulders and went back for another one.

Giggling hysterically, the other guys replaced his muffin. Dan came back and they all howled with laughter. Dan just sighed.

They also thought the Billy Bass fake fish on the wall was hilarious. He could swivel out from the wall and croak "Take Me to the River" half a dozen times a day, and still someone would want to sneak over and push that little button to make him sing still more.

Nine of the kids came from solid, well-fed, two-parent homes. The tenth was Sergey, the wild card in the deck and the puppy in the henhouse. A tough, wiry little 12-year-old from Moscow, he spent the summer with another camper's family and memorized his verses in Russian.

Sergey's vague history included abandonment, hunger, and fighting for survival. As frenzied and pesky as a fly in a tent, he was nevertheless a lovable child.

The boys "crabbed" from the dock one day while the girls took their turn out in the boat. Paul helped Sergey tie his rope to the dock and toss out the crab ring. "Wait at least five minutes before you haul it in," he said.

"Five minutes? How much is five minutes?" Sergey asked. Obviously, almost forever. He paced up and down the dock, grabbing my wrist every 15 seconds to check the time. "Is it five minutes? Huh? Is it? Yeah, it is, see? It's at the one!"

"No, it isn't," I said. "It's still on the 12."

"But there's a one there! See?"

"That one is part of the 12!"

He dropped my wrist in agonies of impatience.

"What's 'one' in Russian?" I asked, desperate to distract him.

"Ah-deen."

"Two?"

"Dvah."

He counted, I repeated. "Dree, tishtee," and on through the complicated consonants to 10. Then he grabbed my wrist again. "Is it five minutes? Yeah, it's five minutes!"

For the children, everything was an adventure: the edge-of-their-seats memory-verse contest (won by the girls), the sand sculpture contest (won by Emily and Kayla's train coming out of a tunnel), and the late-night charades ("Jack and the Beanstalk," featuring Destinie as Jack).

No one complained about kitchen cleanup, even when Katie, the quietest girl, and Sergey, the noisiest boy, had to wash dishes together.

After camp, Sharon went home, fell asleep at 8 p.m., and slept all night. Paul turned the grass-seed cleaners back on at the warehouse. I filled a box with pillows and socks left behind in our van. Sergey flew back to Moscow.

"Thank you for investing your valuable time in the campers," Katie's mom wrote in a thank-you note. "I know there are many other things you could have been doing."

Perhaps, but I can't think of anything better I could possibly have done with those three days.

Simply Complicated

Sometimes living simply gets very complicated.

The first batch of corn this summer wasn't large, less than a hundred ears. But it was terribly wormy and processing it seemed to take all day.

The children did the husking on the front porch, just outside the kitchen. Every few minutes I heard a shriek as an ear of corn went flying back into the basket and my teenage girls sat rigidly with huge round horrified eyes, their hands splayed stiffly in the air as though they were geckos climbing a wall.

"Oooooh, now that one wins the prize!" they exclaimed, their voices shaking. Then they would draft 11-year-old Ben to drop the offending brown caterpillar down the gaps in the porch floor.

I helped with the husking for a while, gingerly pulling back the silk to check for the brown granules that indicate worms, then quickly whacking off the end of the ear with a sharp knife. When I was too slow, I shuddered just like my daughters as one of the biggest larva specimens I had ever seen humped its way out of the ear.

After the husking came more endless jobs—blanching the corn, batch by batch; cooling it in buckets filled from the garden hose; and then cutting the corn off the cobs.

When the last bag of corn was finally in the freezer, I scrubbed the kitchen, chiseling dried bits of corn from the floor and counters. We counted the day's total; from all that work and anguish, we reaped a measly 11 quarts of corn, only a small fraction of what we need for the winter.

I wondered, Was it worth it?

This is the sort of dilemma I face daily, trying to balance my limited resources of time, energy, and money to serve God, help others, live simply, and provide the best sort of life for my family. Most of us long for simplicity, for a less hectic life with more time, peace, and fulfilment. Often, people see the Amish as living this sort of ideal life.

"I've always thought I would like to be Amish," a man in the blueberry patch told me wistfully this summer. "So far, my wife hasn't been willing, but I would be happy to get rid of our modern things and join the Amish."

These people also see me, with my Amish roots, as uniquely qualified to prioritize my life and center on what's really important. While those roots taught me practical skills and the value of family and community, I find myself somewhere between my Amish past and the modern world.

Many of my mother's choices were defined by her church community and by poverty. Living in a different era, I have to define my own priorities and weigh hundreds of options my mother never had.

I believe in sacrificing lesser things to gain greater, in putting people before things, in family and community over self, in God's kingdom over all. I believe in homegrown over store-bought, in natural over artificial, in homemade over manufactured.

Even with these well-defined priorities, I constantly face tough choices.

Is it okay to buy a fast-food meal if it means more time with a friend? If having a garden means I don't have time to teach vacation Bible school, which do I choose? Is making my own food always better than buying it? Am I insisting on doing things the slow and old-fashioned way long after it becomes pointless? Can I use Bug-B-Gon to keep those disgusting worms off the corn?

And what about those green beans last week? Only about a third of my green bean seeds sprouted this year. The plants produced lavishly, but I ended up with only 10 quarts of beans, about a fourth of what I wanted. I couldn't bear to feed my family tasteless supermarket canned beans all winter, so I found a produce stand that sells fresh beans and ordered 30 pounds. For an extra 25 cents a pound, they told me, they could cut and wash them for me.

"Sure," I said impulsively, thinking of efficiency and time saved, and took home three large plastic bags of stiff, moist, green bean pieces. When I hauled them into the kitchen and set them on the counter, five-year-old Jenny burst into tears. "But I like to snap beans, Mom. Didn't you get any that I can snap for you?"

I tried to comfort her, explaining that I had so much to do, my sister was coming to visit in two days, I really needed to can the applesauce as well, and this was a nice way for me to save some time. But my explanation fell flat. How could saving time possibly matter to a five-year-old when she loves to snap beans?

My state of mind did not improve when I was imprisoned in the kitchen for several hours while I monitored two pressure canners full of beans, terrified that either my absentmindedness or my temperamental stove would blow up the house.

By the time I pulled the last jars from the canners, I still didn't know exactly what I should have done. If my garden beans didn't do well, should I do what my mother would have done and serve extra cabbage salad all winter instead of beans? Did it make sense to buy and can beans that someone else grew, or was that as pointless as making a pie with a purchased pie crust and instant pudding?

Should I buy fresh beans at Safeway every now and then all winter? Or would beans in tin cans ultimately be the best use of my time and money?

I sensed, however, that if I were going to buy beans, it would have been better to buy them whole instead of cut, that the experience of having the family snap them together would have been more important than the time I saved.

Like everyone else, I wish for a defined and tranquil life, but it doesn't look like I'll ever get it. Come to think of it, in many ways my mother's life wasn't so ideal, either. She worried constantly about our finances, and when the pigs got into the garden, Mom was as stressed and frantic as any suburban mother running late in slow traffic. But today she knows that, for the most part, she chose the things that mattered over the things that didn't.

Meanwhile, I still aim for simplicity and face daily dilemmas in how to achieve it, but I allow myself to make mistakes on the way.

Doing the corn, I've decided, was a good idea even though we got only 11 quarts. Years from now, the girls will shudder and laugh together, remembering a goal accomplished, those dreadful worms, and a heroic little brother gently dropping them down the gaps in the porch floor.

Finding Common Ground

My daughter Emily carefully set the bottle of ink on the table in our room at Motel 6. Next, she opened a narrow box and removed an elegant writing instrument, too classy to be called a mere pen—a spiraling length of heavy green glass that narrowed to a clear, grooved tip. Slowly, she dipped it into the ink and began to write on a yellow legal pad.

Sprawled on the bed, I watched her briefly and then returned to reading my book.

Some time later, Emily pressed her new blotter on the words, then slowly folded the paper, walked toward me, and bowed. "A letteh for yew, Madahm," she announced, in a contrived accent.

I opened it and read.

Once upon a time, there was a girl named Emily. Emily had a big family. Sometimes Emily felt that her parents didn't love her. One day Emily came out of school and a robber grabbed her. She kicked and screamed. The kidnapper was her mom! Emily's mom dragged Emily clear across the country. And I don't know what happened next, cause I'm Emily and I am still being held hostage!

Emily Smucker

P.S. I don't feel unloved anymore.

The "letter" was quintessential Emily, an imaginative mix of fantasy and reality, of elegant handwriting and splotches of ink, of clarity and confusion.

We have a custom in our family of taking each child away by themselves—I take them when they're 12, Paul when they're 13. But I had never taken Emily on what the children call a Twelve Trip, since she had serious health issues when she was 12, and at 13 we were preoccupied with going to Africa for the winter.

When she reached 14, the time was right. What should I do with her? A few years earlier, I took her older sister Amy to Portland on the train and went shopping. Emily doesn't like it when I compare her to her calm and responsible sister, and yet she constantly compares my treatment of the two of them and resents it if I don't treat them equally.

I would take Emily shopping as well, I decided, at Woodburn's outlet mall and in the historic town of Silverton. I did the train thing with Amy, so I would do something different with Emily. Something dramatic for the drama queen. I would kidnap her.

Paul made motel reservations and agreed to take care of things at home. I made arrangements with Emily's teacher.

I wore sunglasses and a long trench coat with upturned collar when I arrived at school on a Friday afternoon to whisk her away. I didn't play the part nearly as well as Emily would have. In fact, I looked like a 40-something mom making a fool out of herself. Emily would have snapped into the role perfectly, skulking along with sinister mystery in every step.

She is a born actress—always playing a part—who can whirl a piece of fabric around her shoulders and suddenly become Queen of the Smuckers, tall and haughty. "Bow before me," she commands, so regal that we feel a strange compulsion to do just that. The next day, she impulsively turns a piece of masking tape into a moustache and suddenly she is a science teacher, pompously lecturing in the middle of an otherwise normal afternoon.

Who is Emily, really? I often wonder. What is merely a role she plays and what is reality? Is she a cute little girl or an elegant young woman? Is she simply playing at being a "typical" teenager, moods shifting with the winds, angry and unreasonable one day and thoughtful and understanding the next? Is she actually the wise and witty young woman who has a special sensitivity for older people and small children?

For some time now, our relationship has been the same sort of mixture as the letter she wrote—impulsive affection and arguments, miscommunication, and moments when our eyes meet with an electric current and we instantly understand each other.

The purpose of our trip was not only to affirm and honor Emily, but to get to know her better. We have been through times when our communication looked like a geometry diagram of two separate lines in two different planes, neither parallel nor intersecting, with no shared points.

But slowly, we are finding things we have in common. I am a bookworm; she was the child who struggled to read. And then one day she discovered the delicious thrill of words, reading Robin Hood and quoting aloud, "'Hark! Yonder cometh a gaily feathered bird,' quoth Jolly Robin." She looked at me and grinned, and I grinned back, both of us getting the same buzz from the old-fashioned words.

We both love classic elegance, and fell in love with the glass pens at our first stop that Friday, an antique shop. She couldn't believe I would buy one for her, as much as they cost. "This is your day," I said, deliberately setting aside my tightwad tendencies.

"The owners told me that if someone is deserving, I can add a blotter besides," the clerk told us. Emily chose a blotter with pictures of antique ink bottles and Italian text.

Shopping at Gap was rapture for Emily and torture for me, digging through a wasteland of flimsy scraps of fabric that in my opinion hardly qualified as clothes. But I kept my opinions to myself and amazingly, we found an outfit that fit my strict parameters, and I bought Emily a shirt, skirt, and shoes.

We spent the night in Salem, and on Saturday we wandered around Silverton, admiring the murals and historic brick buildings. We walked around one block twice before we found the tea shop we were looking for, entered it, and found ourselves in the most charming atmosphere we could have imagined. The waitresses wore little black hats and long, full skirts, and the tea was served in miniature pots bundled in quilted cozies. The desserts were pure elegance, lemon tart for Emily and a Belgian chocolate torte for me, complete with a fresh nasturtium on the plate.

One thing we completely understand about each other is our sheer joy in places like this. We savored the flavors and atmosphere for an hour, and then it was time to go home.

"Do you really feel like we don't love you?" I asked, her "letter" gnawing at my mind.

Emily laughed and hugged me. "No, I was just being silly. I know you love me."

She was soon asleep, a tall and lovely young woman curled up on the seat like a small child—no roles, no pretense, just Emily, herself. I drove home in the pouring rain, thinking of how much I love her and how blessed I am to be her mom.

The Indispensable Mom

Erma Bombeck once wrote that if she had her life to live over again, she would go to bed with a cup of tea when she was sick instead of acting like the world would go into a holding pattern if she wasn't there to direct it.

Normally I agree with Erma, but at the time, as I clipped and filed the quote, I wasn't sure. Did we moms choose to make ourselves irreplaceable, or was it part of the job description? Could my family's world keep turning if I stayed in bed the next time I was sick?

I had a chance to test Erma's philosophy. One Friday evening, I first sensed that all was not well when a dull ache crawled up my arms and my head slowly grew five pounds heavier. I went to bed and shivered for half an hour before falling asleep.

Just after midnight, the soft swish of flannel pajamas woke me. Beside the bed stood 11-year-old Ben. "Mom, I threw up."

He was calm and clean. Wonderful, I thought. He's 11. He knows how to run for the bathroom, no big deal.

"Ooooooh, that's too bad," I murmured, half asleep. "Why don't you take a bucket, just in case, and go back to bed?"

"I threw up all over my blankets."

I shook Paul. "Ben threw up."

He slept on, his good ear conveniently down in the pillow and his deaf ear up. Only Gabriel's trumpet could wake him before Ben's bed would be soaked to the mattress.

Erma meant well, I'm sure, but her husband must have been a light sleeper.

We plodded upstairs, and I gingerly pulled the blankets off the loft bed six inches above my head. Walking across Interstate 5 in the dark would feel less risky than this.

Ben was surprisingly eager to help. "I can stuff the blankets in the hamper, Mom," he offered. Holding my breath as I gathered the corners of the blankets to contain the mess, I didn't answer. He tried again. "Shall I put them in the hamper for you?"

So this is the legacy I have left my children—the idea that everything you put in a laundry hamper, even something as unspeakable as those blankets, is magically restored to its clean and rightful glory by some good fairy.

"No, no," I sighed, "just get a clean blanket and go back to bed. With a bucket."

On Saturday, I had a long list of chores to accomplish. I wasn't sick, really, and surely after I had another cup of tea, it wouldn't be such hard work to open my eyes, and walking across the kitchen wouldn't feel like wading in peanut butter.

By noon, I was leaning against the sink, exhausted and chilled. Fourteen-year-old Emily looked at me and commanded, "Mom, just go to bed!"

Was Erma speaking through my daughter? "All right," I said. "I give up." I stretched out on the recliner with a wool blanket around me while Emily, bless her, mopped the kitchen.

My temperature slowly percolated upward, my breathing grew more painful, and I started to fall asleep, an invisible signal for everyone to crowd into the living room to ask me questions.

The three youngest were hungry. Paul was taking a load of donations to St. Vincent de Paul for me. Amy and Emily were going to shop for groceries.

"Mom! What's for lunch?"

"Where's your wallet?"

"Okay, so what besides the old dryer did you want me to take?"

"I'm hungry."

"How much money do we need?"

"Is the brown stove ready to load up?"

"Okay, so to get to WinCo, you go down 99 and then where? Beltline or something?"

"What's for lunch?"

"Have you seen my new jacket?"

"Were there some Goodwill bags or something you wanted me to take, too?"

"Shall I make macaroni and cheese?"

"If I don't get the new dryer hooked up until Monday, are you going to have enough clean school uniforms?"

At last they left me alone and I curled up miserably under the blanket.

My fever was inching higher, I was sure of it. The pain in my chest was getting worse, and if all went well, a full-blown case of pneumonia would send me to the hospital where I could sleep all I wanted and no one would bother me except doting nurses in quiet shoes coming to take my temperature and bring tea.

The phone rang. Amy answered and hollered to me, "Dad's wondering if the Goodwill bags can go to St. Vincent de Paul."

You've got to be kidding me, I thought. "That was the idea," I croaked. Amy repeated it into the phone, and hung up. "Guys!" she muttered.

These people, I decided, would not survive without me.

Sunday morning I stayed home from church, too sick to go away but not too sick to make lunch for my beloved family who always comes home famished after church. Alternately working and resting for 10 minutes, I made my usual chicken and rice hot dish and a salad. I sensed guiltily that this was the sort of heroic-mom stuff Erma regretted at the end of her life.

My heroics did not extend to dishes, so Paul and the children washed them while I stayed in bed. Feeling worse instead of better, I gratefully sank my head in the pillow, closed my eyes, and fell asleep. Once again, this signaled my younger children to swing open the bedroom door, one after another, like cuckoos popping out of a clock.

"Can I have a piece of bubble gum?"

"Me, too?"

"What shall I do? There's no more bubble gum in the jar."

"Mom! Steven took a piece of candy without asking. I saw him hide the wrapper."

"Can I go outside?"

That did it. Since when, I asked them, does anyone in this house have to ask if they can go outside on a Sunday afternoon? And why weren't they pestering their dad with all these questions instead of me?

Dad, it turned out, was taking a nap on the couch. They didn't want to bother him.

I sent them outside and burrowed under the blankets. My lungs hurt, my head hurt, and I could no longer remember why I had ever gotten married, let alone had six children. Don't they put pneumonia patients under a tent in the hospital? How lovely to be all alone under a dreamy white tent with no sound but the burble of Vicks-y steam rising from a vaporizer.

On Sunday evening, someone found a box of ice cream sandwiches left to melt on a kitchen chair. Emily couldn't remember if she had a clean uniform for the next day, and Jenny's nails, I discovered, were awfully long because no one had thought of trimming them.

"Paul," I said, "I have failed as a mom."

"You have?"

"I have made myself indispensable. A good mom works herself out of a job, but you guys can't function without me."

Paul looked at me like my fever was higher than he had realized. "You're supposed to be indispensable."

"I am?"

"We need you. If we didn't need you around, what would be the point of being a mom?"

"I don't know," I said.

Nevertheless, when Ben threw up again a few nights later, I elbowed Paul until he woke up. "Your turn," I smiled, and went back to sleep.

Erma Bombeck would have approved.

Holding On, Letting Go

*M*y daughter Amy called me from the top of the Empire State Building early this week. She sounded breathless and cold.

"Hi Mom! Guess where I am?" I wanted to ask a hundred questions, but the connection was bad. Before long, Amy cheerfully ended the conversation, leaving me clutching the phone, hungry for more.

Amy at 16 years old is a young senior, having condensed four years of high school into three. Going on a mission trip is a graduation requirement at our small church school. This year, the three seniors, one junior, and two sponsors flew to New York City—where a multinational Mennonite church thrives in the heart of Brooklyn—for a week of training in cross-cultural ministry.

While she is mature for her age, Amy also is tiny and innocent. What were we thinking to send her from our idyllic country setting to the big city, home of the Central Park jogger, the Mafia, Bernard Goetz, Son of Sam, terrorist attacks, and gangs?

I tried not to hover over her in hand-wringing apprehension, limiting my advice instead to occasional calm suggestions such as, "Make sure you never go anywhere alone! I mean it. You stay with the group."

From the time Amy was conceived, my instinct has been to protect her, to keep her close. For us moms, the near and familiar seems safe and the distant and unfamiliar does not.

When our children were smaller, we lived in the "bush" in Northern Ontario. There were plenty of dangers—bears, drowning in the lake, getting lost in the woods, freezing to death—not to mention that the nearest doctor and hospital were hundreds of miles away.

I came to be at peace with all this, took necessary precautions, and felt like we could hardly live in a safer place.

One summer, a family with four children came to visit. We were down by the lake one evening, and the children played on the dock and walked at the edge of the water. The visiting mother was so nervous she could hardly carry on a conversation.

"Be careful! Not so close to the edge! You hang onto your sister, I don't want her to drown! John, do you see what they're doing?"

I thought, Dear me, Woman, relax. They're perfectly safe.

A few weeks later, we took a vacation and went shopping for the first time in about a year. Getting out of the van and heading into a store, I was terrified.

"You get back here! Don't you wander off like that; somebody could grab you, and we'd never see you again. Watch for cars! Matthew, you hang onto Amy's hand. Look both ways before you cross here. If someone tries to kidnap you, you fall to the ground and kick and scream as loud as you can."

Some distance into this yammering, I realized I sounded exactly like the woman at the lake. No doubt, despite her behavior back then, that mother was perfectly calm when she took her children shopping.

Last summer, Amy and her sister Emily took a walk in the woods and ended up near a cow pasture where an angry bull pawed and snorted at them and tried to break down the fence.

No doubt my jaded New York friends would laugh at me and say that an angry bull rattling the fence is far more dangerous than some dreadlocked crack addict with low-slung trousers lurking in the subway.

Amy called me one day. "Mom, you know what you said about these dangerous dreadlocked guys with baggy clothes? Well, we all got on the subway today and this guy with a really baggy sweatshirt and pants got up and offered his seat to Phebe and me."

And she mentioned another day they were lost on the subway and a dreadlocked stranger was really nice and gave them directions.

Oh.

Amy's almost-daily reports were perky and enthusiastic. She loved her classes, she was meeting lots of nice people, she had a very interesting conversation with a Jewish woman.

"Mom, New York is not dangerous," she assured me one day. "At least in this section of town. We girls walk outside at night."

"Alone?" I yelped.

"Well, the three of us stay together."

That was a relief—sort of.

Amy was doing fine, I had to admit. Sensible and level-headed and well-supervised, she was ready for this. The problem was, I wasn't.

"You have to let them go," another mom told me recently, "if you want them to come back."

Intellectually, I have known this all along. But this time, with my daughter traveling across the country, it was painful and difficult. It meant deliberately going against the primal instinct of all these years to keep her close by, safe, right beside me.

The group flew to Seattle and spent the night driving back home. I was sitting on the couch with my Bible and a cup of coffee in hand early on a Wednesday morning when the front door opened and a small and very pale, ghostly figure glided in, weighed down with a suitcase and backpack.

I enfolded Amy in a hug, laid her on the couch, and dashed off to bring ibuprofen for her headache, a glass of water, and two slices of toasted homemade bread with lots of real butter. This was pure, exploding joy: to have Amy home and to serve her like this. My chick was back in the nest and all was well.

Thankfully, this trip to New York was only a brief flutter from the nest, and Amy isn't leaving for good—yet.

Now, she is busy finishing her courses and planning for graduation. She talks about what she wants to do next year—maybe get a job as a nanny. After that, college; someday she wants to travel or live overseas.

The future is calling my daughter and she's eager to meet it. My job as her mom is to walk this delicate line of holding on and of letting go, of protecting her and of releasing her into the dangerous world out there to find her own path, her own life, a place she finds familiar and safe.

Grace without Limits

Our middle daughter Emily was baptized last week. Our family sat on the front pew that Sunday, a fine vantage point for observing the three candidates—15-year-old Emily, her friend Stephanie, and an older girl Phebe. They sat on chairs directly in front of us, looking deceptively serene and almost grown up as they listened to the sermon, the story of Jesus baptized by John the Baptist.

We Mennonites practice believer's, as opposed to infant's, baptism. It is a symbol, a public way to acknowledge a personal decision to follow Jesus Christ. For young people growing up in the church, it means that their pilgrimage of faith is now their own rather than an extension of their parents'.

Baptism requires a measure of maturity, since young people are then expected to be responsible for their choices and to contribute to the work of the church. In the weeks leading up to that Sunday, Stephanie's mother and I wondered if our daughters were really ready for this. It wasn't that I doubted Emily's faith. She has been tuned to spiritual things ever since she was small. If I couldn't answer her questions, she repeated them as though I was half deaf and not too bright.

"Does God have blue eyes or brown eyes?" she asked me at age four.

"I don't know," I said. "See, the Bible says that God is a spirit and...." She heaved a sigh.

"Mom! Does! God! Have! Blue! Eyes! Or! Brown! Eyes?"

"Blue eyes," I said, figuring that God understood.

At age seven, she made a Valentine's card for Jesus, telling him how much she loved him. She opened the upstairs window and tossed it in the air, certain that he would catch and read it.

More recently, she got a study Bible for teens and read it daily, finding answers to her questions. For instance, she found that God's eyes are neither blue nor brown: "I read in Revelation that he has eyes of fire," she told me. On her own, she found verses to fit her life—on friendship, forgiveness, love, and much more.

While I felt Emily's faith was solid, her maturity was another matter. She seemed much too young for this level of responsibility.

Riding in the van that morning, Emily gave a far different impression than she did sitting erect in her chair at church. Then, she had munched an apple, since she had gotten up too late for breakfast, and rhapsodized dramatically about her new dress that turned out exactly how she had pictured: "This silllllky bluuuuue with sweeping Grecian sleeves." She tossed her head and swept a hand through the air.

I especially had misgivings after the birthday party a few weeks before. This year, Emily chose to spend an afternoon going to garage sales with three friends. As the driver and chaperone, I got an eye-opening insight into Emily and Stephanie's capacity for silliness.

As we drove around town on that hot afternoon, the girls had a staring contest, shrieked about bugs, insulted each others' handwriting and long fingernails, and pinched one another in revenge. Then, seeing horses in a pasture, they instantly dropped the nastiness and, all in unison, burst into a chant: "Four. White. Horses. Standingbyariver."

Descending in a flutter on one garage sale after another,

they noisily admired old gloves, fur collars, and anything impractical. A cute little swivel chair with a wrought-iron back brought a brief argument and silent glares until one of them finally said the other could have it.

Stephanie began a story on Belt Line Road and said "like" 14 times before we reached Highway 99. Then, abruptly, she yelled in my ear as a Willamette Ag truck passed. "Kurt! Hey Kurt!"

"Who's that?" the others asked.

"Kurt. He works with my dad."

"Him? He's old!"

"He has some cute kids, like, boys."

By the end of that exhausting day, I thought Emily and Stephanie needed about four more years of intense parenting before they were ready to appear in public again, let alone get baptized.

And yet, these same girls stepped up to the microphone that Sunday morning and shared articulate and moving stories of God's call and their choice to follow. "I've had many questions," Emily said, "and God has helped me find answers for them. I'm far from perfect, but God is daily changing me."

Stephanie read a poem about giving her imperfection to God and receiving love and forgiveness in return.

Next came the vows. "Do you believe in one true, eternal, and almighty God, who is the creator and preserver of all visible and invisible things?"

"I do."

"Do you believe in Jesus Christ as the only begotten son of God?"

They did.

"Don't let anyone look down on you because you are

young," the Bible says. Who did I think I was to limit God's grace to the mature and proper?

Emily, I reminded myself, is the one who can keep a carload of little kids mesmerized with the story of Rapunzel, and the one who taught summer Bible school and persuaded a squirming bunch of eight-year-olds to put on a well-organized skit of Daniel in the Lions' Den for their parents.

They knelt to be baptized. One minister held a bowl of water; the other dipped up a handful of water and gently poured it on each girl's head.

My job, I decided, was to give Emily and Stephanie permission to be young, to bless and encourage them, to celebrate.

"Arise and walk in newness of life," the pastor said. I imagined angels all around, rejoicing with us.

The Mystery of Marriage

Somehow, it all came together in that moment: lovely bride, tall groom, attentive guests, and wiggly flower girl. Candles burning, bridesmaids watching teary-eyed, a holy hush, and the vows—"to have and to hold until death do us part."

"This," said my husband, "is a great mystery."

It was no wonder that Rosie's wedding affected everyone in her large family. My husband's youngest sister, she has always belonged to all of us, freely sharing the drama of her life so we felt like we were up on stage and part of the action.

Rosie kept us updated on her life as she discovered her musical gifts and developed them, first training at Westminster Choir College in New Jersey, then returning to Oregon to teach music.

She also kept us updated on her frustrating love life. Rosie didn't want just anyone, just to have a man in her life. It had to be the right one, for all the right reasons.

As a succession of young men appeared on the scene and then left, Rosie entertained us with vivid descriptions of them.

"Bill" seemed awfully nice, and they dated for a while, but he finally decided he liked her, but not *that* way. Plus, says Rosie, he had self-esteem issues.

"Mark" seemed promising, a wealthy medical student, but he was into feelings. When they visited his uncle in Portland

203

one weekend, he didn't help Rosie carry her luggage into the house because, after all, he didn't feel like it. Rosie didn't figure there was much chance he'd ever feel like helping out with a sick child in the middle of the night, either, so that was the end of Mark.

"Daniel" was resurrected out of Rosie's past and came to Oregon to see her. A nice guy—maybe this would work out. But, no. "He kept trying to be witty," Rosie said afterward, "and I kept saying 'Duh!' in my mind. I didn't want to spend the rest of my life saying 'Duh' in my mind."

We romantic sisters-in-law ached with her disappointments, and we kept hoping she would someday meet someone as special as her brothers.

"Loneliness has been an issue for me in the past year," Rosie wrote, with characteristic honesty, in her 2001 Christmas letter to friends and family. She went on to describe her gradual acceptance of loneliness as a part of her life. "I am still lonely at times, but the heaviness is gone."

And then, suddenly, there was Phil.

Rosie had slept overnight at our house soon after Christmas so she could stay with the younger children while the rest of us went to the airport early the next morning. She sat cross-legged on the bed, typing on her laptop while I did last-minute packing.

"Oh, I should tell you," she said, "I'm going out with a guy tomorrow night. I've never met him, but he's from Albany. Remember Don Smith, the farmer I worked for a couple of summers? This guy is a friend of Don's and Don thought we should meet. We've e-mailed a couple of times. His name is Phil Leichty."

"Ah," I said, and promptly dismissed it from my mind. Two weeks later, I came home from my trip and my children were bouncing with news—"Mom! Aunt Rosie has a boyfriend!"

Now that, I thought, was quick.

We first met Phil when he and Rosie came over for supper the night of the big storm in February. I had to do my observing by candlelight since the power was out, but Phil impressed me as having the same unassuming confidence that my husband has.

Plus, he talked with the children and put them at ease. "Phil is a phish you should keep," I e-mailed Rosie afterward.

She seemed to agree. "Phil just comes through," she told me. "Over and over. We'll be in some new situation and I'll wonder how he'll react, and he just comes through."

Soon, Rosie had a new light in her eyes and her nieces and nephews were talking about marriage.

"Aunt Rosie, I don't need another Uncle Phil," Ben moaned one evening when she stopped in. He already had two, since Paul and I each have a brother named Phil.

"She won't be our Aunt Rosie anymore!" Emily wailed, and decided she didn't like Phil, and never would.

Phil, who learned a few things while working with kids over the years, asked her to write a poem for him. Emily loved him instantly and soon churned out a masterpiece that said, in part: Leichty was a teacher / Leichty was a coach / I was glad he did not think / my aunt was a cockroach.

She also wrote an ABC poem, touching on Phil's mustache and other important details: N is for nose, right over his fuzz / O is for old, Amy knew that he was.

My girls were stuck on Phil's age for a long time. "He's so old," Amy sniffed, with typical teenage emphasis. "I mean, 41. That's like Dad!"

"Aunt Rosie is 29," we reminded the girls. "It's not like she's your age." But they were unconvinced.

A noisy discussion erupted one day: How are we going to distinguish between all these Uncle Phils?

"They all have different last names," I said. "Why bother with fancy nicknames?"

They tried to be polite, but their faces all read "Duh, Mom. How boring." So, they finally decided, it's Uncle Phil Glasses, Uncle Phil Loud-Voice, and Uncle Phil Big-Socks.

Big-Socks? "Yeah, because when Phil and Rosie took us to the coast, he was wearing these big basketball socks. I mean, they were like knee-socks."

"Over-the-knee socks!" Ben added.

I thought, Uncle Phil Big-Socks. Please.

They announced their engagement in March. Rosie was immediately swept into a whirl of planning and shopping, and, true to form, she swept the rest of us with her.

Our three-year-old Jenny was to be a flower girl, dressed in a miniature version of the bride's dress. Sewing her satin and lace dress was like stitching cotton candy to cobwebs. Whenever I needed to rip out a seam, it felt like the whole thing was disintegrating.

Jenny, sensing my busyness and distraction, grew increasingly naughty. She would sneak out of bed at naptime and squeeze Blistex onto a pillow or shake a thick layer of baby powder on the windowsill.

"Jenny, why do you do this?" I wailed one day. She smiled sweetly, turning on all her Aunt-Rosie/get-out-of-trouble charm. "Cuz I'm a little kid!"

In the weeks before the wedding, I nagged my procrastinating husband about preparing that wedding sermon. "Sermonette!" Amy always added. "Remember, Dad, no more than 15 minutes!"

Paul would pop into the house and find me frantically hemming up dresses, cleaning the house, or mixing potato salad. "Does it have to be this much hassle?" he kept asking. "I mean, we have three daughters. Are we going to have to go through this three times?"

Before we knew it, we found ourselves crowded into the church nursery while a stream of guests flowed into the sanctuary. Zelma the seamstress adjusted bridesmaid dresses and finally resorted to holding the necklines in place with double-sided tape. Jenny kept trying to yank the wreath of roses off her head. In desperation, I grabbed a needle and thread and literally sewed it to her hair.

Then, miraculously, it all came together. Jenny floated up the aisle at the right moment, looking far too angelic to ever dream of rubbing hand lotion into her mother's best quilt. Paul delivered a well-prepared sermon in spite of all my worries, and stayed well under 15 minutes.

"Marriage is a mystery," he said, quoting from Ephesians. "God designed it, and we know it works, but we really don't know how.

"You'd think we'd have everything figured out after 18 years," he went on. "God has blessed me with a wife who is committed to making our marriage work, but we are still discovering the mysteries of love and sacrifice and commitment and how they make a relationship work."

Afterward, we divided up dozens of sandwich buns and gallons of leftover potato salad. Paul was on his hands and knees with a can of WD-40, trying to get sticky residue off the floor where someone had taped down the cord leading to the punch fountain. Someone asked Jenny if she was the flower girl and she said, "No, I was a princess!"

This is the beauty of marriage, and the mystery—that even though two people are happy and successful, they are somehow incomplete without each other. That their joy becomes ours as well. That after 18 years of marriage, my husband can slip a compliment to his wife into a wedding sermon.

And that when I see him scrubbing the floor in his brand-new suit, I can fall in love with him all over again.

"Too Busy for You"

No one knows why my husband's grandfather built his grass-seed warehouse on the other side of Muddy Creek when he had plenty of land on this side.

One theory is that he was copying his brother Herman, who had built his warehouse across the creek a few years before. My husband Paul runs the warehouse now, and Paul's brother Steve owns a pellet mill nearby. Both of them are tired of the bridge over the creek.

A concrete slab 30 feet long and 15 feet wide, the bridge might be adequate if visibility were good on both sides of it. While there's a straight stretch on the north side, the south side involves a tight squeeze between the old barn and another building, then a sharp angle, down and left, then the bridge.

More than one piece of equipment has ended up in the creek, and many of us have had the terrifying experience of finding ourselves nose to nose with a seed truck just as we crossed the bridge.

In my case, I had a minivan with four children in it, hurrying home to make supper. Just as I came to the bridge, Uncle James in his ancient seed truck appeared on the other side. I slammed on the brakes and felt the back of the van sliding sideways on the bridge, which of course had no rail of any kind. James's brakes were a bit uncertain, I found out later, but we managed to stop with our radiators about three feet apart.

So I was delighted to hear that they were putting in a new bridge. Nice and wide, guardrails, coming in straight from the road.

The only reason I took time to go watch the process was that my mother-in-law called and asked me to take a message to her husband, who was at the site. When I got there, two men were attaching cables to a tall tree leaning out over the creek, hoping, I was told, to guide it onto the creek bank as it fell.

Part of me wanted to protest, to keep this beautiful tree from being cut down. But then I thought of the new bridge, the convenience for everyone, the vast improvement in safety.

Watching the loggers added to the feeling I've had, lately, that there's something I'm supposed to learn. There is a parallel between the trees in my life and my constant busyness: Sometimes, a good thing needs to go in order to make room for something better.

I love trees. While I am too busy to be a Julia "Butterfly" Hill and sit in a tree for two years to protect it, I am fiercely protective of the trees in my care. I love their stability and grace, their shade in summer and their bare branches against an evening sky in winter.

Except for one huge oak tree, the trees around our house are still adolescents, and I am a long way from my dream of having a house nestled among towering trees like a duck's nest in tall grass.

So I react with mother-hen protectiveness whenever anything threatens my trees. I protest noisily when the county sends a postcard telling us that they're going to trim the branches overhanging the road, or when my husband wants to trim the limb of the walnut tree that's scraping the roof on the back porch.

During a fierce winter storm, I stood at the window and watched the oak tree as the branches bobbed in the wind and even the massive trunk seemed to bend and sway. Silently, I begged it not to fall.

Ever since we moved into this house, my husband had been telling me we should get rid of the two pear trees by the back fence. "No," I said. "Let's keep them. They're trees, and we need trees. Plus, they're fruit trees."

He also wanted to get rid of the anemic maple tree. "Somebody dug it out of the woods and planted it here," he said. "It wasn't particularly healthy to start with, and then someone gashed it with the lawn mower and it's had this big scar ever since."

"It'll be okay," I insisted. "Think of how long it would take another tree to grow this tall."

For some reason, I am often just as protective of my obligations and possessions, all the things that conspire to keep me frantically busy.

"Yes," I say, "I'll take your extra apples. And that bag of plums? Sure, why not?"

"Yes, I think I could teach Sunday school."

"They need boys' pajamas at the Eugene Mission? Maybe I could sew some for them."

"Well...yes, I think we could manage a table at the farmers' market."

"A writers' conference? Sure, I'll go with you."

"Oh, look!" I say, admiring a garage-sale bargain. "This huge piece of fabric for only a dollar, and a rubber stamp for only 50 cents!" I bring them home and they become another obligation, something to store, organize, and use.

Before I know it, I am too busy, with too many commitments and too many things, in addition to the daunting job of running a household.

My three-year-old daughter Jenny learned a Veggie-Tales song this summer. She has a way of singing it when I am at my busiest, like an innocent little prophetess calling me to repentance.

"Busy... busy...," she sings. "Frightfully busy. You won't believe what I have to do."

Describes me exactly, I think.

"Busy, busy, shockingly busy. Much, much too busy for you."

And I flinch. This is the peril of being too busy: Meeting a deadline becomes more important than playing with Jenny, and letting the tomatoes spoil seems like a greater sin than failing to visit Uncle Milford after his surgery.

I was digging iris bulbs beside the house several days ago. I wanted to rescue them before my husband builds a new porch there, and I also thought they might sell at the farmers' market in Harrisburg. As I yanked away a handful of leaves, I found a delicate little oak tree growing among the matted irises.

This is how the obligations come into my life, I decided, like an acorn sprouting silently in the iris bed, small and innocent. But cutting things out of my schedule is another matter, like removing a full-grown oak, involving heavy equipment and cables and permits from the county.

The trees by the fence that I defended so staunchly turned out to be "winter" pear trees. I found that I didn't like winter pears, and getting rid of hundreds of yellow-jacket-infested pears every fall was a dreadful job. Even then, I couldn't quite bring myself to get rid of those trees, even after I admitted that they were ugly—sort of stubby, with dead branches poking out awkwardly.

One of the pear trees blew over in that winter storm. To my surprise, I was relieved to see it go—enough so that I gave my husband permission to get rid of the other one. Now, instead of tolerating second-rate trees, we can choose—flowers, shrubs, or leaving it bare. Or maybe we'll decide to plant more trees, carefully selected to fit that particular spot.

I gave Paul permission to take out the maple tree and replace it with something stronger and healthier. I'm hoping a new oak tree grows by the creek, maybe over by the old bridge.

And I think I'm ready, finally, to do what it takes to cut some good things out of my schedule to make room for the things that really matter, to hear my daughter singing and to know that this time, I'm not "much, much too busy for you."

Gifts and Gratitude

Apple Gratitude

My husband's second cousin Leroy Kropf is our near-est neighbor to the east, right where Muddy Creek and Powerline Road curve to the north. Some years ago, an awk-ward little wedge of Paul's grandpa's land butted up against Leroy's, and Leroy asked if he could plant apple trees on it. Grandpa agreed.

Ever since then, Leroy has shared the bounty of those apple trees with Grandpa's descendants. Every fall, brown paper grass-seed sacks, bulging with apples, appear unan-nounced under the west bins at our warehouse.

Like chickadees to a feeder, we flutter to the warehouse to pick up our share. There are red Priscillas, plump Jonagolds, and best of all, bags and bags of Yellow Delicious apples.

I haul mine home and then, rapturously, choose a large, smooth yellow apple, admiring its perfection and feeling its healthy heft in my hand. And then I pause reverently to say thanks.

You might say there are two approaches to giving thanks. The general: "For health and food, for love and friends, for every gift thy goodness sends...." And then, the specific "my-favorite-things" approach—"Doorbells and sleighbells and schnitzel with noodles."

I lean toward the second. Not that I'm not deeply grate-ful for good health and a warm house and a wonderful family, but what really makes me give heartfelt thanks are those apples.

My children like the apples as well, and take the smaller ones to school in their lunches every day. But they think I'm just a bit weird to rave like I do over a mere apple. That's because they don't remember what it was like to live in Canada and do without.

From 1990 to 1993, my husband Paul and I taught at a school for Native Canadians in an isolated reserve in northwestern Ontario, where the lake was frozen over from October until the end of April, and the groceries at the little Hudson Bay store had to be flown in. Milk cost more than $10 a gallon, and the few fresh fruits and vegetables looked tired and cost a fortune.

So, naturally, we seldom had fresh fruit. Grapes and peaches I could do without, but it was apples that I craved, and the few times when I did manage to get some, I was so protective of them that I went just a bit crazy when my supply was threatened.

One winter day our mission director Eugene was flying in from civilization to see us. I had contacted his wife a few days before to ask if she could send some apples along. Sure enough, he arrived with a bag of Yellow Delicious apples. I was thrilled.

After Paul took Eugene to go visiting in the village, I arranged the apples in a basket in the middle of the table and warned the children that I was going to admire them for a few days before any of us took a single bite, and anyone who ate one of them without asking would be in serious trouble. The rest of the day, I gloated over those beautiful apples and anticipated that first bite.

Paul and Eugene returned that evening. As Eugene walked past the table, he noticed the apples. "Hey, those look good," he said. "You don't mind, do you, Dorcas?" Without giving me a chance to answer, he casually picked one up and took a satisfying bite.

I don't know if I looked as stricken as I felt, and I still don't know how I stayed calm when I desperately wanted to scream and weep and pull on his arm and beg him to spare my apples.

Something worse happened two years later. I forget who brought them that time, but again the apples were flown in and I arranged them in a bowl on the kitchen table.

Traditionally, the Cree don't knock before they come inside, so it wasn't a big surprise when two 11-year-old boys from our street burst in the front door one afternoon.

Laughing, they each grabbed an apple out of the bowl and ran back outside.

Oh well, I thought, trying not to panic. I guess I don't mind sharing. Or maybe they're just teasing me and will bring them back.

I looked out the kitchen window, and there were the boys, smashing my apples. Deliberately, they threw one apple and then the other as hard as they could against a tree, then picked up what remained and threw them again and again until they were obliterated.

I felt something terrible and violent boiling up inside of me. So angry I could hardly breathe, I wanted to go out and strangle those two boys with my bare hands.

Before that I sometimes had trouble believing that I was actually the sinner by nature that the Bible said I was. But that murderous rage over two apples properly humbled me, and I knew I had valued my right to those apples far more than my relationship with the two boys.

The Bible also says that all things can work together for good. My deprivation back then has led to a deep gratitude today and a guarantee that I will never be able to take apples for granted.

I know that apples in themselves can never make me truly happy, but as gifts from God and Leroy, they bring a special bonus of joy.

Today, I can hardly comprehend the lush abundance of these seed sacks, bulging with apples, in my pantries. I have enough to give away, to make into apple crisp, to supply the children's lunches, and to replenish the blue-speckled enamel bowl on the kitchen counter.

I admire the pile of yellow against the sharp blue, and then I select a perfect apple and slowly take that first crisp, juicy, delicious bite.

And I close my eyes in reverent gratitude. Thank you, thank you, and thank you again.

Escapes for Mom

I enjoy my job as a mom—most of the time.

On those overwhelming days when the groceries fill two carts, the preschooler asks a hundred questions, everyone talks to me at once, and the phone rings constantly, I think, like the Psalmist, "Oh, that I had wings like a dove. Then would I fly away and be at rest." Or, less reverently, "One more person yells 'Mom!' and I'm outta here."

Maybe that's why I found a recent library book so intriguing. The main character was a 40-something woman, married to a busy man and ignored by her three teenagers. One summer day, she went on a walk down the beach, and without really thinking it through, she simply walked out of her life and started a new life somewhere else. Of course, she soon took in a stray cat and befriended a motherless child, and after all the necessary epiphanies, she was back with her husband and children.

"Every mother's fantasy," the book jacket said. Yet, while most of us moms share these feelings at times, very few of us ever actually abandon ship.

What keeps me from doing something so extreme, I believe, is that I make sure I take miniature escapes. These little indulgences repair the leaks in my canoe, so to speak, bail out the water, and keep me on course downriver.

The first of these is my daily cup of black tea.

During our years in Canada, like so many British subjects, I became addicted to tea. On winter mornings, as frost clung to the windows and the woodstove popped and ticked,

I brewed a large mug of Red Rose tea and warmed myself from the inside out.

My tastes were refined during our months in Kenya, another former British colony, where bushes growing on lush hillsides are said to produce the most richly-flavored tea in the world.

How downright luxurious, now, to wake up early to a silent house, put the kettle on to boil, and brew a steaming little pot of Kericho Gold imported Kenyan tea. I set it on a napkin-lined tray and whisk it to my sewing room, where I sip tea, read my Bible, and feel like the Queen herself.

All too soon, I hear my younger children pounding downstairs like a herd of migrating wildebeests. Cupboard doors slam, chairs scrape, and soon the first "Mom!" of the day ends my quiet retreat.

Fortified with tea, scripture, and half an hour to myself, I'm ready to face whatever the day brings.

By evening, I am ready to collapse soon after the children go to bed, but every now and then I escape into a good old-fashioned novel and stay up until some dreadful unmotherly hour—even past midnight at times.

Last week, I wandered through L.M. Montgomery's *The Blue Castle*. Curled up on the couch, with the children asleep, I immersed myself in page after uninterrupted page of Valancy's transition from browbeaten old maid to strong, assertive woman. The household slept as I followed her right to the utterly satisfying end of the book.

The next morning I was groggy, of course, back in the real world where one never knows how things will turn out the next minute, much less at the end of the story. But what a fun excursion into a world where everything comes out perfectly.

My favorite escape is an evening with friends.

Our first Girls' Night Out was my friend Sharon's idea. She and I have a running joke that one of these days we really need to get together and have a nervous breakdown. We've both earned one several times over, but neither of us is quite sure how to go about it.

Sharon has the good sense to know that even if life is difficult, you still need to have fun. In fact, the more stress you have, the more humor becomes a necessity rather than a frill.

One day, she asked if I'd be interested in joining her and a few other women at Applebee's restaurant in Springfield.

Would I ever. I was excited all day, and as evening approached, I was downright giddy. After Sharon picked me up, I found out I wasn't the only one. "Today was such a long day," one woman said. "I was so looking forward to this."

Another said, "It felt like a first date, trying to decide what to wear and everything."

Naturally, our children thought we were a bit crazy. My teenage daughter sniffed, "The thing is, you guys make such a big deal out of it. I mean, if it were us, it would be just like, whatever, you'd just call people the day of, and say 'Do you want to go out tonight?'"

The seven of us figured out that all together we had 31 children, 29 of them still at home, as I recall. When you have this many children, you don't just like, whatever, go out tonight.

At Applebee's, we talked nonstop, ate, and laughed. I was sputtering and wiping tears and having a wonderfully therapeutic time when suddenly my glass slipper fell off and I realized it was 10 p.m. How did this happen? We couldn't possibly have been there for more than an hour.

Since then, we make a point of fitting these dinners into our schedules. We need them.

Somehow, among the stories and silliness and long discussions, we all grow stronger, fortified for the demands we face every day.

Today, I still need to trim the petunias, weed the garden, cook supper, keep Steven from climbing the basketball post, listen to Jenny read, keep the kitten off the screen door, and try to convince my teenager that a driver's permit is not an inalienable right unrelated to her current behavior.

But I know that tomorrow morning I can sit down with a hot pot of tea, and that some evening this month I can stay up late with Nicholas Sparks's *A Walk to Remember*. And tonight...ah, tonight, I'm off to Ping's in Albany for another night out with the girls.

Daffodil Queen

Once again, I am the unofficial Daffodil Queen of Powerline Road.

My daffodils are the first in the neighborhood to bloom, and they outdo all others in sheer quantity. They march in a vast army under the grapevines and spread in lavish thousands in Mark Smucker's clover field just across the fence.

This happens with no effort or intention on my part. For completely mysterious reasons, these flowers conspire to make me shine. In my other flower beds, blackberry vines grow among the roses, rhododendron plants turn yellow and refuse to bloom, and petunias turn leggy and brown.

The daffodils, in contrast, burst out of the ground in the middle of winter, form buds with frost on their noses, and explode in yellow profusion by Valentine's Day. Strangely, I get all the credit for this, as though I fertilized in the right proportions and coaxed these flowers to bloom their hearts out. In reality, I did absolutely nothing.

No matter how many daffodils are picked, there are always more to replace them. My house is awash in bouquets the children have picked, and their teacher and grandma have been blessed as well. My friend Rita, whose mission in life is to take care of everyone, picked some one day for her children's teacher, her husband's secretary, and a neighbor. She stopped in the next day for more, and the next, profusely apologizing. "I feel so greedy, but I keep thinking of more people to give them to, and they just cheer people up."

"No, Rita," I insisted over and over. "We have plenty. Take a hundred. You don't even have to ask." Finally, I persuaded her to take a bouquet home for herself.

My mother-in-law popped in for a bucket of daffodils, distributed them to her friends, and came back for more. Rita's friend Emily came by to pick some. "Do you mind? Rita said you have lots."

And still, my daffodil supply is undiminished. If anything, it has increased.

Driving toward Harrisburg the other day, I noticed that the long line of daffodils on the west side of Highway 99 is blooming again. How sweet, I thought, of whoever it was who went to all that work to cheer up this stretch of road.

Later, I found out that those daffodils actually came from our place. When she lived here, my mother-in-law explained, she dug up hundreds of bulbs, put them in buckets and garbage bags, and delivered them to an older gentleman in Harrisburg. He would plant them along the highway, and his goal was to have a line of daffodils from Harrisburg to Halsey, a distance of nine miles. Unfortunately, he died before he accomplished his goal, but I notice that he made it at least halfway, past Cartney Drive. Amazing, this one man's labor of love. And how astonishing that he could take that many of our bulbs and not diminish our supply a bit.

I never appreciated the daffodils' dependability as I did this year, when they proved to our new son that the seasons really do change in Oregon. Steven came from Kenya, where the temperature ranges from warm to hot and the bougainvillea blooms all year long. He arrived in December, when the view was bare and brown, and ice covered the puddles one morning. "Now it's winter," we told him, but it won't always be like this. In the spring, it's much warmer. And see out there where that fence is? There will be lots of flowers blooming there. Really."

Steven always looked skeptical, as though he expected Oregon to remain as cold and drab as when he first arrived. But now the daffodils, reliable as sunrise, are proving us right. Steven picks enormous bouquets for me, convinced that if a little is good, more must be much better.

There is a bit of the divine in daffodils, I believe, of grace to the undeserving, of love that multiplies when it is given away, of dependability one can count on, and even a touch of the miraculous.

Back in our first year of marriage, before children and the clarified priorities that come with them, I found Paul to be a kind and affectionate husband with one unacceptable flaw: he never brought me flowers.

I compared him to my friends' husbands who regularly bought roses. I hinted, of course, not yet realizing that hinting to a Smucker was like poking an elephant with a twig. And one lovely spring day after Paul left for work, I sat down and cried.

Realizing that God does not approve when we fail to appreciate his gifts, I called to mind all the things Paul did that I liked, from washing dishes to encouraging my interests to taking care of our finances.

There at the table, I made a vow to God and myself that I would never again hint or nag about flowers. If Paul never brought me flowers for the rest of my life, I would love him anyhow without resentment.

The rest of the day I felt, simultaneously, the terror of great risk and a deep sense of peace.

Then, the unbelievable. Paul came home from work that day and presented me with a bouquet of daffodils. Stunned, I hardly heard him as he explained that he had stopped in at Strubhars to buy fresh milk as he did every week, and Maxine had such a nice bed of daffodils in her yard, so he asked if he could pick some for me since I like flowers so much.

Twenty years later, I still feel the awe of being part of a miracle. Every spring, when I am again transformed from a busy, blue-aproned housewife to Daffodil Queen of the neighborhood, I catch another glimpse of grace and glory and God.

The Perfect Porch

The city of Kisumu, Kenya, where we lived for almost four months, was hot, crowded, noisy, and dusty. Combined with the culture shock of a Third-World country, it was a stressful place to live.

"You need to go to Rondo," the other Americans kept telling us, with a dreamy, almost reverent, look in their eyes.

So, one weekend, we did, driving an hour and a half to the Kakamega rain forest. We turned off the highway onto a one-lane dirt road, where the forest closed in above us, tangled bushes brushed against the car, and skunk-colored monkeys hopped across the road.

After nine miles, a sign appeared indicating the Rondo Retreat Center. The gates opened and we entered a lovely enclave of green lawns, scattered cottages, and ravishing flower beds, all surrounded by the enormous trees of the rain forest.

My husband checked in at the office and we were escorted to our cottage, a quiet, yellow, wood-sided house, so different from the endless concrete buildings of Kisumu. Our rooms were decorated in the dark, understated style of colonial British days and, best of all, a long, low porch ran the length of one side of the cottage.

We set our luggage in our room and then, while the children set off to explore, I felt drawn to the porch, where I settled into a comfortable wicker chair and absorbed the wonder of that place—the cool air, the quiet, the green beauty. Monkeys scampered through the treetops as though I had personally ordered them for my entertainment, and the stresses of Kisumu seemed a million miles away.

Then, to add the final touch of perfection, a black-vested waiter came up the brick walk with a large wooden tray in his hands, which he set on the little table in front of me. I assured him that he didn't need to serve us, so he left, and I rapturously poured tea from an elegant pot into sturdy white teacups. Then, settling back in my chair with my tea and a piece of cake, I informed my family that I had officially died and gone to heaven.

The exquisite aura of that moment on the porch at Rondo has stayed with me, and I hope to duplicate it in my new porch here in Oregon.

Every house needs a proper porch, I believe, a special place not quite inside and not wholly outside either, yet more than a transition between the two. A destination in itself, a retreat.

We had a porch like that when I was a small child. An old church pew took up one end, a metal lawn chair sat at the other, and morning-glories twined up the posts. We shelled bushels of peas in its shade and snapped green beans by the hour, our add-a-paragraph stories getting sillier as the beans in the bucket diminished. When our work was done, my sisters and I played on the porch, dressing up the cats in dolls' clothes and collapsing in laughter when a kitten tired of our games and took off for the barn with a sunbonnet tied under its chin and a fluffy pink skirt bobbing up and down.

Back then, the front porch was where we met the outside world and talked with people we didn't know well enough to invite inside. The Watkins salesman, for example, would sit there to show us his products, cracking English jokes that I comprehended only enough to be embarrassed. It was also a place for other Amish women to sit and visit with

Mom in Pennsylvania German while we children played in the yard.

Through nearly 20 years of marriage and 10 different houses, I have wanted a porch. A real, old-fashioned front porch, painted white, with hanging ferns and comfortable chairs. Not a deck—too modern. But with a nice sturdy rail, to avoid the carport look.

Instead, I have had a series of small structures with ragged-edged plywood or peeling two-by-six floors. True, they served well their purpose as transitions from outside to in—the children thumped across them hundreds of times and Jehovah's Witnesses knocking at my door found a bit of shelter under the roof. But I always hoped that someday I would have a real porch.

We bought my in-laws' house in 2000, and like all the other houses of my married life, it had a small, fraying-at-the-edges entry. "Someday," my husband promised, "you'll have your porch." So I merrily planned and designed. I wanted the porch to look like it was built in 1911 like the rest of the house and not added on 90 years later, so I took photographs of other houses from that era and studied the porch posts and roof lines. I sketched pictures of the old porches in Ohio villages when we went East one summer, and on the long drive home I planned my perfect porch.

It would wrap around two sides of the house, I decided, east and south, from the main living-room entrance at the front to the kitchen on the south side, where we would replace the windows with sliding patio doors. The posts would taper and the rail would be a small wall about two feet high, solid and authentic.

And then I waited. A new bathroom took higher priority, and then business expenses, and later a trip overseas.

I kept the sketches and my husband frowned as he figured our finances.

Finally, over a year ago, Paul announced that when we rerouted the driveway we would also begin the porch. I was delighted—less so when I came home and discovered the front yard torn up with World-War-I style trenches, and more so when the foundation was built and the floor of the porch began to take shape.

"Now, when is the roof getting built?" I asked impatiently when the floor was done.

"The roof?" Paul said cheerfully. "I told you, didn't I? We can't build the roof till next year."

He had probably told me, but I hadn't wanted to hear it. So I kept waiting, grousing now and then that this roofless porch was worse than no porch at all, like a sidewalk turning the corner and going nowhere.

We went to Kenya then, and Paul arranged for his carpenter nephew to build the porch roof while we were gone. Meanwhile, near Lake Victoria we found a man who gathered reeds from the shore and wove beautiful wicker furniture just like the chairs I had admired at Rondo. "British Airways lets you take furniture as luggage, since it's a souvenir," someone told us. Sensing that my wait was almost over and I was getting even more than I had hoped for, I bought two tables and six chairs for my new porch halfway across the world.

Sure enough, the roof was in place when we came home. It was perfect—hipped at the ends, just as I had ordered it, and it balanced the look of our boxy house, just as I had planned.

The rail is still being built and the posts aren't finished, but I have my porch at last. Sometimes, on warm days, I sip tea in my wicker chair, its curving arms encircling me protectively. The Huns may be invading in the form of nesting starlings in the rafters, and upstairs it sounds like the peasants are revolting, but I am a queen on my regal throne, serenely surveying my kingdom.

"Hope deferred makes the heart sick," the Bible says, "but a longing fulfilled is a tree of life." This is my tree, and I hope to sit in its shade for many years to come.

The Best Gifts

Gift certificates for our warehouse employees, miniature flashlights on key chains for my Sunday school boys, maybe a new hot water bottle for my mom. My Christmas list has more than 60 people on it this year, and I am deep into the fun but exhausting job of choosing gifts for them all.

While I want the gifts to be appropriate and useful, I also hope I am giving another kind of gift—a present as special as the one I received years ago from two unlikely people.

Looking at him, no one would have guessed that my Uncle Ervin liked pretty dishes. A large, burly man, with a voice somewhere between a raven's caw and a hacksaw, he operated heavy equipment for the city of Hartville, Ohio. It was said that when he drove the snowplow down the street, mailboxes popped off one by one like a child pulling off dandelion heads and tossing them aside.

That may have been because Ervin had only one eye, having lost the other one when a horse kicked him. He enjoyed removing his glass eye and false teeth to terrify the little cousins.

And yet, for all his unrefined ways, Ervin liked pretty things, especially glass. Every couple of years, when we gathered at Aunt Vina's in Iowa, we knew that at some point, Ervin would show up with three white boxes, stiff and new, for me and my two sisters.

Inside, hidden under layers of rustly white tissue paper, we would find something delicate and beautiful. One year, it was milk-glass goblets. Another, little blue glass Cinderella slippers. Once he gave us all miniature china teacups, and another year it was "real" teacups and saucers, made in England, fine bone china.

The teacup and saucer set was given to me during those awful, awkward, adolescent years. The set is on a shelf in my kitchen, reminding me of the other gift Ervin gave me, something much more valuable.

Back then, I felt like I was a nuisance to my older brothers and a frustration to Mom and Dad. My older sister despaired of ever teaching me any social graces.

I think my family loved me, and I loved them. But our relationships were complicated and tangled. Ervin, on the other hand, with the closeness of an uncle and the distance of Ohio, loved me simply because I was his niece. He never mentioned my behavior or analyzed my attitudes.

Instead, he gave me beautiful, delicate glass as though he believed that I, too, were beautiful, delicate, and special. When I dust the teacup he gave me, the gift I remember is the feeling that he loved me for who I was, that I mattered.

Turk Kofstad gave me a similar gift, but in a very different way. I think about him early on Thanksgiving or Christmas morning, when I'm wrestling with the enormous turkey I bought at Safeway. Grunting, I heave the turkey onto the kitchen counter. Then, somewhere between peeling off the plastic wrap and putting the turkey in the oven, I start talking to it.

"Here, Turk, let's pull that neck out of there, and let's tuck that wing under THERE and this one right HERE...and now let's see if there's room for your hind legs right there...."

Talking to Turk the turkey always makes me think of Turk Kofstad, so I turn to whatever child happens to be in the kitchen: "Did I ever tell you I went to school with a guy named Turk?"

"No. What about him?"

"Well, he was a grade ahead of me, and his name was actually David, but he lived on a big turkey farm north of town, so they called him Turk."

"What was he like?"

A good question. Turk was not the kind of guy you reminisce about 20 years later. "He was nice," I say. "Friendly. And funny."

"Did you have a crush on him?" my daughter asked me once. A crush? It never occurred to me to have a crush on Turk. He was neither cool nor cute (today's criteria, my daughter says).

Instead, he was skinny and his teeth were crooked, and he wasn't athletic. But he always seemed to be grinning about something.

Our small-town high school in Minnesota was innocent and benign in many ways. But, as in any high school, it was difficult to be different. Among hundreds of Lutherans in blue jeans, I was an Amish girl in dresses. The kids were kind, for the most part, but I felt like a nun among them, treated with respect but never quite included, never quite acknowledged as a person.

Chemistry class was serious enough whenever Mr. Torgerson was lecturing, but when we went to our lab stations at the back of the room, the class turned into a mad-scientist atmosphere of protective goggles, strange mixtures bubbling in test tubes, and teenage craziness.

I was respectfully asked for help with formulas, but I was not included when people fried all kinds of objects, such as flies, that were never meant to be heated over Bunsen burners.

Turk was in my chemistry class, and one day he held a key in a pair of tongs and heated it above a Bunsen burner. Then, impulsively, he turned and tossed the key onto my chemistry workbook. I shrieked as the key immediately burned down through about 30 pages.

Turk laughed, I laughed, everyone laughed. For the next few weeks, every time I handed in a paper with a key-shaped hole at the bottom, I relived that warm sense of being included, that brief episode when I didn't feel different.

And on Christmas morning, preparing the turkey, I remember the gift Turk gave me of treating me like I was a real person.

At this time of year, gift certificates and hot water bottles serve as visible tokens of my love and gratitude, but the gift I want to give all year long is much more important.

I picture one of my chubby Sunday school boys 10 years from now, tall and rangy and packing to leave for college. In the back of a drawer, he finds a little flashlight on a key chain. If he remembers where it came from, I hope he can also remember the kind of gift I received from Uncle Ervin and Turk: of feeling special, loved, and included, like someone who really mattered.

Mice and the Power of Nature

This is nothing like living through a hurricane, I know, but out here in grass-seed country we are getting our own little taste of nature out of control.

Only afterward do I think philosophically like this, not while I am crawling around my sewing room with a flashlight in hand, having a desperate conversation with an unseen mouse.

Me: Where is that trap? I know I set it right here. Really, I did.

Mouse: No, you didn't. You're all mixed up. Beginning of Alzheimer's, you know. Bwa-ha-ha-ha-haaaaa!

Me: Listen, I know good and well I set that trap right there. At least I think I did.

This is the second time in two days I've been through this. I clutch my skirt around my knees and survey the room, then get down on the floor and cautiously look in the corners.

Then I spy it, under the ironing board one day and behind a basket the next—a floundering, squeaking mouse dragging a gray plastic trap.

"AAAAAAHHHHHHH there it is! MATT! Where are you?" Matt is my oldest son and frequent rescuer, but he's not at home.

I call my husband with shaking hands. "Paul? C-c-c-can you p-p-please come home ss-s-oon?"

I can't take much more of this.

238

Normally, I am not squeamish about unwanted animals, having lived in the country most of my life. I have dealt with a bear in the backyard, skunks under the house, raccoons in the corn, nutria in the tomatoes, rabbits in the lettuce, birds in the chimney, bats in the attic, and a squirrel on my kitchen counter. I swat flies with precision and smack spiders with my bare hands.

Here in the Willamette Valley, mice have always been a fact of life. They raise families in the grass fields and run away when the combines come through.

After harvest, I hear mice skittering away in the dry ditches every few steps when I walk down Substation Drive. When the rain begins, they move indoors and we fight to keep them out of the pantry all winter.

Living in old farmhouses for the past 10 years, I have encountered hundreds of mice. I don't enjoy this, but the only time I actually lost my composure was the morning I was pouring Cheerios into my bowl and a fat gray mouse dropped out of the box, scampered out of the bowl, and disappeared behind the peanut butter.

My 12-year-old son was impressed. "Wow, Mom, I didn't know you could scream that loud."

But none of us have ever seen anything like this year—the unbelievable numbers, like a biblical plague.

Most winters, the cold weather inhibits reproduction and the rain drowns out the nests. But a dry, mild winter last year encouraged the mice to proliferate in astonishing numbers.

In the spring, our farmer friend Larry first noticed patches of grass grazed down. By June, we heard reports from alarmed growers of large areas of dead grass, of decimated fields, and of grass moving eerily as hundreds of mice moved through.

Harvest brought more stories. In some annual ryegrass fields, the yields were down as much as 75 percent. Loose dirt from tunneling mice got mixed with the grass seed and made cleaning difficult.

The mice were everywhere. A man near Albany told us he counted more than 100 road-kill mice from one telephone pole to the next. My friend Anita saw two mice wiggle under her screen door in broad daylight and had to close her garage door to keep the mice from running inside. By the end of harvest, otherwise gentle Mennonite girls were climbing off their combines at the end of the day and nonchalantly stomping on mice with their flip-flops.

Our cats feasted on mice and left half-eaten offerings lying in the carport. My six-year-old daughter heard my jaw clicking as I ate a slice of bread and announced, "Mom, you sound like a cat eating a mouse."

Then, after harvest and long before we got any rain, the mice began moving indoors. I set a trap under the kitchen sink and found a mouse the next morning. My son emptied and reset the trap, and an hour later we had another one.

So it went until midnight, when 15-year-old Emily burst into our bedroom and announced hysterically that a mouse was banging around under the sink.

Ten mice in 24 hours, and then Matt bought a spray can of foam insulation at Hurd's Hardware and Paul sprayed it in all the holes under the sink.

This solved the problem, briefly. But this is no ordinary year and these are no ordinary mice. They tried a new tactic, not only moving into new territory, but also messing with my head and disappearing with the trap until I could no longer trust my own mind.

While I do not take any pleasure in killing mice or in seeing them suffer, I believe this is a just battle. I don't want them in my house, eating my precious stash of chocolate, nibbling on the potatoes.

I don't want their germs and droppings around my family. But they're welcome to live outside. I'm not going to put poison in the garden or bother them if they run across the yard.

I once wrote an essay for a New York editor and mentioned my son emptying a mousetrap. The editor felt like this gory detail was too much for her sensitive city audience. Perhaps New York mice are wise and clean individuals like Tucker Mouse in *The Cricket in Times Square*, who lived in a drainpipe, appreciated classical music, and did not produce 2,000 descendants in his lifetime like Oregon mice.

"We thought we had farming pretty well figured out," says a farmer north of us. "This new growth-regulator spray came out a few years ago and was better than anything we'd ever had. We figured, 'Hey, we really know what we're doing.' Then this year we did the same things and got half as much seed. It never occurred to us that nature would throw us a curve and we'd have all this trouble with mice."

When nature has the last word, there's not much you can do. At my house, I pray for better days and am grateful for the people around me who sympathize, empty the mousetraps, and reassure me that I really did set the trap where I think I did.

Since we seldom have extreme weather here in the valley, maybe it's good for us to be reminded now and then how very little power over nature we actually have.

Help Wanted: Finder and Clucker

A combination of factors led me to take stock of my skills and abilities this last month. There was the self-evaluation that comes naturally with the new year, and my occasional worries about what I would do if, God forbid, something terrible happened to my husband and I had to support the family.

Also, I helped my brother's wife find aptitude tests on the Internet when she wanted to change jobs, which made me wonder about my own aptitudes.

And I turned 40 this past year. According to author Jean Lush, I will soon be beyond the sheer-survival mode of a busy mom, and I need to start planning now for new worlds to conquer.

What I found was that I have a long list of dubious skills that could earn me little admiration and less money. I began to wonder what I would ever put on a resume.

I started by asking my family for ideas, and first on their list was my ability to find things. I have a knack, they said, for finding a homework slip at 8:10 a.m., or a microscopic hand for a Lego guy, or the screw that was lying on top of the furnace yesterday.

My daughter said she's amazed at how many phone numbers I have stored in my head, and my son admires my ability to quote a Bible verse for every occasion.

"The people who sat in darkness have seen a great light," I'll tell him, turning on a lamp when he's reading in eye-straining semi-darkness.

242

I also know every word to every verse of dozens, maybe hundreds, of hymns. My children would find this more impressive if I didn't try to sing them all. "But tim'rous mortals start and shrink, to cross the narrow sea...," I warble.

Recently, I bought two recorders, hoping my home-schooled daughter and I could learn to play together. My kids immediately started picking out tunes.

"Hey, there's do-re-mi-fa-so," my daughter said. "Do you hear that, Mom?"

No, I didn't hear it. I do try to sing in church, although I lip-sync when sitting beside my operatic sister-in-law so she won't hear me, and also because I like to pretend that those beautiful sounds come from me.

At least I'm not like my brother, who refuses to join in the singing at all. "Why don't you just pretend?" I asked him once.

"I used to," he said, "until I realized that I was obviously inhaling while I was supposedly singing."

I'm sure I have no future in athletics or law, as I am terrible at sports, strategy, and logic. I refuse to play basketball, chess, or the mind games my teenagers try on me.

My husband learned years ago that I don't think well on my feet and that we are all happier if he doesn't take advantage of it. We had dated for less than a year when at lunch one day I asked him, "Why don't you eat your broccoli stems?"

"Why should I?" he shot back. "Do you eat tree trunks?"

"No, but...," I stammered, thoroughly confused and filled with a vague, bewildering sense that somehow the logic here was all wrong but I couldn't figure out how or why. A quicker person would have snapped, "No, and we don't eat tree leaves either," but I didn't think of that until about two days later, after he had apologized and I had decided to keep dating him after all.

The only table game I am good at is Boggle, in which you find words in a tray of letters. This has not been a huge benefit to my life, but it was very satisfying the time I played at a New Year's Eve game-night and thoroughly trounced the guy who bragged that no one ever beat him.

I do well at sewing and baking, but am average, at best, in all the other aspects of housework—cooking, decorating, canning, and so on.

However, I feel I am unusually gifted at imitating. This is fine when I read to my three-year-old and cluck like the hen and moo like the cow.

Unfortunately, I am also good at imitating eccentric speakers, not a good hobby for a minister's wife.

If I were filling out an application, the aptitude page would still be empty. What could I write? "I can do a J-stroke in a canoe." "My friend Frances was amazed at how well I drive a stick shift." "A cashier once complimented me on how fast I can write out a check."

At 20, my lack of skills bothered me. Competitive by nature, I felt compelled to be good at everything, embarrassed about the things I couldn't do, and intimidated by everyone who could. Somehow, I was blind to the fact—more obvious to me now at 40—that no one can do everything, or do everything well.

My husband's Aunt Orpha, for instance, seems like a paragon of domestic virtue. But I found out that she had never quilted in her life until just recently when she took a few stitches in a quilt at her nephew's house.

My mother-in-law, who can easily cook a dinner for 20, hires someone to do her sewing. And my husband, computer whiz and businessman, is a poor speller.

Only recently did I begin to understand that our value does not depend on our abilities. God gives each of us specific talents to use to bless others. The more I accept my own limitations, the more I see how all of our talents can complement each other.

A friend and I put on a baby shower some time ago. She is terrified of speaking in front of people, so she planned the menu and I was in charge of the games. My husband's sisters have taught our children all they know about music. I sew for them occasionally, and my husband gives them advice on buying cars. My husband fixes the computer for me when it freezes up; I edit his important letters.

I have even found that my teenagers, for all their delight in confusing me with their twisted logic, will go to bat for me and supply a snappy answer to a stranger's rude comment when I am too tongue-tied to think of one.

Life is short, and I will never learn to be good at everything. Thankfully, however, I am surrounded by family and friends who, collectively, have all the skills I lack. And even my shaky skills can bless their lives in return.

My husband insists that even if something happened to him, we would still be well provided for, and I wouldn't have to get a job if I didn't want to.

He's probably right, but still, sometimes I wonder if there are any openings out there for someone who can convincingly cluck like a chicken.

Your Land, My Land

The letters to the editor in *The Register-Guard* were running about 10-to-1 against President George W. Bush and his policies the week I left to speak at a women's retreat in Georgia. At the conference, I stood in the lunch line next to a woman whose close-set eyes looked vaguely familiar. "I hope you don't mind my saying this," I said, "but you look like President Bush."

"No, Ma'am, I don't mind," she said. "I believe that man was chosen and anointed by God."

I love this country.

I never realized how much America meant to me until five years ago, when I visited my sister in the Middle East for two weeks. When the plane landed on American soil again, I was surprised by the intense emotion I felt. It was more than a sense of safety and more than the relief of coming home. It was a deep fondness and gratitude.

Last week, as I hopscotched from Eugene to Greenville, South Carolina, and back again a few days later, this appreciation was renewed. I don't often fly, and I still have a sense of wonder at being up above everything and seeing the vastness and beauty of this nation.

The morning I flew out of Eugene, mist hung over the harvested, plowed grass fields as the mountains slept in the background. In Seattle, huge container ships loaded up at the docks in the harbor. As we prepared to land in Detroit, I looked down on the intriguing juxtaposition of a sprawling city, two Great Lakes, and peaceful Canadian farmland across a narrow strip of water.

Descending in South Carolina, I studied the crops below, bumpy-textured and still a deep green. Corn, maybe, or possibly cotton.

We have much to unite us in this country: identical Taco Bells from coast to coast, a common language, and an attitude of embracing change and improvement. At the same time, we have tremendous variety in food, dialects, and interests.

On the way to Seattle, the flight attendant served us Starbucks coffee. In the kitchen at the conference center in Georgia, a 30-gallon plastic garbage can had a sign on one side: ICE TEA ONLY, and sweet iced tea was ladled out in pitcherfuls at mealtimes.

In South Carolina, a homemade sign on the back of a pickup truck announced, "Dale Earnhardt lives!" A large poster in the Eugene airport advertised a new and improved bicycle.

The accents changed as I crossed the country, from the efficient English of Microsoft employees discussing software, to the drawl of the former Minnesotan who sipped his orange juice and said, "It's a bit tricky to hit yer mouth," when the plane hit turbulence, to the warm accent of the South, where each word is stretched out and savored.

I appreciate the fact that it's okay to love your country, and show it—or not. In Canada, where we lived for eight years, being patriotic was not considered in good taste. I believe it was during the 1993 election when a candidate was asked, "Are you patriotic?" and he answered with a roundabout, "If I were accused of being such, I would not deny it."

Mennonites are a bit like Canadians in their discomfort with flagrant patriotism, believing that their heavenly citizenship takes precedence over any they have here on Earth. Yet it is biblical to love a place, I believe, judging by the psalm written when the Israelites were in captivity in Babylon and longing for home: "By the rivers of Babylon we sat and wept, when we remembered Zion... If I forget you, O Jerusalem, may my right hand forget its skill."

This affection is not a political loyalty, necessarily, since I don't agree with many government decisions, and the affairs of politics are like birds that twitter and fly far above my head.

But it is something more solid, grounded in the land itself and in the people who live here, the warm community spirit of sitting on the riverbank in Harrisburg at dusk on the Fourth of July, listening, with a thousand neighbors, to the Knox Brothers singing gospel songs in the gazebo.

My sister's twice-weekly updates from the Middle East the past 10 years have made me appreciate this country more, in much the same way that I appreciate my husband more when women confide in me about their marriages.

Most Americans, I believe, don't comprehend the level of chaos rampant in much of the world. It may be simple things, such as knowing that if you take a package to three different post offices in a foreign town, you will get three different answers as to how much it costs to mail it. Or the constant expectation of bribes to get anything accomplished, from getting a package through customs to getting a license plate for your vehicle.

And, of course, there are much deeper things, disturbing stories of strange disappearances, shadowy crimes in high places, and elections that are rife with corruption. Even the simplest elections turn dirty, my sister sighs. A nurse, she held a clinic in a tiny village and treated the family of a man who was running for mayor. A rival candidate, they said, had poisoned the family's well.

When "Jill" confides in me about her awful, disappointing husband who buys her flowers and does laundry, but he just won't talk about his feelings, I want to introduce her to "Nancy," who has suffered unspeakable abuse in her marriage for 20 years, just to make Jill realize how nice she actually has it.

Similarly, I am troubled by people on every part of the political spectrum who seem to think that this is a terrible country, one step away from completely going to the dogs. While I don't deny them the right to their opinions, I sometimes wish I could put them on a plane and let them live somewhere else for six months or so. Sudan would do nicely, or Myanmar, or a score of other countries.

America is not perfect, yet for all its diverse elements, it works. However frustrated we may be with a current situation, there is always hope for change.

Packages and people and political processes move across the country with amazing efficiency. We are free to think and express whatever we wish about President Bush, and we are blessed to live here.

The Kindness of Strangers

"**E**veryone is always so *nice* to you, so polite, like you're a nun or something," my friend Kim used to say. She liked to go shopping with me, she said, just to see all the cashiers being nicer than normal.

"How do they treat you when I'm not around?" I asked her once, a bit skeptically.

"They're curt and rude," she said. "Not like when I'm with you."

Kim may have been correct in her observation that my Mennonite garb makes people respond more politely than normal, but I still encounter plenty of unkind people. Drivers cut me off. The soulless pencil-pusher at the passport office acts disappointed when I have the right documents with me and can actually get a passport.

An acquaintance, Queen of the Subtle Insult, pokes me verbally where it hurts most. Taken off guard by this behavior, I respond with shocked silence. Then I obsess over it, and, three days later, ironing shirts, I finally think of a brilliant comeback, so wise and witty that it would surely have brought the offender to his knees in humble repentance, if I could only have said it at the time.

But thanks to a comment from my daughter, I think there may be a better response.

Accustomed to the freedom of country roads, I don't enjoy driving in Eugene. It was especially stressful the summer day I found myself on West 11th Avenue with a car full of children, in heavy traffic, searching for the place on the left side that tests the gauges on pressure canners.

A couple of wrong turns found me in a parking lot, and there was no way to get to my appliance store without returning to West 11th. Four lanes of endless traffic zipped by as my desperation grew, and I was sure I would never make that left turn safely.

As I waited, I noticed a bike about two blocks away, piloted by one of those grim, lycraed, helmeted, sunglassed, hunched-over bikers, pumping rapidly down the sidewalk, right toward our car, which had its nose across the sidewalk. I sensed it would not be wise to block the biker's way, but it was impossible to pull out into the street. In my rattled and desperate state it didn't occur to me to simply back up the car.

Soon, the biker braked to a stop at my door, blowing a whistle and yelling angrily. He dismounted, walked his bike around the car, stood by my daughter's window, savagely cussed us out, then shook his helmeted head in disgust, mounted his bike, and went on his way.

Stunned, I wanted to burst into tears, leave town, and never come back. But with this traffic, there was no hope of escape until maybe midnight. And then, miraculously, a minivan slowed down, the woman inside smiled and motioned at me to turn, and a gap in the traffic opened up. I slipped out into the street and fled.

From the back seat, my daughter Emily asked, "Okay, Mom, which one are you going to remember—that nice lady or that mean man?"

She knew I was already stewing about how I should have handled the situation. ("We had homemade cookies in here...why didn't I open the window and give him some as a peace offering?") Emily's words brought me up short, and I immediately made a decision. I would deliberately attempt to remember the woman's kindness whenever the memory of that dreadful man popped into my mind. I would not honor his behavior by forgetting hers.

I want to show my appreciation to all the nice people in my past by making sure their deeds are firmly stuck in my memory. Especially, I want to salute a man I encountered at the Department of Motor Vehicles.

My 15-year-old daughter Amy announced one morning that she was finally ready to take the written test for her driver's permit, so after school we hurried in to the DMV, hoping to get there by the 4 p.m. deadline.

We couldn't find a parking spot until I swooped over and nabbed one on the left side of the road. Just as quickly, I realized that this is not the sort of thing one should do right in front of the DMV. So we tried again, and finally rushed in the door a minute before 4 p.m.

We pulled our number from the red machine—32—and glanced around. Twenty-eight was being served, a few people sat waiting—did we have a chance? I hurried to the counter and asked the gentleman behind it if we were on time to take the test. He glanced at the clock, then at my number, then shook his head.

"You have to be at the counter by 4 p.m., and you're what? Number 32? There's no way you'll make it," he said blandly, without the slightest sign of sympathy.

Amy looked crushed as we turned to leave.

We were about 20 feet down the sidewalk when we heard running footsteps behind us and a man's voice calling, "Wait!" We turned around and saw one of the men who had been sitting inside. "I'll trade you!" he said, waving his number. "I'm number 29, and maybe if we trade, you'll still have a chance."

Amazed, we quickly switched numbers and hurried back inside. Number 28 had just finished and we arrived at the counter as the clock hit 4 p.m. Amy passed her test with a 93 percent.

I thanked the man profusely before we left.

"I saw how disappointed your daughter was," he said. "My daughter took her test a few days ago, and I know how much it meant to her, so I wanted to help if I could."

When Amy left the DMV, she had a new permit in her pocket and a triumphant grin on her face.

I guess my friend Kim was right: people really are nice to me. I want to thank them by remembering.

And, if I have a chance, I want to pass their kindness along at a moment when giving up a few minutes of my time can make all the difference to someone else.

Heritage and Hope

Connecting Generations

"**D**o you want to call home and see how things are going?" I ask my daughter Amy.

"Sure," she says, and reaches for the phone, then pauses. "Could someone show me how to use this?"

I teach her how to use a rotary dial, and she makes the call. The two of us are at my parents' home in Minnesota for a week's visit. Amy is 14 and almost inseparable from her cousin Janet, who is 15 and lives next door. My parents are in their 80s, and I feel like I am the uncertain link between two generations, as though I am trying to connect a rotary-dial phone and the Internet.

"Who is Tommy Hilfiger?" my mother asks the girls, who are into brand names.

Dad adds, "Is he your boyfriend?"

Amy and Janet double over, laughing, then Janet gives him a short, shouted lesson in fashion, hoisting up her foot to show him the Hilfiger logo on her sock. Dad looks mystified, either because he can't hear or can't comprehend, or both.

"Come on, we need to see Dad's animals," I tell Amy one afternoon, and we head to the barn.

"Ewwww, that smell!" she shrieks when I open the door. I am dumbfounded. Complaining about a barn smell is like fussing because garden dirt is such an ugly brown.

Amy and Janet are confident and talkative, strong in their opinions and finding lots to laugh about. I wonder what Dad thinks. He always valued decorum and country life, saving his harshest criticism for the times my sister and I acted, as he put it, like silly town girls. If Amy and Janet's behavior irritates him, he doesn't let on, but the girls freely let us all know that the dentist-drill squeal from Dad's hearing aids drives them crazy.

For a while, I feel like I am the only link between these disparate generations, constantly trying to explain them to each other. But as the week goes on, I find to my relief that there are many connections between these girls and their grandparents that go far beyond my groping attempts to find common ground between them.

Amy might turn up her nose at the barn smell, but we are all intrigued by the small flock of nervous goats and calm, heavily wooled sheep that wanders the property at will. When Mom steps outside the back door with a bucket of old vegetables from the grocery store, the sheep all come running, and Amy takes photographs from the window as Mom tosses bunches of broccoli at her flock.

Later, one of the sheep finds a five-gallon bucket out by the barn and somehow gets the bucket over its head and can't get it off. Dad and I circle in slowly over the frozen grass as the sheep baas pathetically inside the bucket. Then we perform a dramatic rescue while Mom and the girls cheer us on from the dining-room window.

In addition, we are all bookworms. No matter where we sit down in my parents' house, there's a stack of reading material within reach. And all of us, I notice, have the same tendency to pick up a *National Geographic* or *Reader's Digest* and be lost to the world within seconds.

The night we look at the quilts, I decide that what connects us most is the history we share, the stories that each generation passes to the next. After the dishes are done, we descend to the basement—Mom and I, Amy and Janet. First we sit on the couch and Mom shows us a stack of pictures almost two inches high. Each one shows a sample of her handiwork.

"This was Matthew's baby quilt, and this one was Jason's. I made this for Rebecca's wedding."

"This was the first quilt I made after our fire," she says, her voice tinged with sadness, remembering. A tragic fire in 1987 destroyed their house, almost all their possessions, 25 quilts-in-progress, and all of Mom's desire to ever make a quilt again.

It was Aunt Vina, Mom's sister, who came to the rescue, driving up from Iowa some weeks later with a new sewing machine, a rotary cutter, and a box of fabric.

"We're going to make a quilt," she told Mom, guiding her, still dazed and shocked from her loss, through the familiar rituals of selecting the colors, spreading out the fabric, cutting, and sewing.

Something that was frozen in my mother slowly thawed, and after that she trusted her instincts again, gathering scraps of fabric, cutting and sewing them. Today, she has this two-inch-high stack of photos documenting her recovery, and her fabric collection spills out of boxes and drawers.

Our family's history has been marked by fires, and the girls seem to understand Grandma's loss. Janet's family also had a house fire, seven years ago, and Amy remembers losing her clothes and favorite doll in a van fire when she was five years old.

Mom hands me another picture and I immediately notice the flaw toward one end of the quilt—a small square is a quarter-turn "off." Mom says, "Would you believe no one noticed the flaw in that quilt until the picture was developed?" And this leads to another story about Aunt Vina.

"She was making a quilt for some rich lady," Mom says, "and when she was almost done, she noticed that one of the squares was turned the wrong way. She didn't know what in the world to do, because it would have been almost impossible to fix. So she finished it, and when the lady came to pick it up, Vina said, 'There's this Amish custom to have one flaw somewhere in the quilt to keep you from being too proud of it. So this quilt has one little mistake in it somewhere.' The woman was all excited. She said, 'Oh, I hope I find it!'"

The girls giggle, and I smile, thinking of the same determined resourcefulness I see so abundant in Amy and Janet. In fact, Amy is here only because all summer and fall she found creative ways to earn money to pay for her own plane ticket.

The last picture is laid aside and it's time to look at the quilts Mom is working on. Racing against glaucoma, Mom is trying to piece a quilt for each of her 16 grandchildren before she loses her eyesight. She disappears into the spare bedroom and returns with a stack of quilts on her arm.

There is ceremony to viewing a quilt, and ritual, like handling the flag at a military funeral. One by one, Mom selects a quilt off the stack and carefully unfolds it. She holds two corners and I hold the other two, and we all admire that sweep of colors and shapes.

There are Grandmother's Fans, Log Cabins, and combinations of the two. One quilt is an Autumn Leaf, and we all gasp in admiration as it unfolds into a scattering of leaves drifting down on a sunny day.

Janet grows a bit impatient with the process and starts unfolding the next quilt while Mom is still folding the last one, a serious no-no in the unwritten rules of viewing quilts.

Will these girls really appreciate their quilts? I wonder. Only Mom knows how much work is invested in each one. I have a pretty good idea, but the girls, I'm afraid, have next to none.

"How do you think we should decide who gets which quilt?" Mom asks. We suggest having each grandchild list three favorites and having someone outside the family decide. Mom still looks worried. "Some of them are nicer than others," she says. "Like this one. It's nothing special, just scraps."

Then, to my vast relief, both Amy and Janet speak up at the same time, saying exactly what they ought to say.

"It doesn't matter, Grandma. They're all pretty. Whatever we get will be special because you made it."

A generation from now, my grandchildren will no doubt think me hopelessly old-fashioned, with an obsolete computer and one of those funny cordless phones from the '90s.

But I am saving up quilt scraps and stories, confident that as long as we love each other, we will somehow find ways to connect.

Lasting Memories and a New Humility

*I*t wasn't a typical Mennonite memorial service. Less formal, for one thing, with more reminiscing, and we laughed more than usual. But then, as someone pointed out, Don wasn't a typical Mennonite man.

I have no idea what attracted Don to our church 15 years ago, but I like to think that there was a divine plan behind it all. I used to picture God looking down at our church in Brownsville and thinking, Hmmm...a bit too proper, maybe a little too buttoned-up. They need to learn a little more spontaneity, more love, more humility. I think I'll send them, let's see—yes—Don McGarry!

So there he was, a hot-tempered McGarry among placid Kropfs and Smuckers, a World War II veteran among conscientious objectors, and a history buff talking about Joan of Arc among farmers discussing grass seed.

At the memorial service, I tried to put my finger on what it was that made him so exceptional. Why was it that guests visiting at church soon forgot everyone else but remembered Don, even years later?

"I guess Uncle Don never quite grew up," a niece said. I thought of Jesus' words, "Anyone who will not receive the kingdom of God like a little child will never enter it." I think it was this childlike quality that best explains what made him special.

Like a child, Don was utterly honest, humble, and loving. He was easily angered, but he never held a grudge, and minutes after an angry outburst, he would be in tears, apologizing.

It was said that a childhood injury had damaged Don's brain. He never quite recovered, and this was his weakness, resulting in black moods, confusion, and a lack of social skills. But it was also his strength, because it meant that he loved us all with a warm exuberance and displayed a refreshingly genuine honesty in everything he said. One minute he could irritate us to death, and the next minute he would say something so profound that we felt, for all our practiced Christianity, that he was the one who really knew what it meant to follow Jesus.

None of us will ever forget how much Don liked to talk. Anyone who was willing to listen heard long monologues whose subjects jumped from Billy Sunday to Don's cats to rambling recitations from the Bible to that awful government inspector who was coming to see Don's house that week. He buttonholed my nine-year-old son in the restroom and railed about that terrible Mexican bologna he bought that tasted like dog meat.

He left long, meandering messages on his friends' answering machines. He dominated Bible studies while the teachers tried, but seldom succeeded, to tactfully cut him off and steer the discussion back to the lesson at hand. When we shared our concerns at prayer meeting, there was no stopping Don as he rumbled on and on, hardly pausing for breath or punctuation.

"Let's pray for Bill Webster, too, that God'll get him off of that dope he's on; he got madder'n a nest of hornets one time; that dope'll do that to ya. And we won't need to pray for Mrs. Reed, the one we was prayin' for, I believe she passed away. And pray for us to keep close to Christ you know and talk about him so people will call us a fanatic. That's what we wanna do, just talk about Jesus. That'll get 'em, won't it? And pray for me that I'll abstain from all appearance of evil with my tongue, that's my greatest enemy."

At prayer meetings, most of us prayed two- to four-minute prayers with all the right phrases and the occasional thee or thou. Not Don. "I pray for Sharon, Lord. She demolished that little car of hers just like I did that little Datsun I used to have. But I wasn't hurt bad, and I sure hope she wasn't either. Thank you that Sharon never got killed in that accident, Lord. And I pray for my neighbor, Lord. He just flies into a spasm you know when I start talkin' about you. But I do see a change in 'im. He's not gettin' worse. You know the Word says the wicked will wax worse and worse."

The children in church cringed whenever Don started praying. Rumor had it that they used to time him and his record was 14 minutes. Just when I would start feeling really annoyed at him, he would break down and cry. "Jesus, I just love you so much. Thank you for dyin' for a sinner like me." And, I would feel, again, like the arrogant Pharisee in the Bible story, who thanked God that he was not like the weeping publican.

The rest of us waited for someone else to speak first when the minister asked if anyone had a "testimony" to share. But Don would bounce to his feet instantly, pushing up his thick glasses. "Yeah, brother, you know, the Lord's just been so good to me and my asthma's doin' so much better, you know, and I just wanna say I'm through with sin and livin' for the devil, but sometimes I think the devil's in my cat Salem, you know, oh, he just goes wild...." A long time later, he would finally wind to a close and sit down.

If Don liked someone, he showed it. He met me in the parking lot after church one Sunday and said, "Hey, Dorcas, your husband can sure preach! He sure don't lack for words, does he? He just goes and goes like a Gatling machine gun, don't he?" It was probably the only time in history that a Mennonite preacher was compared to a Gatling gun, and I will never forget that unique and genuine compliment.

He also loved his houseful of cats and "A Capella Harmony," the young men's quartet from our church that was gaining a measure of fame in the community. "God is sure honoring our quartet!" Don told me one evening.

"He is?" I said.

"Yeah, my cat had four kittens last week! Just like the quartet!" He chuckled, amazed at this coincidence.

"Are you going to name them after the guys?" I asked.

He grinned. "Hey, yeah, maybe I should!"

And that was how Don came to have four cats named Tom, Byran, David, and Konrad.

Don spent lots of time reading his Bible, and often quoted an amazingly appropriate verse for the occasion. But sometimes he read things into scripture that no one else had ever seen. I was helping him scrub his kitchen one day, trying to ease his mind about the HUD inspector coming the next day. When I wiped the coffeepot, Don said, "Do you like coffee?"

"Yeah, I like coffee," I said.

Don laughed. "Well, me, I'm just a surfer when it comes to coffee."

I stared at him. "A surfer?"

He nodded. "You know, the Bible talks about surfeiting and drunkenness, and I don't get drunk no more, but I sure do like coffee, so I guess I'm a surfer with coffee!"

"I...guess...so," I managed as I went back to washing the stove.

They found Don on his living room floor one Sunday morning in April. His exhausted heart and lungs had finally quit altogether.

Since then, I sit in church and glance over at his aisle seat, expecting him to jump to his feet with fresh news about what God has done for him lately. I wait for his rumbling voice at prayer meeting, and it never speaks.

But I sense a subtle change in the rest of us—a new openness, perhaps, and a new humility. Soon after Don's death, my husband Paul asked the congregation, during a Sunday service, if anyone had a testimony to share. Many of us talked about what Don's life had taught us. "I've never seen people get to their feet so quickly and speak so freely," Paul told me afterward.

This, we're learning, is the paradox of God's kingdom— that the least will become the greatest, that the one who humbles himself will be exalted, and that a little child will lead those of us who think we're all grown up.

Seven-Foot Brothers

My youngest daughter, four-year-old Jenny, likes to jump on our trampoline, but not by herself. "Can you jump with me?" she pleads. But her siblings never want to because they're not allowed to "jump wild," as they put it, because she can't keep her balance.

One day, however, Jenny sweet-talked her oldest brother Matt into jumping with her. I looked out the window and saw, not both of them jumping separately, but six-foot Matt holding three-foot Jenny in his arms, her arms around his neck, her legs wrapped around his waist. Slowly and gently, he bounced her up and down and around the trampoline in a strange and quiet and beautiful dance.

Watching, I prayed: Please, may this always be what she remembers about being his little sister.

When I first came to Oregon, I lived near Halsey with a family who owned a grass-seed warehouse. One evening, I went up to the flat roof of the warehouse, some 40 feet high. Then I climbed up a ladder another 10 feet to the top of a little platform, where I had a great view of the sun setting behind Mary's Peak, and I snapped a few photographs.

When I descended the ladder, I was startled to see the warehouse maintenance man on the roof fixing something. "Good evening," he said. "I'll bet you have three brothers."

"Yes, I do," I said.

"And they're all older than you," he went on.

"That's right," I said. "But how did you know?"

"Just the way you went climbing up there," he said vaguely, chuckling to himself, and that was all the explanation I got.

Two of my brothers, Marcus and Phil, were at my house overnight recently, here to celebrate our son's graduation from high school. The next morning, we worked our way through three pots of coffee, the newspaper, and a few subtle family jokes. And, as I always do when I'm around them, I pondered my role as their sister.

It is a strange and solemn thing, this dance of big brothers and little sisters. First, we idolize our brothers and then, disillusioned, we turn away. And finally, if we're fortunate, we develop a new and healthier relationship. Years later, we find they have influenced us in ways we never imagined.

As a child, I thought my brothers were like gods: about seven feet tall, all-knowing, utterly confident. I believed everything they told me and did anything they asked me to do. On the night in 1969 when men first landed on the moon, my third brother Fred knelt at the bedroom window, gazed at the full moon, and convinced us all that he saw little black dots moving around on it. My sister and I looked, and sure enough, pretty soon we thought we saw them, too.

He also convinced me that pig feed was good to eat, so I'd often munch on a handful of pig pellets while I was doing chores.

When he told me that the "FD" on the little Fisher-Price fire engine stood for Fatty Dorcas, I believed that, too, and thought I was fat, even when we went to the principal's office in sixth grade for "height and weight" and I weighed only 67 pounds.

When one of my brothers told me to put my hands in front of me and lace my fingers together, I promptly obeyed. He then grabbed my fingers and squeezed them together, a painful experience that, I later read, was sometimes used as a Communist torture.

I believed Phil when he told chilling stories at night back in the days when five of us slept in one room. Cold fingers scratched at the windows as he spoke, the attic door slowly opened, and terrible ghostly forms waited in the closet.

When my brothers repeatedly told me that I was ugly and disgusting, nothing but a crybaby and a tattletale, I was sure they were telling the truth. That was more painful than anything else they did, so much so that it colored all of my memories of that time. When my children were old enough to ask for stories from my childhood, I was unable to remember the good times my brothers and I had shared.

As a child, I tried all kinds of inappropriate ways to get their attention and approval. By the time I was out of high school, I decided that I meant nothing to my brothers, and never would, and it was time to move on and make my own choices whether or not they noticed or approved.

In the strange way that these things work, when I had given up trying, it started happening. An occasional phone call, just to talk; a birthday card; a late-night conversation when the family was together.

I hardly knew how to handle it, some years later, when one of them wanted my opinion on a big decision he was making. "Do whatever you want. It doesn't matter what I think," I told him, repeating the lesson he had taught me so well.

I wondered when this happened—where in our long journey as brother and sister did our paths reverse to such a degree that now he not only wanted to know what I thought, he also wanted my approval?

One day last year, in the middle of a phone call, Fred

abruptly asked, "Dorcas, how mean was I to you when we were kids?"

"Um...well...," I stammered, caught off guard and trying to be tactful.

"Okay," Fred said, "I was mean. Really awful. Well, I just want you to know that I'm sorry. I really am. And I apologize, for everything."

I didn't realize how much I had always wanted to hear those words until I heard them, or how much I wanted to say, "I forgive you, I really do, for everything" until I said it, my tears mixing with the words to wash and heal a wound somewhere deep inside that I didn't even know was there.

Fred went on, "I've been doing some thinking and realize that I've believed a lot of lies."

He started me down the road of examining my beliefs as well, what is true and what is false. At Matt's graduation, we took a picture of him with his two uncles. I was startled to see that he is taller than both of them, and I realized that the seven-foot giants of my memory were actually never all that big.

Nor were they very old. The time Fred pushed me, fully clothed, off the dock and into Lake Koronis, he was only about 14 years old. I thought he was almost grown up, but he was just a kid, coping with a difficult adolescence with the only tools he had.

"Phil remembers you as this cute little sister that he was very fond of," his wife told me. This puzzled me, until I remembered that Phil, though he may have been emotionally distant, was actually not unkind. I had unfairly associated the painful memories with all of my brothers.

And I no longer see them as being utterly self-confident. They have normal bouts of self-doubt and regrets.

More and more, I remember the good times. The time I was sick and Marcus bought me a bottle of orange pop, a rare treat. The times Phil taught me English words so I would know more than Pennsylvania German when I went to kindergarten. The times Fred took me exploring in the woods.

My children think I harp endlessly on how their behavior toward each other now will influence their relationships 30 years from now. It is only because I want their memories to be of encouraging words, of good times, of being held in a big brother's arms and gently bounced.

But since they are kids, after all, I also teach them to say those miraculous words of healing and restoration: "I'm really sorry. And I apologize, for everything."

I will never know all the ways my brothers have influenced me, but I like to think that, despite the hard times, I have climbed ladders in life that I would never have attempted if I had not been their little sister.

A Patchwork of Personalities

It had been 15 years since my five siblings and I were all together, but last month we assembled in Minnesota to celebrate Mom and Dad's 50th anniversary. Two weeks later, my husband's family gathered for three days at a retreat center in the Coast Range.

One would think, at first glance, that these two families are similar. Six siblings in mine, the Yoders; seven in Paul's, the Smuckers. Silent grandpas and indulgent grandmas. Ladies and girls in long skirts or dresses. An Amish/Mennonite heritage with its thrift and hard work and high-carbohydrate food. All of us followers of Jesus Christ. All the children from solid mom-and-dad homes.

However, somewhere among the coffee and conversation, I realized again that these two families are fundamentally different. We used a gallon percolator at the Yoder gathering and brewed coffee twice a day, sometimes using Mom's drip coffeepot in addition, for batches of decaf. At the Smucker reunion, I got up early every morning to make a glass pot of coffee in the restaurant-style coffee machine, but ended up pouring most of it away when, by afternoon, only four or five cups were gone.

My family is creative but not terribly organized, which is why my mother pieced 16 patchwork quilt tops—one for each grandchild—but we didn't know until Saturday morning that she wanted to distribute them that day. My brother's wife and I hung the quilts on the clotheslines, forming a stunning kaleidoscope of colors and shapes and moods rippling in the breeze.

The family assembled, and suddenly Mom had a panicky look on her face. She turned to me.

"How will we decide who gets which one?" she whispered. "Shall we go oldest to youngest?"

"Sure. I mean, I guess so," I said, since no one else seemed to be taking charge. "But let's let the older girls go first, since the guys don't care what they get."

Each of the older grandchildren gathered his or her quilt off the line, and the youngest ones took what was left. While all the quilts were beautiful, some of the colors were less attractive to modern fashion-conscious kids, and these were the last ones chosen. This sent me into a flurry of anguished second-guessing. If only I had known about this ahead of time and done more planning so that everyone could get his or her favorite. But then, I am a true Yoder, given to excessive reflection and regret.

Had this been the Smuckers, the quilt distribution would have been planned with more strategy than a political convention, with each quilt numbered, three ballots for each grandchild, and no time wasted on hindsight.

Grandma Smucker hates to sew, so distributing quilts wasn't an issue. However, every detail of their reunion was organized months in advance through lively e-mail discussions and then finalized in a four-page e-mail from Rosie. Final Reunion Notes: Sunny-Day Schedule, Rainy-Day Schedule, Things to Bring, Duties, Free-Time Activities Available, and Stories and Ideas for Reminiscing Sessions.

The Yoders love language—puns and subtle jokes and mimicry. We remember personalities more than events, and imitate aunts and neighbors from long ago.

When Emily flicked her long ponytail across the kitchen counter, I instantly repeated the German command Mom always told us, literally translated, "Fling not your hair the kitchen around!" The granddaughters tried to repeat it, stumbling over the guttural r's.

We recounted my brother Fred's famous joke about the bank teller named Patty who didn't think she should let a frog borrow money since all he had for collateral was a ceramic swan. Hillary, my niece, figured out the punch line and started giggling 30 seconds before she was told that the manager said—naturally—"It's a knickknack, Patty Wack, give the frog a loan."

Unlike the Yoders, the Smuckers are athletic and competitive, thriving on activity. Tournaments were arranged and posted on the wall at the retreat center: table tennis, horseshoes, and basketball.

Paul played his 11-year-old niece Stephanie in the ping-pong tournament, and barely beat her, which meant that next she would play Uncle Phil. I was in the kitchen a few minutes later when Stephanie's mother Bonnie burst in, laughing.

"You should have seen it!" she hooted. "These two big uncles were discussing how to beat skinny little Stephie. Phil was actually asking Paul what her tricks are, and Paul was warning him that he can't beat her by putting a spin on the ball because the paddles are worn out." Bonnie left, still chuckling, to watch the game.

Stephanie won, 21-17.

We reminisced at both gatherings—spontaneously among the Yoders and at a scheduled time with the Smuckers. The stories gravitated toward past disasters and near-misses: the time Paul nearly chopped off Phil's fingers with a hatchet, the time a snake bit my brother.

The Yoder catastrophes often resulted from our uneasy relationship with motor vehicles, having been Amish for so long that Dad seemed to feel that repairing brakes was optional and you could always pull on the steering wheel and yell, "Whoa!" This resulted in my brother Marcus losing control of a tractor on a steep hillside, and Dad crashing the car into a pump at a gas station.

Most of the Smucker disasters resulted from plunging headlong into danger, a trait that seems to contradict their tendency to plan and organize. There was the time Paul rode his tricycle on the flat bed of his dad's truck and fell off, and the winter night when Phil drove a snowmobile into a field and hit a barbed-wire fence.

At the Yoder gatherings, Paul tends to fade into the background, reading old *Reader's Digest*s while the rest of us forget he's there and lapse into German. With his family, I mostly listen to the hubbub because when I try to say something, no one hears me.

Yet somehow Paul and I, coming from these two disparate families, have formed a combination that works—my bright ideas with his practicality, his aggression with my caution. I drink coffee; he drinks milk. I laugh aloud at James Herriott books. He frowns intently over John Grisham.

Like red and blue combining to make purple, his fiery family background and my contemplative genes have merged in the vivid characters of our five biological children. Our daughters are fearless and creative. Both of our biological sons love sports, and both have also been known to lie awake at night worrying about house fires or cougars prowling along Muddy Creek.

Our kids grow up on Grandma Yoder's stories and Grandma Smucker's potato salad. A few are organized;

the others let life happen as it will. They all know bits of German, but none of them likes coffee.

Each of our children is unique, like a block on Grandma's quilts, distinct and separate, yet blending into the vast and beautiful patchwork of family, a rippling kaleidoscope of color and personality and love.

Fearing the Fatal Error

I always thought my dad had a strange relationship with his vehicles.

He relied on a Farmall M and a John Deere 720 to plow and plant and bale hay, and on a series of large old cars to transport his family. But he never seemed to understand how they worked, and when they broke down, he seemed to take it personally. Mystified and frustrated, he had no clue what to do except haul them to the shop.

To this day, Dad has a tentative, deliberate way of fastening his seat belt, turning the key, and putting the car in reverse, like a new pilot on a solo flight. He avoids freeways, preferring back roads and familiar routes.

I see that same deliberate caution in myself when I use a computer, the same reliance on the machine but with no idea of how it really works. When I venture off the familiar roads of Word documents and Juno e-mail to try something new, I fearfully click here and then over there and sigh with relief when nothing blows up in my face.

In contrast, my children grew up with electronics and seem to have a oneness with them, the keyboard an extension of their hands, the computer somehow connecting directly with their brains. My son grabs the mouse and clicks recklessly—moving this, dragging that, opening something else. Watching him feels like skidding down an icy road at 60 miles per hour.

Coping with today's electronic devices helps me understand my parents just a bit better. After a week of aggravation, our computer is working again. Microsoft Word opens when I double-click the little picture and Juno brings messages from my sister and daily decluttering tips from FlyLady.

Such a remarkable machine, so convenient, so efficient— what would I ever do without it? But only last week I thought it was an arrogant invention that refused to listen to me and had no mercy on my desperation. As icons disappeared and Fatal Error messages popped up, I wanted to throw it in the garbage and go back to being Amish.

I know basic first aid in such cases—hit control-alt-delete, restart the computer. Beyond that, I panic, certain that all my files are lost forever.

Thankfully my husband Paul can perform minor computer surgery, even raise the dead at times. While I hover restlessly in the background, wringing my hands and praying, he pops in CDs, pushes buttons, reformats the hard drive, and (oh, the relief) miraculously puts everything right.

At these times, I have a new sympathy for my parents. Computers and cell phones stymie me at age 42, but Mom and Dad were in their 50s when they left the Old Order Amish church and joined the modern world with its cars, tractors, electrical appliances, cameras, and phones.

It seems to me that young minds are wired to understand new technology and older ones are not. Somehow, teenagers understand how things work, why they break down, and how to fix them. They incorporate new inventions into their daily lives and use them as casually as a toothbrush. Past the age of 35 or 40, the mental switches start to turn off, and gadgets and machines become a mystery. We need them, we rely on them daily, but they are impossible to understand and often frustrating beyond belief. Sometimes, we fear them.

My husband is an exception to this rule, but it has proved true for my parents, myself, and my children, each generation embracing the technology of its youth but developing a fearful awe toward the gadgets introduced later in life.

Telephones, for instance. None of my grandparents ever had a phone, and when my parents first got one, it was a jangling affair, with a two-foot cord, right in the middle of the house. Thankfully it didn't break down like the car often did, but Mom and Dad still seemed half afraid of it. They made phone calls ceremoniously, cautiously picking up the receiver and turning the rotary dial. "It's already ringing!" Mom would announce, amazed.

My sisters and I had no trouble learning the art of chatting for hours on the phone, but Dad never has. He is still back in the era when a long-distance call meant that someone had died. "Hello? Dorcas?" he says. "Yes. Well. How are you? Do you want to talk to Mom?"

Unlike my parents, I use the kitchen phone so much some days that it feels attached to my ear. But I am not nearly as blasé about my cell phone, a lovely little device that came into my life a couple of years ago. How convenient—how modern and chic, really—to whip it out of my purse in the bulk foods aisle at WinCo to call home and ask how much cinnamon we have left.

However, I use the cell phone only for basics. My children pick it up in the car and casually punch buttons—saving numbers for me, changing the ring tones and backgrounds, hunting for games. "Now, make sure you get it all back to how it was before," I harp nervously. "I have no idea how to undo what you're doing."

They chuckle. Poor Mom, still half Amish.

Recently, I gained a new understanding of the changes my dad faced when he left the Amish. Over lunch with Dad's brother John a few days ago, my sister asked what my dad was like as a young man.

"Your dad was the best horseman in the county," Uncle John said. "He could take a team of horses and plant the straightest rows of anyone. We all thought he was the expert. Your dad used to say that horses were better than tractors because tractors rounded off the corners of the field and horses made them nice and sharp."

My sister was astonished, and so was I when she told me. We had never heard this before. To think that Dad, so inept and bumbling with anything mechanical, had been the community expert on horses when he was young.

What was it like for Dad, I wonder now, to trade in horses for tractors, to lose expertise to gain efficiency, to see his sons more capable at fixing machinery than he would ever be? We knew Mom and Dad left the Amish because they felt it was best for their family, but we had no idea of what Dad had sacrificed in the process.

I suppose this is how it will always be—the young will be the experts and older folks will struggle with change. I expect that my grandchildren will someday use technology that will completely bewilder my children, and Matt or Amy will call me on their old-fashioned cell phone and tell me that they finally understand.

From Baby to Bride

When I left home at 19 to come to Oregon, my parents and two sisters took me to the airport. "The ride home was really quiet," my sister told me later. "Even Dad had tears in his eyes."

Why in the world, I wondered at the time, would anyone be sad, let alone shedding tears, at my going away? Kids are meant to leave home someday, after all, and my parents' lives would be easier and quieter without me.

Life was all future, then. The present was endurance and impatience; what mattered was the next door to open, the next adventure.

Now, on the other side of 40, the present matters most. Some days, I would give almost anything to slow down time and to make things stay exactly as they are. Especially after a month full of travel and change, I understand those teary eyes all too well.

It began with my niece Annette announcing in a gleeful e-mail her engagement to a Lancaster County, Pennsylvania, dairy farmer.

Three weeks before the wedding, my younger sister Margaret, also from Pennsylvania, gave birth to her third child. She would have a houseful of guests over the wedding, so I put my 17-year-old daughter Amy on a plane and sent her ahead of me to help her aunt for two weeks.

My parents are in their 80s, but my siblings and I felt that they needed to be at Annette's wedding. We decided that I would fly to Minnesota, pick them up, and escort them to Pennsylvania.

It was a strange journey that week, of tears and laughter, of bumping into the past and being pushed into the future, and of the present overlapping with both until it was hard to remember what was now or then or still to be.

Seventeen years ago, my sister Margaret was a petite and cheerful teenager who came to help me when Amy was born. She did my housework, took my two-year-old on walks, and deliberated over which watch and socks to wear with which outfit.

Today, Amy looks remarkably like Margaret did back then, and as Amy washed dishes in Margaret's kitchen, wrestled toddlers in and out of car seats, and wore her fashionable Aeropostale sweatshirts, I had an uncanny sense of the past and present telescoping into one.

At the wedding, I had the same sensation of the past intruding on the present. Annette, the bride, was the baby who first made me an aunt, and my old photo albums are full of pictures of her—posing with the cat, opening Christmas gifts, dressed up in whatever strange costume her three aunts concocted.

As Annette floated up the aisle in a beautiful shimmer of white, my sister and I, through our tears, had a sudden sense of deja vu, of the little niece she used to be, and of an old photo of Annette at four years old, dressed like a bride with an old organdy curtain on her head and silk flowers in her hand, standing in front of a refrigerator box turned into a playhouse, grinning at the camera and her indulgent aunts.

When did this happen? I thought. When did I blink and that day became this one?

It was in my parents, however, that I saw the most pronounced results of time passing.

When I was small, Mom was the one who took care of me, firmly holding my hand to cross the street. Later, she always made sure I locked the car doors before I drove anywhere alone.

When I had small children, she loved to do my laundry and pamper me, knowing the difficulties of babies and sleepless nights.

But this time, I took care of them. At home in their farmhouse, they still seem competent and self-sufficient, but in the vastness of airport terminals they seem small, frail, and lost. Long ago, they took me to the airport and made sure I had my ticket. In a complete and jarring reversal of roles, I drove to the airport, got our boarding passes, and then hovered, worried, and reminded: "Do you need a bathroom?" "Are you hungry?" "Do you have your bag? What about your heart pills?"

To navigate the long distances in Detroit's airport, I put both Mom and Dad in wheelchairs. Seldom have I wanted to reverse time as much as I did then, seeing the parents that were once healthy and hardworking being helplessly pushed along by others.

Two weeks after we came home from Pennsylvania, Amy traveled, all alone, to the United Arab Emirates for a five-month project of teaching the three daughters of an American family.

We watched her as she waited to go through security. Then she looked back at us, grinned, and marched jauntily off to her gate as my husband held me and I cried out the savage pain of letting her go.

When time and change make daughters leave home and

parents become older, I want to clutch the present and never let go. And yet, only when the present dissolves into the past can little girls grow up to help others, teenagers find their calling, parents become grandparents, and grandparents see a beloved granddaughter walk up the aisle on her father's arm.

I don't know the sort of life I would have led if my parents had refused to let me go to Oregon. I hope it would have been good and full, but I know I would never have been blessed with this particular life—this husband, this home, this amazing reddish-haired daughter off to welcome a future of her own.

Changes and
a Child

The Turkey and the Vine

*P*erhaps our decision to go to Africa can best be explained by two stories, one involving a turkey and the other a vine.

The first story began with a typical Christmas ritual, probably repeated in a million American households. Half a dozen siblings, parents, and in-laws surrounded the island in the kitchen to transfer the turkey from the roaster to the platter.

My friend Liz was among the people gathered around the island as the process began with someone spreading an old newspaper over the counter to catch the drips. As her father-in-law prepared to pull the enormous bird out of the oven, Liz began to read a few paragraphs in the newspaper spread in front of her.

Suddenly, a small news item caught her eye, and she read with a growing sense of horror. A family (possibly Kurds from Iraq; I don't recall) was escaping over the mountains into Turkey. A husband, wife, and three or four children were locked in the back of a truck that was carrying them to, they hoped, a better life. It was bitterly cold, and one by one the children succumbed to hypothermia.

The parents desperately pounded on the walls of the truck and shouted for help, but apparently no one heard them and the truck kept going. By the time they reached their destination and were released, the children were all dead.

"Listen to this!" Liz exclaimed, and read the story aloud.

"Hmmm. Yes. Terrible," the others said. "Now, where's that pot holder? Here, careful with that platter. Hand me a fork, will you?"

"I stood there," Liz told me later, "and I was just overwhelmed with the sorrow of those parents in that story. But I felt like, to the people around me, their suffering had no meaning and no significance except as a little bit of newspaper to catch the drips from the Christmas turkey."

And then, there was the vine. My husband recently wrapped up a series of sermons based on the book of Jonah. We all discovered that this book is much more than a fanciful children's story about a man who was swallowed by a whale.

After Jonah was deposited back on dry land, the Bible says, God gave him a second chance and told him, again, to go to Ninevah to tell the people they were going to be destroyed for their wickedness. Jonah gave his message and then sat on a hill outside the city, waiting expectantly for judgment to fall on these enemies of Israel. As he sat in the hot sun, God made a vine grow to give him shade.

Jonah was grateful for the vine and the benefit it provided. But to his disgust, the people of Ninevah repented and were not destroyed after all. Worse, a worm chewed through the vine and made it wilt, so his shade was gone.

As Jonah sat pouting in the sun, God showed him that he had cared more for a temporary physical comfort than for the lives of thousands of people that God loved as much as he loved Jonah.

This is why we are taking our family to Africa for four months.

Like most Americans, we enjoy our comfortable and insulated lives. Reading a newspaper article about some terrible car-bomb explosion on the other side of the world, we scan the paragraphs to see if any Americans were hurt or killed. If there were not, we unconsciously feel that maybe it wasn't that bad after all, and we are still safe and all is well.

My husband and I have often wondered how, in all of our comfort and affluence, we can give our children an accurate perspective on how blessed they are in relation to most of the world. How do we teach them that their blessings come from God with a responsibility to use them wisely and share with others? And how do we teach them that other cultures have much to teach us, and that every person in the world is as valid and valuable as they are?

The best way, Paul and I decided, would be to show them firsthand.

So, a couple of years ago, we began to pray about a family service project in another country. We wanted something that the whole family could be involved in, in a place that was reasonably stable politically, where English was the main language.

Once we decided that we really wanted to do this, things began falling into place. Paul suddenly had requests for custom work at his grass-seed warehouse, enough to finance the whole project. We found someone who could live in our house, take care of the warehouse, and process orders for my new book.

Our daughter Emily, who had been in poor health for a couple of years, was diagnosed with allergies and gradually regained her health. And through a friend of a friend, we found a place to go: a small organization in Kisumu, Kenya, that takes in orphaned street boys and provides them with a home and an education.

As a former British colony, Kenya fit our language criterion. And, as African countries go, it is quite stable politically. However, like much of Africa, Kenya has been ravaged by AIDS, with roughly one million of its children orphaned by the terrible disease.

Rick and Audrey McAninch, originally from Washington state, started the Into Africa Foundation to work with boys who have been orphaned by AIDS. Girls, they tell us, are more likely to be taken in by the extended family because the women do much of the physical work of the family and also have value as brides. Boys often are turned out into the streets at eight or nine years old.

While we expect to involve the whole family in our work, we still have a somewhat vague picture of what we will actually be doing with the boys and for the organization. We do not have grandiose plans or agendas. We don't plan to change a culture or rescue a thousand orphans. But maybe we can make a small difference in the lives of one or two.

We want to go with a teachable attitude. We would like to get acquainted with the land, people, and cultures of Kenya. We want to learn more about the world and our place in it.

Most of all, I want us to learn the lessons of the turkey and the vine: We are blessed with privileges and comforts such as shopping at well-stocked stores, enjoying a Christmas turkey, and living in the safety of rural Harrisburg.

All of these are wonderful, and we appreciate them. But the lives of people, whether from Oregon, Kenya, or anywhere else, are eternal rather than temporary and infinitely more worthy of our time and resources.

The Sound of Dignity

Back in Oregon, a train whistle often wakes us up in the morning, or the oil furnace rumbling to life rouses us.

In Kenya, we wake each morning to the sound of swishing brooms. The windows have screens to deter mosquitoes and iron bars to deter thieves, but no glass. So the morning air glides in around the curtains, and the morning noises filter in with it. Roosters crow, dogs whine, children yell, and the brooms swish.

The swishing begins before dawn, before the sun leaps over the edge of Kenya with hot intensity. As I lie in bed, savoring the brief coolness, I can picture Martin, a former street boy, or Simon the groundskeeper, bent double, sweeping the sidewalks all around the house with a bundle of stiff straw.

First the sound is a dry swishing, sweeping off yesterday's rust-colored dust, wilted flowers, and pieces of gravel. Then the swishing is wet, as he makes his dutiful round again, this time with a basin of water, dipping his broom in and washing the long sidewalk and our front steps, leaving them wet and clean when we get up and unlock the doors to let in the morning light and air and begin our day.

We are still raw newcomers in Africa, slack-jawed at the sights, feeling our way around, overwhelmed with the differences.

Yet, in little ways it is becoming like home. Every day, I

see small things that remind me of Oregon, and the strange and new are gradually becoming familiar.

My husband Paul and our five children and I began this four-month project—helping a small organization called Into Africa with its work with orphaned boys. Rick McAninch, the director of Into Africa, drove us the 200 miles from the airport in the capital, Nairobi, to Kisumu.

Along the way, gasps from the children alerted me to two baboons squatting beside the road, and farther on, a herd of zebras grazed nearby. We drove through the famous Rift Valley, where it seems a giant knife sliced down the western third of Kenya and pried the two sides far apart.

As we drove through villages, women sat patiently beside the road, hoping to sell us carrots stuffed into plastic bags or potatoes stacked in neat pyramids.

Trees grew on many of the hillsides, their shapes familiar from a lifetime of *National Geographic* photographs of African sunsets with silhouetted giraffes among flaring, flat-topped trees.

About halfway to Kisumu and still in the hills, we started seeing what looked like vast fields full of bushy plants in a vivid spring green. It's tea, Rick told us, first cultivated here by the British and now a major export.

In Oregon, a field that size would probably be harvested by a big John Deere combine, but here, the tea fields are all harvested by hand, the workers picking off the newest leaves and putting them in baskets on their backs.

After a jarring five-hour ride on some of the worst roads I have ever seen, we reached Kisumu and our new home.

With nearly a million people, Kisumu is the third-largest city in Kenya. Located just south of the equator, it hugs the north shore of a small arm off Lake Victoria, the second-largest freshwater lake in the world and the source of the Nile River.

Having viewed it from across the bay, I would guess that the area of the city is far less than Eugene, with its 140,000-some population.

The only way to describe Kisumu is as I first saw it—a series of vivid impressions coming too rapidly to process them fully. Swarms of people—walking beside the road, milling down the sidewalks—the crowd at the Harrisburg parade repeated every day.

Very few cars in relation to the number of people on foot. Tiny little stores packed next to each other, selling electronics or dishes or bread.

Crowded white minibuses called *matatus*, careening down the street, their musical horns honking wildly. Small rickety fruit stands on street corners, the roofs consisting of skinny parallel branches.

Feverish beggars pleading, "My mother in Mombasa is very sick. Please, I need money for food for her." Street boys slinking up to your car, hands extended.

Women in bright dresses carrying umbrellas to shade them from the sun. Bicycle taxis whizzing by with each passenger straddling a seat behind the driver much like you probably used to ride with your big brother.

For most people in Kisumu, life is very difficult. Blue-collar wages run between one and three U.S. dollars a day. Malaria is so common that the U.S. Center for Disease Control does much of its malaria research here. The AIDS statistics are vague but terrible by all accounts, with an estimated 20 to 25 percent of the population inflicted with HIV or AIDS.

Corruption robs people of a fair chance to get ahead, and bribery is so rampant that public places such as airports are festooned with signs: "You have the right to be served. DO NOT OFFER A BRIBE."

Our three-bedroom apartment is an escape from the over-whelming realities of the street. It is part of a sprawling concrete house that contains the office and library of Into Africa, the directors and their family, and half a dozen staff members.

Surrounded by high walls and hedges for security rea-sons, our home is located in a lovely middle-class section of town with American-sized houses, well-kept flower beds, palm and mango trees, and neat driveways where garden-ers slowly sweep the flower petals off the gravel in the hot afternoon sun.

This part of Kisumu is where little familiar touches of home pop up unexpectedly—a philodendron just like my potted plant at home, a prowling cat. Paul and I went on a walk one day and came up behind a herd of cows ambling along the street exactly like the cows in Minnesota used to meander home when I rounded them up at milking time.

Just a few blocks away, in stark contrast to our manicured section of town, is one of Kisumu's three slums, a vast field of tightly-packed makeshift shacks, dirt paths, old galvanized tin roofing, painted advertisements, and people, people, people.

A hundred thousand people live there, they say, but I wonder who could ever get an accurate count. Here, more than anywhere else in the city, the poverty reaches out and slaps us in our sheltered American faces.

Every morning, thousands of people walk from this slum, past our gate, to their jobs downtown, a mile away. To our amazement, they are, almost without exception, neat and clean—the men in slacks and buttoned shirts; the women in pretty dresses or well-pressed skirts and blouses.

And when I meet them, the people are friendly, smiling, and nodding. From my perspective, it seems impossible.

Still a newcomer, I wonder if I will ever really understand these mysterious images of Kenya: clean and friendly people somehow emerging from a horrifying slum. A thousand strange new sights mixed with a dozen dear and familiar.

And waking every morning to sweeping brooms—the sound of a strong and quiet dignity refusing to give in to dirt and despair and desperation, the sound of daily swishing bravely on.

Making a Difference

*I*t was said, in the concentration camps of Europe in World War II, that among great cruelty and inhumanity one could also find great kindness and sacrifice.

Here in Africa, where daily life for many people is somewhere between difficult and horrifying, one finds small flames glowing—people willing to sacrifice to make a difference. Compelled by what they sense as a "call" from God, they do what they can, undaunted by the enormous suffering around them, content to make a difference to a few. We have been honored to get to know some of these special people and watch them at work.

According to our new friend Vincent Okello, a walking almanac of Kenyan statistics, all the indicators of poverty in Kenya are up in the past five years.

"More people than ever are living on less than one U.S. dollar a day," he says. "And it is always the children who are affected first. More of them die before the age of five, fewer get an education, and girls marry younger and carry on the cycle of poverty."

We asked Vincent about the street boys we see downtown. "How do they get there? Are they dumped like abandoned puppies at the age of eight or 10?"

"No," he says. "There is a three- to five-year pattern of increasing neglect before they end up on the street. Often the father is sick first, and the mother is increasingly preoccupied with his care, perhaps leaving to visit him in the hospital. Then after he dies, she is preoccupied with earning a living and getting food, and the child is left alone more and more, and perhaps the mother also dies. The child begins to make forays to the neighbors to ask for food, then he goes farther afield, then to the nearest town, then to the next one, and finally he ends up here on the streets of Kisumu."

Vincent is a college graduate—a rarity here, as fewer than one percent of Kenyans earns a degree. "I could easily leave and get a job in Europe or America," he says. "All of my friends have left. But I feel called of God to stay here and help my country."

He has a good job doing research for a non-government organization working with technology development. In addition, he donates his time to a number of causes, serving on committees with the Kenya Bureau of Standards and Save the Children UK. He also is the administrator of Into Africa, helping Rick and Audrey McAninch and the 30-plus street boys in their care.

Rick McAninch was a successful sales manager for a wholesale plumbing company in Seattle before he and Audrey came to Kenya in 1995. Now, he takes care of a hundred nuts-and-bolts details for Into Africa, and she oversees the boys' daily care and education.

At the Timothy House, the boys' home and school, the boys cook on a fire outside and sleep on no-frills metal bunk beds.

"We don't want them to get accustomed to an American lifestyle," Audrey says, "because they will probably never be able to maintain it in this country after they're grown, and there's almost no chance they can go to Europe or America. So we want them to know how to survive in this culture.

297

But mostly we try to build the character and practical skills that can make them leaders, so they can be like David in the Bible, who started off as a shepherd but had what it took to be a king when the time was right."

Kenya's educational system and widespread corruption make finding capable teachers and trustworthy staff difficult. The rewards, says Audrey, are seeing a boy who people think would never be anybody and watching him become somebody, and seeing the change in boys' eyes, from the vacant look one sees on the street to "happy eyes."

When we first arrived in Kisumu, and were still sorting out all the new faces, Audrey said, "Jonas is gone right now, but you'll know he's back when you hear singing."

Sure enough, a few days later, I heard a gospel song in a rich baritone, vibrating around a corner. Behind it came a tall young man, all knees and elbows, with a big smile. It was 25-year-old Jonas, who grew up in a nearby village and has been helping the McAninches for nearly eight years.

Jonas helps to screen the boys who come to Into Africa. He gets to know them on the street and travels to their home villages to determine if they are really orphans and if family members could care for them. While he would love to make a living performing gospel music, Jonas's calling for now is with the street boys, teaching music and serving as a houseparent at the Timothy House.

He also goes downtown early in the morning, when the boys are waking up from their night on the sidewalks, to let them know help is available. At times he rounds up several dozen, takes them to a restaurant, and buys them bean-and-corn porridge.

Once a week, Jonas goes to the Remand Center, a government-sponsored rescue/juvenile detention center. My husband accompanied him one Friday and watched, amazed, as Jonas sang and talked for two hours and kept the full attention of 60 kids.

One day, we heard a commotion at the gate and found that it was Jonas and five new boys just off the street. Soon Audrey, a drill sergeant of a woman with a big heart, was behind the house "interviewing" them.

"Can you work? We don't want boys here that don't work!"

Yeah, they could all work, they said. She handed each a garbage bag and told them to prove it, so they trooped out the gate and down the street to fill their bags with garbage. After a while, they returned, looking like tired, raggedy Santas with packs on their backs.

We went outside to meet the boys, and it was like an Aid-for-Africa brochure come to life. Imagine a boy, perhaps your 10-year-old son, in an ancient pair of shorts and an old T-shirt, five sizes too big, gray with dirt, shoulders ripping out. Imagine the look in the eyes of a boy with no mom, no dad, no home, no love, no bed to sleep in, no food in the fridge; a boy who regularly sniffs solvents to forget his troubles; who has spent the last year fending for himself on the streets at the mercy of the weather and older boys preying on him in the sickest ways imaginable.

It was those eyes that stuck a knife in my gut and twisted it.

Thankfully, Audrey decided they could all stay, and Jonas escorted them to their new home and got them settled in. Within a few weeks, the boys' vacant eyes began to change into the eyes of normal, mischievous 10-year-olds.

Jonas also helped our family get acquainted with Kisumu. A few days after we arrived, he offered to show us the neighborhood. We wandered around the block and down another street and ended up at New Life Home.

Some years ago, a British couple saw the need for a place in Nairobi for abandoned babies and those with HIV/AIDS, so they opened the first New Life Home. Later, they wanted to start satellite homes in other cities, so Rick and Audrey offered part of their house. Two years ago, the babies were moved to a new building about a half-mile away.

We entered the gate and signed in with the guard. Then, a nurse named Prisca showed us around.

"We have 16 babies now," she said. "We find them everywhere—in garbage cans, in latrines, left beside the road, abandoned at hospitals and police stations. We keep them here until they're six months old. Most of them get adopted out—over half to Kenyans and the rest to Europe and America."

We entered a breezy room and saw a receptionist's desk, couches for visitors, and half a dozen babies in infant seats. The place was clean and neat and sunny and well-furnished— but I took one look at those beautiful babies and felt an enormous and terrible sorrow rising up inside of me, and I burst into tears.

Prisca was still talking, but I was drowning in tears and trying to find a tissue.

"I'm sorry," I told her. "I can't help it."

"I understand," Prisca said kindly. "It's very moving. I've lived in Kenya all my life, and I still see things that move me to tears."

Four years ago, Prisca had a good job at the best hospital in town. But, she says, "I was reaching the end of the road

300

with stress. All the deaths, all the HIV...I saw that I couldn't take it anymore. Then our friends Rick and Audrey asked if I would help with the babies, and I felt called to this work. The pay is less, but it's much more satisfying. The babies come in so sick, and after a few days they perk up. You see them grow, then you see them get adopted into a family, and the parents bring them back to visit. It's so rewarding."

Prisca's husband John was a banker with Kenya Commercial Bank, but after Prisca began her work with the babies, he says, he felt called to help as well. He is now the administrator, overseeing the finances and general operation of New Life Home, Kisumu. "When you do what God wants you to do," John and Prisca say, "you are always at peace."

Kenya has nearly a million AIDS orphans, Kisumu has 1,500 street boys, and the AIDS infection rate is still increasing. Somehow undaunted by the statistics around them, these ordinary people are quietly making a difference in people's lives, one by one.

Another Tiny Grave

One Sunday, we got a taste of life—and death—in an African village.

There are Mennonite churches in five villages surrounding Kisumu, so we decided to attend the one in Rabuor, about 15 minutes away, on the main road leading to Nairobi. When we called the pastor's wife to get directions, she said that they were having only a short service at church that morning. After that, they would all be going to a funeral at the home of one of their church members, a young family whose five-month-old son had died the previous Friday.

After a brief service in a simple, concrete-block building, everyone piled into all the available vehicles as only Africans can pile into vehicles. Our family sat in our dusty Peugeot station wagon's two seats, and three grown men squeezed into the back. We made a small caravan as we headed down the main road.

After a few minutes, we turned off onto a dirt road and bumped along for a few more dusty miles, then parked beside a swamp.

Our group of 30 or 40 gathered at the bridge that crossed the swamp. It was probably 50 feet long, and we inched across, picking our way cautiously along the haphazard collection of branches and boards, careful not to step on the end of a board for fear it would plunge down, seesaw style. Thankfully, there were fenceposts every 10 feet or so to grab onto, and to my relief the pastor picked up Jenny, my four-year-old daughter, and carried her across.

After we had all safely crossed the swamp, we walked across a large cow pasture—dotted with thorn bushes and, here and there, a spindly tree—over to a circle of houses in a *dala*, or family group. Traditionally, the husband has a house, and each wife has a house, and later, the sons add houses as they are married. There is a complicated hierarchy, and a specific way each house has to face in relation to the others.

The parents of the deceased child were Tom and Goretty. They had a total of seven children, and this one, little Merle Beachy, named after a Mennonite bishop, was the fourth to die. He was sick for four days, they said. They assumed it was malaria.

First, we went to Tom and Goretty's place, crowding into the dark interior of their 20-foot-square house with its thick mud walls and corrugated metal roof. We stood around the little coffin and sang a few hymns in the Luo language.

Next, we were told to go outside to a makeshift shelter about 50 feet away, where old metal chairs and couches with foam rubber cushions were arranged in a semicircle. Three or four posts had been stuck in the ground, and a few ropes were strung between them and a thorn tree. Then, reed mats and burlap were laid on the ropes to make a bit of shade.

Our family was ushered to the best seats, the little coffin was placed on a small table directly in front of me, and the mother was seated in a chair nearby.

Other people filtered in—more church people, neighbors, family. They found places under the shelter or under the thorn trees nearby. There was no wailing, no noise, almost no talking.

The service began, again with Luo hymns. As the funeral proceeded through a sermon and testimonies and more songs, I sat there with the sun burning hotter and hotter through the thin burlap above me, and felt like I was tasting a little bit of this family's suffering.

There was Goretty in her blue dress, sitting calmly nearby. And there in the center of the canopy lay the body of her precious little boy in a cheap wooden coffin with a window in the top that allowed us to see him without smelling the odors of a two-day-old unembalmed body in the dreadful heat. Across from us sat Tom, on a couch with a few other men, his face deeply sad but also calm. Their three-year-old son laid his head on his mother's chair and fell asleep.

Far away, near another *dala*, a small boy chased his cows among the thorn bushes. The sun burned relentlessly. A rooster crowed. Once in a while, a slight breeze whiffed through the shelter; otherwise, the heat surrounded us like a smothering cloud. A sick-looking brown dog, with open sores on his back and all his ribs showing, crept under the pastor's chair and fell asleep.

I thought back to the night before, when our family had driven out to Lake Victoria. On the way home, we were talking about mosquitoes, and Jenny, with her usual vivid imagination, was devising ways to get rid of them.

"I'm going to draw a picture of a lizard, 'cuz lizards eat mosquitoes, and then I'll show it to the mosquitoes and say 'Rarrr!' to scare them away."

"But lizards don't say 'Rarrr!'" her sister said.

"I know. But I'll just say it to scare the mosquitoes," Jenny said.

It was completely unfair, I decided, that by virtue of where I was born, I could enjoy my daughter and watch her grow up. And, if the mosquitoes didn't all get chased off and she did get malaria, we had the city's best labs and doctors and pharmacies at our disposal. Goretty, by being born in an out-of-the-way African village, could never get her hopes up that her babies would live long enough to talk or draw pictures or grow into adulthood. Indeed, something as diagnosable and curable as malaria had just killed her baby.

This, I thought, is a tragedy.

The service was very quiet. The funeral processions that often pass our house in Kisumu are noisy with screaming, wailing, and what sounds like people banging pots and pans. There were tears at this funeral, but no screaming. To my amazement, both Tom and Goretty stood up and spoke for a few minutes. I couldn't understand what they were saying, but their voices were calm and they seemed to be filled with a supernatural grace.

The service drew to a close, and it was time for the burial. There are no cemeteries as such in the villages; family members are buried in the *dala*. We filed solemnly by Tom and Goretty's house, and there, 10 feet behind their house, was a four-foot-deep hole in the black dirt, with the coffin already in it by the time we got there. The bishop for whom the baby had been named said a few words of comfort to the family and encouraged the church to support them.

"Ashes to ashes," he said. "Earth to earth." And he dropped the first handful of dirt in the grave. It landed with a hollow thump.

I thought, Four times. Four times, now, this mother has buried a child. I am 41 years old, and I can't even remember ever attending the funeral of a child. And this young woman has now personally buried four.

The group dispersed after the burial, waiting, subdued, for lunch. The food was served on plastic plates and eaten with plastic spoons—a scoop of white rice with another scoop of boiled pinto beans. We sat in the scant shade of the houses and ate, then left for home, a long line of us filing across the cow pasture in the blazing sunshine.

We crossed the dubious bridge and piled into our vehicles, this time squeezing five grown men in the back of the Peugeot. We dropped the men off along the way and before long, we were home again, where our apartment had never seemed so cool and welcoming, and we had cold drinks and showers and naps. By evening, most of us were glowing with radiant pink sunburns.

Looking back, I think what I will remember even more than the terrible heat and sadness of that place are the faces of Tom and Goretty. In spite of their losses, they still held firmly to their faith, with a look of calm, quiet trust that God is with them and knows what he's doing.

When life and hope flourish in Kenya, I believe it will be God and people like Tom and Goretty who bring it about.

Bubbles and Paper Airplanes

There is a saying, "Be careful what you wish for; you might get it."

Before I was married, I taught in a church school. One of my worst "hardships" was those pesky parents. One mother thought I was too hard on her child, another thought I wasn't teaching good penmanship, and another didn't like the stories I read to the children. I would share these woes with my friends and conclude, "I wish I could just teach a bunch of orphans! Then I wouldn't have to deal with parents."

Twenty years later, my wish came true, and of course it wasn't at all what I thought it would be. Teaching African orphans turned my assumptions upside down. At the same time, the boys blessed me in ways that jaded American kids could never do.

The 30 former street boys at Into Africa's Timothy House in Kisumu range in age from approximately 10 to 17. They attend school right on the premises, and those who are unable to read are put through a phonics course before joining the main classroom.

During our months in Kenya, my husband Paul taught the larger group of boys and trained two teachers to take over when he left. I helped two or three hours a week with the six boys in the learning-to-read class. First, the teacher wanted me to help him teach phonics, but I soon found out that with the Kenyan rolled or silent R's and all-purpose

307

"ah" sound for vowels, it made no sense for an American to teach them sounds. Instead, I introduced them to a variety of crafts and activities, a good way for them to learn English, motor skills, and much more.

We painted a color wheel on the first day and I found that as long as the boys understood my English, they followed directions very well. "Blue in this section, yellow in that one, and then we mix blue and yellow...."

"Iss gdeen!" hollered Steven, the youngest, his face lighting up with joy.

This, I found, was the most rewarding part of teaching—their sense of discovery, their exuberant wonder. I had assumed that every 12-year-old boy on the planet had at some point made a paper airplane and tossed it across a classroom. But these boys had never heard of paper airplanes, and they frowned intensely as they tried to follow my example, folding this corner down to that line and pressing it down. Then they stood in a line and tossed their planes, a look of priceless amazement on their faces as the planes swooped away.

We made three sizes of airplanes—tiny, medium, and huge—and I told them to guess which would fly farthest. This was their most difficult challenge—thinking for themselves. Their scant education in the Kenyan system had all been rote memorization, and it seemed that no one had ever asked them questions to really make them think.

But they remembered well and even taught the older boys, because Paul told me later that after that lesson, he sometimes confiscated an errant paper airplane in the main classroom.

We mixed dish soap, water, and glycerin one day, I gave each boy a piece of wire to bend into a bubble wand, and then we went outside for their first experience with blowing bubbles. Little Jentrice swished his wand through the air and hollered "Thdee!" as three bubbles wafted through the air. Some of the older boys, 16- and 17-year-olds, watched curiously. I gave them pieces of wire and soon they also discovered, for the first time, the thrill of sending a glistening soap bubble through the air.

I also had assumed that all children know how to use scissors. But the first time we had a paper-cutting project, I was shocked to see two of the boys awkwardly chomping the blades at the paper, their fingers stiff and straight. So I found myself showing a 14-year-old how to use scissors, curving his fingers this way and his thumb like that, all the while thinking, This can't be.

Lurking behind the joys of teaching was the dark awareness that these boys were orphans with terribly painful pasts. One day, I decided to teach them "people" words with stick figures on the blackboard. Man, woman, boy, girl. "The man is the boy's father," I said. "The girl is his sister."

And then I turned around and for the first time saw hard and haunted looks on the boys' faces. What was I thinking, to wander into this minefield, talking of dads and sisters to boys who had lost their families?

"I don't know your stories," I finally said, "but I know you have had hard times and your lives have been sad. But in the Bible, God says that he loves you and he will be a father to you. So when you are sad, you can tell him all about it, and he will hear you." And then I wrapped up the class and fled, burdened with their collective grief.

When I had taught in other schools, we made trivets for the kids' mothers, and most of their artwork went home to hang on the refrigerator or be mailed to Grandma. What do you do with an orphan's artwork?

Well, they had other caring adults in their lives such as houseparents and teachers, so one day we rubber-stamped thank-you notes. Following my example, Lawrence tapped a stamp on the ink pad, carefully pressed it on his paper, and lifted it off. "Caht!" he shouted, thrilled with the image on his paper.

"When people do things for us, we thank them," I said. "It makes them happy. So on these cards, we will write a message saying thank you to the people who take care of you." Jentrice waved his hand in the air and desperately tried to express himself in English. "I thank *you*, Teachah, for coming to teach us!" he exclaimed.

That was supposed to make me happy, but instead, whenever I think of his words, I cry. I am now back in my normal American routine, but my heart is still back with "my" street boys. In my vast abundance, I remember how little they had, how much they gave, and how blessed I was to know them.

Bread on the Waters

 $\mathcal{I}$ first noticed Steven the day he limped into class. He was about nine years old, the youngest in the learning-to-read group at the boys' home in Kisumu. Steven was limping, it turned out, because he had an oozing, open wound near his ankle.

This child, I thought, examining his foot, needs a mother.

He continued to catch my eye with his quiet smile and little bursts of enthusiasm, such as his delighted "Iss gdeen!" when he mixed blue and yellow paint.

Before we went to Kenya, we had talked about adopting a baby. Helping for an hour once a week at the babies' orphanage, I wanted every baby in the place. Yet we never felt that deep-inside "yes" necessary for such a decision.

Then one day while my husband and I were driving to school, I said impulsively, "Maybe we should adopt Steven."

Where did that come from? I wondered afterward. I really hadn't planned to say it.

To my surprise, Paul thought it was a wonderful idea, and our five children were just as enthusiastic. They soon thought of all kinds of reasons we should adopt.

Some were silly: It's so much easier to cut a pie into eight pieces rather than seven, and just think, a package of eight hot dogs would come out even.

Other reasons were practical: Our house is big enough for another child. He would fit neatly into the five-year empty slot between Ben and Jenny. He needs a family, and we have the resources to provide one for him.

311

Fundamentally, we all sensed that we could not experience Kenya's orphan crisis firsthand and not do something tangible about it, something beyond giving our time for a few months.

Ideally, we would have found a Kenyan family to take Steven, and helped with his ongoing expenses. But the AIDS situation is so advanced that the system is saturated, and anyone with any means is already taking care of nieces, nephews, and other relatives.

Even though adoption had been my idea, I had the most misgivings. Was it wise to make a poor black Kenyan Pentecostal city child part of a comfortable white American rural Mennonite family? Steven was a happy child; was it right to uproot him? Did I have enough energy to meet the needs of six children, and was Paul too busy to be a dad to another child?

"What if we adopt him and I don't like him?" I asked Paul one morning.

He snorted. "Do you always like me?"

"No," I admitted. End of discussion.

"Think of the future," suggested our Kenyan friend Vincent. "You know the Smucker family will still be a family in five years. No one knows if this boys' home will still be here then."

One morning, Paul read from Ecclesiastes 11:1, 2 for our family's Bible time: "Cast thy bread upon the waters: for thou shalt find it after many days. Give a portion to seven, and also to eight; for thou knowest not what evil shall be upon the earth."

Fifteen-year-old Amy's face lit up. "That's it! There's our sign!" I assumed she meant the part about casting bread on the waters, but I was wrong. "See?" she said. "It says, 'Give a portion to seven' and we're seven now, 'and also to eight,' and if we get Steven, we'll be eight!"

At first we laughed—such twisting of scripture. But the more I thought about it, the more I felt like that verse was meant for us that morning. Casting your bread on the waters meant investing your resources even when the outcome is uncertain. We didn't know "what evil shall be upon the earth" and how, at some point, we could bless Steven's life, and he ours. We returned to the United States in March, determined to pray and ask for advice before we made a decision.

One week in April, we specifically asked God for "no's" and closed doors if we shouldn't do this. All we got were resounding "yes's" and doors flying open.

Steven's AIDS test came back negative, and an investigator was unable to locate any relatives at all (we didn't want to adopt unless he was a "total" orphan). I had an unexpected conversation with two adoptive moms at a garage sale, where I mentioned what we were thinking and my uncertainty about it.

"Do you remember his eyes?" one of the women asked me, a wise and knowing look on her face. And I immediately started crying; I remembered his eyes all too well.

We e-mailed Paul's African-American cousin for advice and he responded enthusiastically, offering to help in any way he could. "If any family can do this successfully, the Smuckers can," he wrote.

Other people cautioned us with chilling unsuccessful-adoption stories and wondered how we would deal with racial issues. How can we do this? I would ask myself, panicking. And then I would wonder, more calmly, How can we *not* do this?

Eventually, we knew this was the right thing to do, a deep-inside "yes" that would give us strength for the long process ahead.

We waited to tell him until the home study and other paperwork were completed, then the home's director informed Steven and e-mailed his response. "I'm happy. I feel good—to live with you. I want to be their son. I want to be with brothers and sisters. I feel good to have them."

And then, finally, it was real—Steven was going to be our son. My birth-children began with a seed in my womb; Steven became my son through a seed planted in my heart the day I looked at his foot and realized how much he needed a mother.

I once heard a woman say that joy and sorrow travel on the same track and arrive at the same time. We completed the paperwork to adopt Steven and bought a ticket for Paul to fly to Kenya. At the same time, Paul's dad fought his battle with cancer, enduring four weeks of daily radiation. As Paul's departure date drew closer, his dad grew weaker, and our lives were a strange mixture of anticipation and dread.

Should Paul go or shouldn't he? we wondered. The all-important court date was set and we both felt we shouldn't cancel it unless we absolutely had to.

On the day we were preparing to leave for the airport, I was dashing around looking for books Paul could read on the plane. Then the phone rang. It was Paul's youngest sister. "Dad's gone," she said simply.

Instead of flying off to meet his new son, Paul was canceling his flights and appointments and making funeral arrangements for his father.

We grieved for Paul's dad, for our plans, and for Steven's hopes—he had been so excited about seeing his new dad. It would be several months, we figured, before a new court date could be arranged.

To our surprise, our lawyer in Kenya arranged for a new court date only two weeks later. From that point on, we had an increasing sense that God was in charge of this script, writing the story, and that we were only characters in it, woven in with circumstances and miracles far beyond our control.

On the Internet, we had found a group of parents who adopted in Kenya. "It can take months," they warned us. "You'll never get those documents without bribing. I had to give this guy $200 in a men's restroom with the lights off." "The people at the embassy are heartless—you'll be their lowest priority and they really don't care what happens to you." "An embassy inspector has to travel from Nairobi to Kisumu to do an investigation. That can delay things for weeks."

Nevertheless, Paul bought tickets for both him and Steven to return to America on Christmas Eve, three weeks after he left.

Here in Oregon, the church youth group gathered at 11 p.m. to pray at the same time the court hearing was taking place in Kenya. The judge approved the adoption, and Steven was officially ours.

Our lawyer, we found out later, was astonished. The day before, he had appeared before the judge and presented what he thought was an open-and-shut adoption case—a Kenyan couple wanted to adopt the wife's niece. But the judge refused to approve the adoption. There was no chance, the lawyer thought, that the judge would let this American man adopt a 10-year-old Kenyan boy.

A woman at the American embassy took a personal interest in Steven's case and did all she could to get his visa. She also did the investigation.

"My family is from that area," she said. "I have to attend a funeral near Kisumu on Saturday, so I'll come by and do the investigation on Sunday."

Doors opened at the right time, planes flew to Nairobi on schedule, and a vast network of friends kept praying that Paul and Steven could be home for Christmas.

Five years ago, after our daughter Jenny was born, I told Paul, "You can have the next baby!"

In a very real sense, that was exactly what happened. While I stayed at home and encouraged from a distance, Paul labored through regulations, forms, waiting in lines, and computer glitches that threatened delays—all without bribing anyone.

He also bonded with his new son, telling me excitedly about the first time that Steven called him "Dad" and Steven's reaction to seeing giraffes for the first time, out the window of the train.

At the Portland airport, on Christmas Eve, we met Paul and Steven in a flood of hugs and tears.

Since then, Steven has been learning what it means to be part of a family. He feeds the cat every morning, colors pictures with five-year-old Jenny, and hugs me goodnight.

Every day, he makes new discoveries—riding a bike, seeing fog and frost for the first time, sticking magnets to the refrigerator, and picking out "Joy to the World" on the piano.

"He sounds exactly like a Smucker," says my friend Arlene.

Of course he does—that's exactly who he is.

Normal, with a Twist

Every six weeks, the guys in our family get haircuts. I roll up the bathroom rug, set up a wooden stool, clip a garbage bag around their shoulders, and snip. First, Paul's thinning blond hair falls to the floor. Matt's thick auburn hair is next on the pile, then Ben's dark brown locks.

Steven was 10 years old and bald when we adopted him in December—they shaved the boys' heads at the orphanage as a precaution against lice. We let his hair grow, letting it form a soft black fluff and learning how to care for it from helpful people at Sally Beauty Supply.

Finally, Steven's hair began to gather in untidy clumps, and it was time for his first haircut. We followed the same 20-year-ritual of setting him on the stool and clipping the garbage bag with a clothespin. But what should I do then? With the others, I always flip tufts of hair up between my fingers with a comb and then cut them off. But each strand of Steven's hair was like a tightly-coiled spring. There was no way I could use the same technique.

Finally, I pushed the comb into a clump of hair, flat against his head, and cut off everything above the comb, repeating the process all over his scalp. Instead of feathery strands drifting to the floor, little black wads of fluff dropped down, and I pronounced his slightly-uneven trim a success.

Since we save samples of each first haircut for the baby books, we gathered Steven's hair into a little Ziploc bag, labeled it, and put it away.

This, I decided, is life with Steven: normal—but with just a slight twist.

For the first few weeks, Steven was alarmingly good. Quiet and cooperative, he ate what was set in front of him and went to bed when he was told. Not that I minded having an easy child, but I worried that he was too damaged by his past to be a "real" child.

Then, the night our church hosted a welcoming party for him, I found out he was a normal boy. Two or three little girls came running down the stairs, shrieking that Steven was balancing on the balcony rail. I nearly fainted, imagining him plunging 15 feet down and cracking his head open on the edge of an oak pew. Even though he had spent the past four years in an all-male environment, Steven obviously had an inborn urge to show off for girls.

He also, it turned out, had the same compulsion that my other two boys were born with to throw balls in the living room. And, like his brothers at age 10, he thought all noisy bodily functions were hilariously funny.

Just as I was convinced that he was a normal 10-year-old Smucker boy, he threw in a little twist, choosing a purple comb-and-mirror set from the merit store in his classroom and proudly wearing the comb in his hair. It was hard to know how to respond—should I let him enjoy the comb and expose him to possible ridicule, or should I disappoint him with an explanation of American gender roles?

It also was hard, at first, to set limits or to discipline Steven. Thinking of his past, with its unimaginable grief and loss, was almost paralyzing. Somehow, I wanted to spare him pain for the rest of his life. So, with sweetness and patience, I explained the family rules: "In this house, we walk around the couch, like this; we do not climb over it, and we do not throw balls in the living room because things can break."

Then, quite suddenly, I was tired of being syrupy. Steven was a member of the family; he ought to get the same treatment as anyone else. So when he threw his red ball in the living room again and it hit the ceiling fan and light with a clanging of chains and fan blades, he got yelled at with all three names: "Steven Ochieng Smucker!"

After that, he was like a lamb let loose in a new pasture—having a wonderful time but determined to test the electric fences and getting shocked every time. He went down to the creek without telling me where he was going. No creek time for two days. He got his church pants muddy. ("I didn't play outside. Really. I only ran around.") No electronic time for two days.

Then, when I thought he was getting causes and effects all figured out, he showed me how little he really knew. He had the good sense to take off his new watch before washing the car, but then he tossed it in the grass and forgot to pick it up. It was run over by the lawn mower and destroyed. I grieved more than he did when he gathered up the broken pieces and brought them inside. How I wanted to rush out and replace the watch, but we knew he would learn faster if we let him experience the consequences.

In matters such as the watch, Steven reasoned like a four-year-old. My other five children progressed through childhood in logical stages—fun babies, exploring toddlers, inquisitive preschoolers, and so on.

Steven still seems to experience every stage of childhood at once. He snuggles beside me to listen to *The Biggest Bear* over and over, just like my kids at age three. He giggled like a six-month-old and begged for more when I showed him how This Little Piggy was done. For weeks, he was like a two-year-old, dashing around the house, grabbing everything he could reach, and pushing buttons on the phone, computer, and CD player while I followed with a chorus of no-no's. He dug a hole in the garden and had a mud fight with Ben like any 10-year-old.

And sometimes, sadly, Steven is about 30 years old.

One day, my daughters were discussing a character in an Anne of Green Gables book. "In the book, the boy dies. In the movie, he lives," one of them said.

Steven, overhearing, got a frightened look in his eyes.

"Who died?" he asked.

"Just a pretend person in a book," I said. Then, on a hunch, I added, "Did any of your friends die when you lived on the street?"

"There was a big boy who wanted to be the leader of the street boys," he answered. "And some of the others didn't like him. So they took a block like this," (demonstrating about two feet by three feet) "and they threw it at him. A lady took him to the hospital and they buried him."

It was the familiar twist, only this time it was a knife twisting in my gut. God have mercy, I thought, how can we ever hope to heal this child's soul? Within minutes, however, Steven was back to normal—shooting baskets, playing with the cat, doing his chores—his happy look back in his eyes.

Our prayer for Steven is that somewhere among the siblings and parents and pets and food and love and friends that make up his world now, the gaps in his life will be filled in and he will emerge as a normal, functional adult. Yet, we also want him to stay just a bit on the other side of normal, with his grief and loss turned into an extra measure of compassion, his pain becoming a greater sense of gratitude and joy.

A Boy and His Dog

Our adopted son Steven is just like the rest of the Smuckers in that he has a noisy sneeze and can argue like a budding lawyer, but he also has a heart for animals like none of us has ever seen.

The girls and I like cats, and in his early teens our oldest son Matt was fond of his lizards in a detached, scientific way. But for the most part we are not animal lovers, and in particular, I am not a dog person.

But Steven loves all animals and has a gentle, mysterious charm with them. Last winter, he found a half-dead rabbit on the road, brought it inside, and tried to revive it. Even though my husband Paul insists that Katzie is an outdoor cat, Steven sneaks out the back door on cold mornings and lets her into the laundry room.

We had the house re-sided last summer, and one day the siding guy, whom I had considered a sensible man up to that point, found two half-grown starlings in the porch rafters. He gave them to Steven, suggesting he keep them as pets. I was unaware of this until I came into the living room and saw two birds fluttering madly in opposite directions and a flustered and guilty-looking Steven trying to chase down both at once.

We finally corralled the birds and put them outside, Steven helped me clean up their deposits on the carpet, and I lectured him about keeping wild animals out of doors. He complied, reluctantly, and after that I would see him sitting motionless on the porch swing with the starlings on his shoulders.

But he always wanted more animals. He begged for chickens, lambs, more cats. Cows and horses would be nice, and goats. Maybe some ducks and turkeys. And a dog. He really, really wanted a dog.

The biggest drawback to having animals is the guilt I endure when the kids lose interest and neglect them. Matt still cringes when I bring up the Dead Hamster Episode that led to the end of his pet career.

The last thing I wanted was the guilt of a dirty, hungry dog yapping at the back door. "I have enough to take care of around here without adding a dog to the list," I ranted, but my protests did not decrease the pleading look in Steven's eyes, or his siblings', who were rapidly being swayed to his side.

"All right," Paul told Steven, "you prove with Katzie that you can take care of a pet, and we'll get you a dog." There wasn't much to prove, I admitted, grudgingly, as Steven had been feeding Katzie faithfully almost from the day he arrived.

Paul thought we should get a dog from a shelter or the "free" ads in the newspaper, maybe after Christmas. But then we heard about Mr. Fenske's dog.

Mr. Fenske was an elderly German man from nearby Brownsville who started attending our church. One Sunday I asked him, *"Wie geht's?"* ("How's it going?") He grinned in delight, and we had a short conversation. I looked forward to practicing my German with him again, but he died only a short time later.

The family asked the church youth group to sing at his funeral. Not long after, we were told that Mr. Fenske had left a dog, and his children wanted to give it to one of those Mennonite families whose young people sang so nicely at the funeral.

Oh, great.

We drove to Brownsville one Saturday to see the dog. Mr. Fenske's son Daniel led us through the house and onto the back porch where we were greeted by a massive beast that looked the size and color of the lions we saw on safari in Kenya.

"No. Absolutely not," I protested mentally. "He could pick up Jenny and toss her like a rag doll. If he planted those paws on my chest I'd be flat on my back in an instant."

"His name is Hansie, and he's real friendly," Daniel said. Indeed. Hansie pranced around us, sniffing impolitely and wagging his tail so hard it nearly knocked us over. To my relief, he didn't lick, bite, or jump up on us, but we soon had dirt and blond hairs all over our clothes from waist to shoes.

"My dad was too weak to groom him much," the son apologized. I could well imagine. Two grown men couldn't bathe this dog against his will, and for sure not frail Mr. Fenske with his walker.

"I suppose he'd eat us out of house and home," I muttered.

"Actually, he doesn't eat that much," Daniel said. "The last time we weighed him he was 180 pounds, so we're cutting down on his food."

We drove home with the kids bouncing up and down in the back seat. "Yes! Yes! Yes! Let's get him!" Paul kept his own counsel, but I could tell he loved the dog and was plotting his strategy for persuading me.

The next few days, Paul organized and the children promised: food, shelter, water, grooming, playtime, cleanup, training. Delicately they chipped away at my resistance until I had to admit that I had no more reason to say no.

Except for one thing: a mental block from my childhood experiences with dogs. Paul never knows quite what to do with a wife awash in feelings, but one evening he patiently listened while I told him my stories. We would pick up a free puppy somewhere and irresponsibly let it fend for itself until it chased cars and we got tired of it, and then we would get rid of it. Worst was the time I saw my brother attempt to put down a dog behind the barn; it didn't die until the second shot. I'm sure Paul didn't have a clue what to say next, but he said exactly the right thing: "I promise we will never shoot a dog."

"Okay. Fine. Let's get the dog."

Paul built a nice fenced dog run. Daniel Fenske and his wife bathed the dog and gave us his doghouse, a leash, and a large bag of dog food.

Hansie came home on Thanksgiving Day. Already, he seems to belong here. His German name fits right in with Katzie's. I go out and talk to him in my native German dialect, and he understands me better than anyone else in the family does. I still am not a dog person, honestly, but I find him a very remarkable dog. I take pictures to post on my Web site, and it looks like I have a normal-sized dog and really little kids.

When we gave Steven the gift of a family, we had no idea what precious gifts he would give us in return. Thanks to him, we have a noble-looking German shepherd named Hansie who lies in his kennel and watches alertly over this new kingdom of his. He and the boys race around the yard together. He goes on walks with the girls and I know that no other dog, human, or cougar would dare come close enough to harm them. He loves us all, especially Steven, with a warm and gentle and mysterious affection.

Downstairs the Queen Is Knitting

Table of Contents

Introduction

Raising a family is like a canoe trip down the Willamette River. You have a pretty good idea of where you want to go and how you want to get there, but the actual journey involves things you weren't expecting: a swift current, dangerous snags, swirling eddies, and lots of seemingly unproductive hard work, as well as the unexpected beauty of leafy sunshine on the water and determined ospreys diving for fish.

This book is a collection of essays about rural life in Oregon's Willamette Valley. It's about the strange, surprising journey of family life, about joy and laughter as well as guilt and grace and grief. It's about legacies and children and travels and marriage and loss.

These stories revolve around my husband and me and our six children. Written over a three-year period, they do not appear in chronological order, so you can open the book at random and peruse a chapter of your choice. Each one, I am told, is as long as a cup of coffee. Some are sweet, some black, some with lots of cream.

Growing Up

Silly Putty on the Quilt: This, Too, Shall Pass

Life is never dull with two preteen boys.

Steven is 11, Ben is 12, and all day, the action never seems to stop. They eat mountains of calories and beg for more the instant the dishes are done. They spring into the air and slap their grimy hands on the door frames every time they walk through. Everything not nailed down, such as eggs or quart jars of green beans, must be tossed into the air and (usually) caught, every napping person wakened, every phone conversation disrupted.

They hold burping contests and comb-and-paper kazoo concerts and karate-chopping-cookies demonstrations. They put rocks in each other's ears, whack each other with canoe paddles, and soak each other when they're supposed to be washing the van. They break their little sister's hoe — accidentally, they insist — and my favorite china saucer. They feed ice cream to the cat, leave their sandals in the yard for the dog to chew on, and try to hatch tadpoles in quart jars of slimy green water. They put a loaf of bread in the freezer, as instructed, then absentmindedly place a three-pound package of sausage on top of it.

Personal hygiene is a foreign concept. The boys would wear the same T-shirts every day until they stood stiffly at attention under their own power.

With Ben's digital camera, they make jittery movies with scenes that plunge sideways and swirl nauseatingly. One boy sweeps to the basket and dunks the ball while the other holds the camera and hollers a commentary, trying to sound like Jerry Allen, the Ducks' announcer. Then they huddle their sweaty bodies in front of the computer and replay each scene backward and forward at high speeds, howling with laughter and shoving each other.

Mothering these boys is an exhausting job, complicated by the fact that I also have three older children and a 7-year-old daughter who thinks too much and never stops talking. "I wonder what I should do," she says, soaking in the bathtub, "if I'm all grown up and there's this guy who really likes me and he wants to marry me, but I don't really like him. What should I do, Mom? I mean, he might be nice and stuff. And I'd feel sorry for him. But if I don't like him I don't want to marry him, you know?"

One day I decided I deserved a break and sat down to eat a slice of pie and read one section of the newspaper. What are the chances, I wondered, that I can get through this pie and this paper without being interrupted? Zero, it turned out. I was interrupted 11 times—twice by the phone ringing, once by someone at the door, and eight times by children who "desperately" needed me.

I spend much of my time averting disaster and dealing with crises, always with the sense that I am forgetting something important and if I only had a moment to catch my breath I would remember what it was. What I need most and seldom get in this stage is perspective, a "this-too-shall-pass" mentality to give me a sense of humor and a wider view than today's broken eggs on the kitchen floor.

The truth, which I normally am too distracted to recognize, is that I have the perspective I need right under my nose. Matt, who is 20, and Amy, 18, are seldom around and make far less noise than their siblings, so I don't notice them as much. They spent hours in their rooms studying until finals week was over, and now they zip through the kitchen, grabbing an orange, on their way to work. Both of them are responsible young adults who take out the trash or clean bathrooms without complaining and call me on the way home to ask if I need milk or fresh fruit. Now and then, my husband and I sit up late with them and have long, refreshing discussions.

And both Matt and Amy, now that I think of it, used to be 12.

I was cleaning the attic recently when I found a stash of books and magazines: *Animals of North America, Encyclopedia of Animal Life, Reptile Digest.* It seemed like only yesterday when I had put them in the attic, and only the day before when they were all over Matt's room and he was consumed with his interest in animals.

I called Matt up to the attic and asked him what I should do with all these books. He looked them over, maneuvered his tall body down the attic ladder, and said casually, "You can give them all to Goodwill."

I wanted to cry. Suddenly I was nostalgic, actually sentimental, for the days when he was 10 or 12, spouting animal facts, arguing incessantly, losing his temper, and placing a jar of meat and flies on his windowsill and watching the entire biomass change into a seething pile of maggots.

Matt, who used to act like he would die if he had to dry dishes, was my lifesaver last week when we threw a surprise party for Amy's 18th birthday at a park in Peoria. He muscled tables, chairs, slow cookers, and pitchers into the cars and then helped me unload them all at the other end and reload them when the party was over. When did he turn into a considerate, helpful young man? I have no idea.

A few days after her party, Amy curled up on the couch with Paul and me for one of those precious late-night talks. "The other day I found my diary of when I was 12," she said. "You guys must have been really worried about me. 'I hate Dad!'" she quoted, laughing. "'He's just so harsh and domineering. I just hate it when he always lectures me. And Mom gets in bad moods and gets mad at people for nothing.'"

Amy was right: We were worried about her back then. She didn't like us, and I feared she never would. "Everything I say to her is the wrong thing," I wailed on the phone to my brother, who had a daughter the same age. I felt that we were losing Amy and I had no idea how to bring her back.

My brother, as I recall, tried to tell me that I was doing the important things right, everything would be OK, and Amy would not always be 12. I didn't believe him. Lost in the thunderstorms of that time, I saw no signs of the sunshine on this side or a laughing young woman sitting up late for a cozy talk with her mom and dad.

At Amy's party, I sat at a picnic table beside my sister-in-law, Rosie. "How are your kids doing?" she asked, genuinely interested as always.

"My big kids are turning into these really nice people," I said. "I'm so impressed with them."

"You sound surprised," Rosie said, amused.

"I never felt like I knew what I was doing as a mom," I told her. "I was always surprised when my children turned a year old because they had actually survived babyhood under my care. And when they turn into good adult people, I can hardly believe it, either."

Today, Steven's denim quilt showed up in the laundry hamper smeared with huge splotches of green Silly Putty. I have no idea how to clean it.

I see that, in spite of my careful instruction, all five of Ben's dresser drawers are open, all at different angles, with tired socks and shirts hanging over the edges and spilling onto the floor.

"This, too, shall pass," I tell myself. "Someday they'll grow up; someday you'll be surprised. Take a deep breath. Stay calm. Believe."

Gifts from a Child

ight on time on a Monday afternoon, my son Steven and I enter the small sanctuary at Emerald Baptist Church. His wet shoes squeak on the wood floor as he finds his seat in the third row. I sit toward the back and wait.

More boys come in, sniffing and cold, with raindrops in their hair. They shuck coats and toss them to their mothers, then bang on the piano, tap the drums, or clamber over the seats.

Tama, the director, takes her place and claps her hands: clap, clap, clapclapclap. The boys repeat the rhythm. Stragglers find their seats. Talkers quiet down. Tama slaps another short series. The boys repeat it.

Then the pianist plays a few notes and the weekly miracle happens as two dozen elbowing, noisy boys suddenly transform, with a burst of clear and beautiful song, into the Junior Boys' division of the Oregon Children's Choir. "Glo-o-o-o-ria," they sing, "Hosanna in excelsis!"

As the music swirls around me, I feel, as always, a mix of love and pride and vindication and awe and strange unnamed emotions. What gifts—this son, his talents, and the blessings he has given our family.

The Christmas story is about God choosing the most unlikely to bring the greatest gifts: a small child, poor and powerless, bringing redemption and hope to the world. God still works in children today, I believe, not in the cosmic sense of bringing salvation as Jesus did, but in subtle and gentle influences that we never thought to ask for.

Steven came home to us from Kenya two years ago on Christmas Eve, a small, shy, tired 10-year-old with a shaved head. It was soon obvious that Steven loved music. He could hear a tune once and whistle it perfectly. Everything became a song: On school mornings, he hopped to the bathroom after breakfast chanting "Teeth, face, hair!" to the tune of "Hot Cross Buns."

"You should develop his talent," my musical sister-in-law said. I took her word for it, since my husband, Paul, and I are not especially musical.

After much searching I found the Oregon Children's Choir and took Steven in for an audition last summer. He scored five-out-of-five on all the little exercises, and the director said she would be delighted to have him in the choir. It was a confirmation, again, of a divine touch on Steven's life—a former street orphan transformed into a loyal member of a children's choir in Oregon.

Today, Steven is six inches taller, 30 pounds heavier, and many times more noisy and active than when he first came. He has a nice crop of hair that clumps when he forgets to brush it.

Despite his arrival on Christmas Eve, Steven does not wear a halo. He fudges the truth at times, absentmindedly leaves scissors in the refrigerator, and is known as one of the Burp Kings at his school. Yet this does not disqualify him from blessing others, both in our immediate family and far beyond it, a comfort to those of us who sometimes wonder if we are too imperfect for God to use in his purposes on Earth.

One of Steven's many gifts to me comes when he sings. I thought I was at peace with my lack of music ability, yet something blissful and healing takes place when I watch

Steven singing in the choir, tall and confident in the back row. I finally feel compensated for a lifetime of failing choir tryouts, having the teacher tell me in front of everyone that I was singing too low, and not knowing how to sing the "shaped" do-mi-sol notes.

Steven has blessed our family in other ways as well.

"Have you noticed that Ben doesn't say 'I'm bored' anymore?" my daughter asked the other day.

She's right. Ben, who is 13, used to flop on the couch and complain that there was nothing to do. Not anymore. Now he has a willing buddy to toss a football with him, canoe down the creek, or practice burping.

Also, I had a troubling sense, a few years ago, that my husband's busyness was calling his heart and priorities away from his family. He traveled a lot and took on enormous amounts of work. When Steven came, Paul quit traveling and made sure he was at home every evening for six months to put Steven and the other children to bed. Paul chose this primarily for Steven's benefit, but I feel that it brought him back to the rest of us as well, and I am grateful.

Perhaps the most remarkable story of Steven's influence involved an inmate at a state prison in Salem. Every year our church helps with a project that delivers thousands of handmade Christmas cards, along with cookies and a small gift, to inmates in various prisons around the state. The schoolchildren help with this as well, coloring and signing dozens of cards.

Some time after last year's project, the director received a letter from a 21-year-old prisoner and read it at church. The young man wrote that one morning, discouraged and depressed, he tried to write a prayer in poetry form, but quit and threw it away. Later that day, he received the Christmas packet from our church. He ate the cookies and opened the card.

Then he wrote, "It made me cry. It said, 'Have a happy time. From Steven, age 10.' "Something hit me and I don't really know what.... It made me feel like there's somebody out there that really does care. I know he didn't know who was going to get it, but I believe with all my heart it was meant for me. Is it coincidence that I started with writing a prayer to God that day which I've never done, gave up, then received a card ... from a little boy that opened my eyes and heart into something I can't explain?

"I would like you to know I feel weird writing all this. I'm supposed to be a tough guy and I'm still in a gang. But you know, I want help, I want to learn a different way of life.

"I ended up picking that poem out of the trash and I finished it. It's my first prayer to God and I owe it to that boy named Steven (who) by a simple card gave me something I've never ever had, a hope for a better way of life."

The prisoner's poem followed:

My First Prayer: Is There an Angel for Me?
(Dedicated to Steven, age 10)

Is there an extra angel, Lord
That maybe you could lend to me
I know this is a lot I'm asking for
While down on bended knee.
I've caused my world to crumble to pieces
I even pushed my family away
Coming up with excuses I called reasons

> Yet still I feel this pain
> With my hands to my face I close this prayer
> God please forgive me for all my sins
> Please show my family love and care
> Help lead me away from this life I live.
> Amen.

At this year's Festival of Trees, Steven stood with the other choristers, all handsome in their navy blue shirts and khaki pants, and sang: "Do you hear what I hear? Do you know what I know? A child, a child, he will bring us goodness and light."

Listening, I thought, "Yes, he does. Both that child and this one. Yes, I hear, I know."

The Blackberries
of Parenting

I have lofty goals for my children. I expect them to grow up equipped with both wisdom and common sense, able to sense and avoid danger, ready to see a need and meet it, and eager to make a difference in the world. However, I have two adolescent boys who are not as enthusiastic about my goals and standards as I am. In fact, their ideas and mine seem to clash on a regular basis. This results not in me lowering my standards, but rather in plunging into despair because I'm sure I have failed as a mom.

A typical example of this is the recent event we now refer to as the Blackberry Episode. Wild blackberries are both a pest and a blessing in this part of the Willamette Valley. Uncontrolled, they take over any vacant area, smothering old machinery and small buildings and anything else in their way. But late every summer, along fence rows and behind old barns, they produce a crop of delicious berries, nestled among millions of vicious thorns, free to anyone brave enough to pick them.

I have found this a good enterprise for Ben, age 14, and Steven, 12, who like to attempt courageous feats and go exploring in jeans and rubber boots. As August turned into September, I sent them out every few days. They always returned with an ice cream bucket or two of berries, which I turned into pies, cobblers, and jars of pie filling for this winter. Their best picking spot was about half a mile away, across the neighbor's fescue field, along the railroad tracks.

One day I realized the rain would be coming soon and the blackberry season was about to end, so after supper I sent the boys on one last expedition, letting them out of doing dishes as a bonus. An hour or so later they came back, but with only part of a bucket of berries. Suspiciously, I demanded an explanation and Ben slowly complied. "Uh, well, you see, it's like this. We picked a full bucket of berries, plus about a third, and then we climbed the fence back into the field and headed home and I was like, 'Hey! Big wide-open field—let's see if we can walk 200 steps with our eyes closed!'"

I thought, "No no no. Please, no."

Steven traversed his 200 steps safely, I was told, and opened his eyes to see that Ben had veered off north toward Substation Drive and a fence. He yelled, but Ben ignored him, figuring Steven had stepped in a hole or something. Shortly after, at step 181, Ben crashed into the fence and spilled his entire bucket of berries irretrievably into the dirt and straw.

"Yeah."

I am not often at a loss for words, but when I heard this woeful tale I opened my mouth to say something, then shut it, shook my head, then opened my mouth again, then shut it again. The boys quickly leaped into the gap and said all the proper things such as, "We know it was really stupid; we're sorry; we'll never try that again; we'll pick more berries tomorrow."

My husband, Paul, then joined the conversation. "See, what you have to do is look around and make sure there's no fence within 200 steps in any direction before you try that."

My silent tongue let loose at this point in a shrill, "What? That's not the point! The point is that you think about the cargo in your hands before you do something that stupid! And you don't walk with your eyes shut with a bucket of blackberries in your hands, fence or no fence!"

Paul and the boys looked at me sympathetically, no doubt thinking, "Poor Mom, off on one of her rants again."

As always, I read far too much into the incident. I was failing as a mom; there was no doubt about that. All these years and I hadn't taught Ben and Steven a shred of common sense. If they lived to grow up they would no doubt someday try to walk 200 steps across a fescue field—or a busy highway—with their eyes closed, only with their first child in their arms rather than a bucket of berries.

Paul, in contrast, was calm and straightforward as always. "Well," he told me, "that's one of the disadvantages of having creative kids." He did not say out loud, but implied, "And I recall you were the one that always wanted creative kids."

My friend, Arlene, when I called her, was far more consoling. "Your boys are nice," she told me gently. "And they're smart, and they really are going to grow up into good people."

Parenting, I have decided, is much like a jaunt to the berry patch, best undertaken with courage and resolve and tall boots. You hope for a bucket of ripe berries in the end, but there are no guarantees. The thorns may be frustrating and sometimes even overwhelming, but the real challenge for me at this stage is to focus on the berries instead of the scratches I get in the process.

Despite the stupidity of the Blackberry Episode, I have to admit that overall, Arlene is right, and my boys are turning into nice people. For example, both Ben and Steven, for all their irritation at 8-year-old Jenny, will make her a peanut butter sandwich before they make their own. They take her swimming in the creek and exploring in ditches and woods. The other day, Steven actually emptied the kitchen garbage without being told. Ben gets himself up early to finish his homework. Both boys are kind to cats—one of the best indicators, in my experience, of a man's character. And the day after the Blackberry Episode, they headed across the fescue field without being told and returned with a full bucket of berries.

Sometimes, I've found, you push aside a large leaf among a thousand irritating thorns and find an unusually generous cluster of berries. Such was a little conversation I overheard recently, proof that despite my exasperation with them, the boys are absorbing the most important message of all—how truly loved they really are. Paul was on the couch one morning, reading that week's Sunday school lesson, a study from the book of Genesis about Isaac and Rebekah and how they each favored one of their twin sons, Jacob and Esau.

"Hey, Ben," I heard Paul saying, "Who's your mom's favorite child?" And Ben promptly replied with the perfect but completely unscripted answer: "It's a six-way tie for first place." As always, I read far too much into this, thinking tearfully, "OK, I can officially die happy now—I have succeeded as a mom after all."

Parenting, like picking blackberries, is a journey into perilous territory. Sticky refrigerator doors and spilled buckets and senseless arguments poke and irritate. But eventually, biting into the sweet steaming goodness of a slice of blackberry pie, the scratches and scars become worthwhile and almost forgotten.

The Mystery
of Family

An episode seven years ago has found its way into our family lore, retold whenever someone is exasperatingly literal.

Jenny was a baby back then, going on 1 year old. I needed to put a hem in a jumper before we went away for the evening, so I plopped Jenny on the floor and asked 13-year-old Matt to keep her entertained for a few minutes. Then I turned to my sewing machine and hurriedly hemmed.

A few minutes later I heard a thud and Jenny started crying. "What happened?" I asked without turning around.

Matt said, "She fell over and bumped her head."

"Well, do something," I said distractedly. "Rub it where she bumped it or something."

Jenny kept crying. I turned around and couldn't comprehend, at first, what I was seeing. Jenny sat wailing forlornly on the floor while Matt, on his knees, had his hand on the edge of my sewing-supplies cabinet and was earnestly stroking it.

"Matthew Smucker, what on Earth are you doing?"

"You *said*, 'Rub it where she bumped it.'"

Not long ago, another of my children had what we now refer to as a Rub-It-Where-She-Bumped-It moment. I was making a huge batch of mashed potatoes, some for supper and the rest for a hot meal at our church school the next day. On the counter, raw sliced potatoes waited in a large pot while I finished mashing some cooked potatoes in the mixing bowl beside it.

Rushing around the kitchen, I handed 12-year-old Steven a large bowl and spoon and pointed toward the counter. "You dish up the potatoes for supper," I instructed. I cut the meat, stirred the vegetables, and turned to get the potatoes. Steven stood there, conscientiously piling chunks of raw potato into a tall heap in the serving bowl.

Once again there was a dumbfounded exclamation from me and a defensive, "But you *said* ..."

Around the table, I once more related the story of Matt "rubbing it where she bumped it," and both Matt and Steven were able to laugh at themselves.

I am endlessly intrigued with the dynamics of family, especially the differences and similarities between siblings. It is understandable that two brothers would both display such unbelievably narrow literalness, but the twist in this plot is that Matt was born to us and Steven was adopted. Steven's skin and hair are much darker than his redheaded siblings', but in matters of personality he is no more alike or different than the other five are to one other. The experts I read on the subject agree that two siblings can be very similar or they can be far more different in temperament and behavior than two people chosen at random.

I find, in our family, the strangest combinations and contrasts: Two brothers with very different personalities have the same heavy tread walking through the kitchen. Three of my children tend to take me seriously when I say something; to the other three, words from Mom are mere fluff in the wind, to be ignored unless something actually happens. The statistically unusual combination of reddish hair and brown eyes showed up in three of the children. The most prolific writer of the bunch had the hardest time learning to read.

The question, for me, is *why* they are the way they are. One would think offspring of one set of parents, raised in the same household, would be more predictably alike. The experts are no help here, droning on about nature vs. nurture, as though the only choices were A and B.

My own theory leans toward a third option, a mysterious force at work that goes far beyond genetics and environment. I think God handpicks children for the families they belong to, for reasons we may never understand. My friends, especially the adoptive moms, agree. "Steven is a true Smucker," they chuckle, referring to the independent, argumentative spirit common to all of my six. I see that trait as a gift: For all our variation, we have a common thread to identify us as a family, a reminder that we will always belong.

Sometimes, siblings seem to be designed to clash in order for them to learn to get along with anyone they'll encounter in the future. My two older daughters have always been so different that I wondered how they could come from the same set of parents. Amy is short and freckled and logical; Emily is tall and dark and dramatic. When they were little, we grew so tired of their fights that my husband once laid a broom down the center of their bed to delineate the two sides. I was horrified, the next morning, to discover this bunch of dirty bristles sticking out of the covers between their sleeping heads.

But somehow, over the years, their rough edges have polished each other and now they are the best of friends. They talk in an abbreviated code that I can't understand. As Emily recently wrote on her Xanga site, "Sisters, I think, have a certain ability to talk to each other using minimum words, and still understand each other perfectly. Amy and I, at least, have this ability. I wish Mom did, but she doesn't." And Amy wrote on her blog, "I love spending time with my sister. She is the most interesting person I know."

In other ways, I see my children with little quirks so similar it takes my breath away. Jenny, born almost 11 years after Amy and with the same red-gold hair and brown eyes, looks and acts so much like her big sister that I often feel like I'm reliving Amy's childhood. Winding up to read me a story that she wrote, Jenny hitches her shoulders back and takes a deep breath, precisely like Amy used to long before Jenny was born. How does this work? I wonder, watching. And why?

I believe God chose the eight of us for each other and did a much better job than if I had filled out the order forms myself. For all my annoyance when two siblings clash or a distracted child again "rubs it where she bumped it," I believe there is something mystical and miraculous going on here, and I am awed.

The Passing Summer of our Lives

I have neither scripture nor science to back me up on this, but I think summer in the Willamette Valley is about as close to heaven as we get here on Earth.

The days begin with sunshine burrowing through the oak trees along Muddy Creek and the curtains by my bed. They continue with the daily predictable combination of warm sun and low humidity, and end with the mountains turning a dusty '90s-decor blue as the sun sets behind Mary's Peak and the clouds hover like thick gold-edged ripples of quilt batting. The dry heat of midday cools to bearable every evening while we finish the supper dishes. Then I get on my bike and wander down Substation or Powerline roads, watching summer progress in the ditches and fields.

Huge flat fields change from green to a rich tan as the tall grass becomes piled windrows, cut and drying in the sun. Then they are harvested with huge combines driven by people who wave at me as I ride by. I sometimes stop by the road for the sheer joy of absorbing the smell of harvest, an indescribable fragrance, dry and seasoned yet tangy and sharp. After the combines whine down the road to other fields, red and yellow balers take over and efficiently bundle the leftover straw into neat bales as the setting sun lights up clouds of dust behind them.

Between me and the fields, the wild roses bloom first, then teasel and timothy and Queen Anne's Lace take over,

351

waving like passing neighbors, and then the blackberries ripen in tangled profusion in the fence rows.

The fresh tastes and smells of summer are almost divine, as well—field-ripened strawberries first, then radishes from the garden. Fat blueberries from neighbor Dot Kropf's patch. Sweet cherries from Detering Orchards. Scents of fresh cilantro and tomato vines cling to my hands when I work in the garden. And one afternoon the children pick a bucketful of blackberries beside the road and I make the first blackberry pies of the season, the flavor so rich and delicious that I don't even mind the sticky purple drips on the bottom of my oven.

Summer is the season of expansion. Fragile petunia plants in my hanging pots balloon into green velvet clouds studded with bright purple jewels. The garden reaches in all directions, the corn leaping upward after a sluggish June, the zucchini growing seemingly overnight from little field mice to full-grown nutria. I turn my back for a couple of days, and the tomato plants become a jungle, tangled and thick, lacking only parrots and howler monkeys. And then one day, quite unexpectedly, when I get in the van and back it out from under the oak tree, I hear the unmistakable rattle of acorns rolling along the roof, a sure sign of fall. And I think, "Aack! Not yet! Summer has just started! Please, not yet!"

So this is my one complaint about summer in the Willamette Valley: It's far too short.

And the life of our family of eight seems to have reached its own summer season, as well: busy, growing, and productive. My boys are sacking grass seed in our warehouse this summer, coming home with dust in their eyebrows and green stains on their T-shirts, arms, and even necks from lifting hundreds of green-printed paper seed sacks.

I savor the tastes of this season—long late-night discussions with almost-adult children, laughter at family jokes. Most days, even during harvest, we manage to gather, all eight of us, around the table for supper. We hold hands to give thanks for the food, and I think, "Thank you most of all that we can all be here, together."

We are expanding in this season, not in number but in appetites and size. The two teenage boys seem to develop new arms and legs that fill the house like Alice in Wonderland when she drank from the magic bottle. Jenny, 8, is rapidly losing and replacing teeth and, it seems to me, determined to outgrow everything in her closet by next week. I cook food in large kettles and buy rice and flour in 50-pound sacks, eggs in boxes of five dozen. Huge pizzas disappear, gallons of iced tea and six-quart Crock-Pots brim full of roast beef and potatoes.

And like an Oregon summer, this season of our lives is passing too quickly.

My father-in-law, who was old, used to take a nap on the couch every afternoon during harvest. This year Paul, who does not at all seem old to me, announced that the time has come for him to do the same. With a cover on the couch to protect it from the warehouse-dust on his jeans, he snoozes with his nose in the air, just like his dad once did.

Jenny gets annoyed when I call her my baby, and she barely fits on my lap anymore. Emily is proud of her new driver's license and freedom. Matt is preparing for his transfer to the engineering program at Oregon State University this fall.

Our oldest daughter, Amy, will soon be off to a new job at a church school in South Carolina. Will Oregon's perfect summers call her back home? I wonder. I have no way of knowing. Perhaps realizing that these seasons will pass soon is what makes them so precious. Maybe this taste of heaven is meant to whet our appetites for eternity. I don't know.

I just know that this summer, while the grapevines snake into the pine trees and the sun shines through the haze of ryegrass dust in the air, I see my son's suddenly huge feet, my daughter's suitcase, my husband's weariness, and I think, "Oh! But we just started! Please, not yet, not yet."

Shooting for Good-Mom Points

I went to my son's basketball game last week mostly out of guilt. Matt, who is 21, has been playing on a church-league team all winter. Even though he insisted it doesn't matter, and I don't enjoy basketball, I was feeling like a terrible mom for not attending his games. So on Tuesday evening I put lots of children in the car and drove 45 minutes to the high school in Lebanon.

Sitting in the cold gym, I tried dutifully to follow the action. What did it all mean—the raised fists, the sudden whistles, the constant motion? I managed to yell an enthusiastic "Yes!" when someone I knew made a basket, but was plunged into confusion when Matt's team suddenly started shooting at the wrong basket. It turns out they switch sides halfway through the game—how odd. At least I learned something new.

In contrast, my sister-in-law Bonnie, mother of the Harrisburg Eagles' Justin Smucker, has attended her sons' games for years and follows every detail with enthusiasm. She even knows what to yell. At the game in Lebanon she sat on the edge of her seat and shouted, not just a timid "Yes!" like me, but deep, insightful instructions such as "DE-fense!" "Wait till it's open!" "Let 'em foul you!" "Pass it!" and again, "DE-fense!"

What would it be like, I wondered in awe, to be such an expert mom that I knew something intelligent to holler at my child's basketball game?

One of the dark secrets of motherhood is that many of us keep "good-mom/bad-mom" balance sheets in our heads, one for ourselves and a smaller one for others. A "good-mom" mark on a friend's sheet generally means a "bad-mom" mark on ours, such as Bonnie and me at that basketball game.

The reverse is also true. A relative of mine told me recently how fortunate she is that the mothers of her children's friends are all terrible cooks, every one of them. This means that her kids and all their friends rave over her cooking, even if it's only a simple chicken stir-fry or spaghetti. I was envious, since my friends are all phenomenal cooks, but I was also happy for her, knowing how often she feels her scales are tipped to the other side.

My sister and I have been known to sit up late and tell endless mom-guilt stories, anguishing together. "I thought I should restrict his fluids since he was wetting the bed, so I didn't let him drink anything after supper for a few weeks, and then he got this terrible pain in his stomach and it turned out to be kidney stones. Oh, the guilt, I can't describe it."

My husband, Paul, walks by shaking his head in disbelief when we go on like this. His decisions, good or bad, are put in the past and left there, and he says I enjoy feeling guilty so much that when there's nothing handy to feel guilty about, I invent something, and then I feel guilty for feeling guilty.

His sister, Lois, reads parenting author John Rosemond and tells me kindly that I'm a classic American mom, constantly feeling that I'm not doing enough for my children. Despite what my husband and a few super-confident friends say, I think our angst is justified: We have invested heavily in this task, but we won't know until years from now what the returns will actually be.

This is the minefield of motherhood: We make a hundred decisions a day, large and small, often on the fly, using the best knowledge we have on hand, which usually isn't much, with only a guess as to the final results. In a classic "Stone Soup" comic strip, 12-year-old Holly yells, "I'm going to bring this up in therapy someday!" And this is our fear, that a moment's decision today will have terrible consequences 20 years from now.

A friend of mine was confronted by her adult son some time ago. She didn't let him get a motorcycle when he was 17, he said, and in doing so she destroyed something important in his soul. He was getting to be a man, and this was a man's decision, the first one, and so significant. She stole something valuable from him when she refused to let him experience this defining moment of manhood. He tried to be kind about this, and my friend tried hard to understand.

"But," she confided later, "how was I supposed to know? It seemed like he wasn't ready for it, at the time, and it wouldn't be safe. I had no idea that one thing would affect him like this, all these years later. And there's nothing I can do now."

My children, knowing my weakness, like to exploit the "bring this up in therapy" line. I laugh them off when the right choice is obvious, but it's the subtler things that keep me up at night.

For instance, I never expected to have children who were athletic, but I married a man whose genes proved dominant to mine, and we had to decide about involving the kids in sports. On the one hand, it takes a lot of time for parents, both in driving and watching. I am not a pleasant mom when I'm too busy; we all know this. We also know there are enormous benefits to having the whole family sitting down to supper every evening. On the other hand, team sports have benefits as well, and should we deny our children if all their friends are playing?

We finally decided to provide them plenty of equipment and chances to play with their friends, but organized sports would wait until they could drive themselves. Naturally, Paul never second-guessed this decision and I agonize regularly over it.

Our 14-year-old son, Ben, patted me on the shoulder after Matt's game and said, "Mom, I just want you to know that when I play basketball you won't have to feel like you're a bad mom if you don't come to my games." Then he added, "Now, it does matter to me if you come to my choir concerts or not." No problem there, at least. I wouldn't miss his concerts for anything.

Who knows, maybe all of Ben's friends will sit in therapy someday, weeping about their frazzled, competitive childhoods and how they always envied Ben for his fun, relaxed life.

Motherhood is a dangerous and dimly-lit path, and there are no guarantees. Some days the good-mom points outnumber the bad; some days not. But I move forward in faith and hope, trusting that my children will someday, as the book of Proverbs says, stay in the way they should go, and maybe even—Oh joy!—rise up and call their mother blessed.

Going Places

Adventures in Letting Go

My husband planned our trip like NASA preparing a shuttle launch. Weather maps splashed across the computer screen: 6 a.m. Thursday—lime-green for rain in Oregon, lavender and pale blue for snow in Montana; noon—the colors shifted ominously to the right.

We needed to leave at 5 a.m. on Thursday, Paul finally decided, to get through Montana's high passes in daylight. Then he researched gasoline prices and planned our course, driving times, and gas stops—down to the quarter-hour—the 1,900 miles from Harrisburg to my parents' house near Grove City, Minnesota.

We knew the risks of driving this route in December. Yet, we felt we needed to have our children spend another Christmas with their grandparents, and flying a family of our size is much more expensive than loading us all into the van and driving.

How we snatch, at such times, at illusions of control. We were "minimizing the risks," we told ourselves, convinced that our charts, cellular phones, extra coats, an emergency kit under the seat, and Paul's expertise at driving in snow would somehow protect us if nature or chance turned against us.

We left right on time, stopping in Portland to pick up my 15-year-old niece, Hillary, then heading east on Interstate 84, conquering the miles. Kennewick, Coeur d'Alene, Butte.

Except for one unscheduled restroom break that annoyed Paul more than all the hours of noise and bickering in the back seats, we kept to the charts, arriving in Minnesota on Friday afternoon.

Coming back home was different. Sudden freezing rain in Minnesota and snow and wind in the Dakotas forced us to change our route. Like rungs of a ladder, the interstate highways cross the column of Midwestern states, and we had to drive many miles south, to the third rung down, Interstate 80 in Nebraska, to escape the storms.

None of our careful planning included creeping down a mountain on the snowy shoulder of I-80 in western Wyoming while the black ice on the pavement reflected the dusky sky. Enormous trucks that had roared past, splashing dirty water on our windshield, now crawled meekly or lay on their sides in the median, lights still on, pathetically helpless and disturbingly twisted. Nature is king in the wilds of Wyoming, following its own course despite all our plans and calculations.

In much the same way, I have found, the people in our lives resist our presumptuous attempts at prediction, at taming, at bending to our will. From the first pregnancy to our parents' last years, we grasp at illusions of control. We gather our tools—charts, research, and all the right books. We convince ourselves, in 1990 or 1995, that we know how things ought to be in 2009, and that with knowledge and discipline we can make it happen.

My mother was always busy and hardworking. I expected her, by age 85, to let others clean and cook and to do only what she does best: reading to the grandchildren, writing letters, sending cheerful cards, and making Bible-verse scrapbooks for people.

Instead, she is determined to work as hard as she did 30 years ago. "No, no, I can do that!" she said when I told our lanky 19-year-old, Matt, to take out the garbage or bring in the card table for Christmas dinner. She labored over the sink, slicing apples for grandchildren who, in my opinion, have perfectly good teeth and can bite into whole apples.

If I resisted her attempts to tell me how to grow up, why do I expect her to listen to me tell her how to grow old?

After Christmas, Matt caught a bus to Indiana to begin a six-week term at a Bible school. He is a smart, responsible young man who is nevertheless a bit dangerous, saying exactly what he thinks, wearing only what's comfortable, and doing stupid things on a dare.

"Behave yourself," I said, telling him goodbye. "Don't wear that dreadful black hooded sweatshirt that makes you look like the Grim Reaper."

"But it's comfortable, and it's going to be cold there," he answered quietly, with that calm, dismissive attitude my husband displays when his mom worries about him sleeping by an open window.

I pictured Matt wearing the same clothes for days on end and wondered what the girls would think. I don't want him to start dating yet, but it was small comfort to know that his clothing habits are not likely to impress any young ladies.

But then, who can predict young ladies? The two 15-year-olds in our van, Hillary and our daughter Emily, chose their words and behavior by some invisible standard that I could neither guide nor understand. Neither one, for instance, wore socks. All of my logical lectures made no difference. They scampered into gas stations over ice, in rain, and through blowing snow with bare feet in tennis shoes (Emily) or skimpy black dress shoes with little bows (Hillary).

Hillary's mother and I have tried to raise our daughters to be strong and confident young women. But at 15, Emily screams and Hillary apologizes. A waitress handed Hillary an ice cream cone. She took it, squeezing too hard, and the cone began to collapse in her hand. Emily screamed. Every head in the restaurant swiveled. Hillary, embarrassed, apologized shyly.

From inside an Idaho Flying J restroom, I heard the loudest scream of the whole trip. I came out and the girls, giggling, pointed to a little brown refrigerator with a big pink sign: "WORMS $1.99"

"What happened?"

"OK, we're out here waiting, and Hillary goes, 'Hmmm, worms?' and opens the door, and there's all these little round blue plastic containers. So she picks one up and opens it, and it's like, full of these live, writhing blueish-purple worms! So I was like, 'AAAHHH!'"

"What did you expect? I mean, it said, 'Worms.'"

"I thought they'd be dead and pink."

"I'm sorry I literally opened a can of worms," Hillary murmured, eyes downcast. She lives near Portland, but I told her she is actually a true Midwesterner, a person who apologizes when someone steps on her foot.

Which is more scary, to see the ones I love choose their own paths or to sit in the front seat, stomach tight with anxiety, wondering if the next quarter-mile of slick highway will send us plunging down a Wyoming mountainside? At that moment, eyeing the overturned trucks was worse.

Paul drove, stiff and grim, and I calculated whether we would hit a truck or roll down the embankment if we lost control right here. Evening descended, cold and ominous. The children were unusually quiet.

Emily's voice spoke up from the back, calm and sure. "The Lord is my shepherd, I shall not want." One by one, the others joined in. "He maketh me to lie down in green pastures; he leadeth me beside the still waters." Despite the danger, a pervasive sense of peace surrounded us.

Signs for a motel appeared in the endless Wyoming wasteland. We crept to the next exit and pulled safely into the parking lot. With its red carpet, extra pillows, and fancy little shampoos, our room was far more classy than the normal motels we patronize.

"This," Emily crowed, exploring, "is an adventure!"

A lesson in faith from my screaming, sockless 15-year-old: a life tidy and managed has no adventure; a tightly controlled relationship no joy. I could loosen my rigid grasp and trust the shepherd to bring us safely home.

And late the next evening, he did.

No Longer Young, Thank God

There's nothing like being surrounded by a hundred teenagers to make you happy to be on the other side of 40.

My husband, Paul, and I were recently asked to speak at a Mennonite church youth retreat in northern Idaho. This annual event drew young people from four neighboring states and even a few from Pennsylvania and Ohio.

Parenting three teenagers is one thing; interacting with dozens of them for an entire weekend is quite another. We talked to them in the sanctuary, ate with them in a noisy cafeteria, and watched them play endless rounds of volleyball.

"This makes me feel young," Paul said, "and it makes me feel old."

All weekend I had flashbacks to the last time I attended a similar event. It was more than 25 years ago, when I was about 17, and two carloads of us from Minnesota drove down to the youth fellowship meetings in Kalona, Iowa. Both then and now, I was fascinated with the complicated dynamics at play in such a group—the rituals, the interplay, the subtle competitions under the surface. I fancied myself an amateur Margaret Mead, analyzing it all. How things change, I decided. And how they stay the same.

The biggest difference was that back then, I was a teenager, and in the middle of it all, obsessing about my hair, evaluating the guys, and feeling dowdy next to the girls who showed up more fashionably dressed than I. Now, in contrast, I could observe, comfortable and amused, from the distance of 20-some years.

The behavior of girls and guys in a large group, I decided, has not changed a bit. Girls meeting long-lost friends go through a little ritual that played out over and over as the carloads arrived: A wild, feminine squeal, "ASHLEEEEEEE!" that could be heard all over the gym and fellowship room was followed by an exuberant hug and shrill laughter.

As a teenager, I nearly drowned in embarrassment when I spotted my out-of-state cousin across a crowded gym and shrieked her name, and everyone turned and—horrors!—looked at me. Such impulsive exhibition—I must be some sort of freak, I thought. This time, as I watched similar scenes repeated in front of me, I wished I could go back and tell myself how normal I actually was, that this simply is what girls do.

In the church cafeteria in Idaho, the guys and girls congregated at separate tables and peeled the foil off their hot sandwiches. The girls ate daintily and engaged in happy conversation while the guys slyly checked out the girls, then wolfed down their sandwiches, wadded up the foil, and threw it at their friends. The established couples ate together shyly at little tables off to the side.

Paul and I seemed very old and very married in contrast. He felt no compulsion to toss tin foil balls to impress me, and I had no need to giggle to get his attention. Usually we ate together, but if he was busy talking with people, I went through the line and ate by myself without feeling any less secure in our relationship.

There's a certain exciting suspense to life, my daughters inform me, until you find the Right One. The Thrill of the

Chase, my sister, Margaret, used to call it, and she wondered if she'd miss it after she was married.

Surrounded by the mostly subtle interaction around us, I exchanged amused glances across the table with Paul and decided that being settled with the Right One and having all that angst behind me is just fine, thank you very much.

Most of the girls at the retreat wore "cape" dresses, the uniform of many Amish and some Mennonite churches, a simple dress with an extra piece of fabric over the bodice from shoulder to waist. I wore capes growing up and was often told that their purpose is to free women from the tyranny of changing fashions. But fashion must be hardwired into the feminine genes because even cape dresses pass through their own distinct trends and phases.

Back in Iowa at the fellowship meetings of my youth, all the cool, intimidating Indiana girls showed up with gathers on their sleeves, their waists, their necklines, and their yokes, and most of these gathers were embellished with little fabric bows. No one from our area had as yet dared to try these, so we looked on in envy and felt backward and plain.

How times have changed. Gathers are as out as polyester doubleknit. The current look is straight and sleek, from neck to waist and down to the hem. "Mid-calf" was the prescribed length for us, back in our day, and we convinced ourselves of very loose definitions for "mid" and "calf" so that most of our dresses were not far below the knee. At this retreat, not a single dress was shorter than the dictionary-definition mid-calf. To my amusement, the cutting-edge girls from the East played volleyball in dresses that brushed their shoetops.

But then, who was I to chuckle at these young ladies? After all, I wore a navy-blue, long-sleeved, polyester double-knit dress with a three-inch-wide belt to the fellowship meetings on a hot, humid Iowa night—because I was convinced it made me look elegant, and it was as cool, in fashion if not temperature, as I could get.

While I still wear dresses, I no longer wear capes on them, and on the first evening of the retreat I cheerfully wore a green corduroy dress that I bought at Goodwill a few years ago. How freeing to know that I now can use a dress until it actually wears out without worrying about fitting in. Looking back, it seems my life was fraught with anxiety, drama, and taking things much too seriously. I was still shopping for a personality, and laughing at myself at 17 was not an option.

Today, I know all too well who I am. With my children and their friends poking fun at my absentmindedness and other quirks, I might as well join in.

I laughed with everyone else when my niece Jessi recounted how their carload passed ours on the way to Idaho. "There was this big van, and there's little Aunt Dorcas, driving and driving, with earbuds in her ears, just ignoring everything around her. We drove beside them for a long time and waved and waved and tried to get her attention, but she just drove and drove and didn't even notice us." Jessi included an accurate imitation: hands on a big imaginary steering wheel, nose up, eyes staring straight ahead, oblivious to the world.

"Your choices accumulate," I told the girls in my hour-long talk to them on Saturday afternoon. "Even the small things add up to a pile that becomes your life when you're my age." They listened, smiling and attentive, 59 young women who seemed determined to choose the right materials to construct their lives.

Youth, I concluded, is nice in its own way—the energy, the exciting opportunities, the freedom, the ability to program a cell phone, the astonishing metabolism. But ultimately I am glad to be on this side of 40, with the big questions answered and the major decisions settled.

I don't plan to dye my expanding crop of gray hair or buy expensive lotions to plump up my wrinkles. I've earned every single one, and I would not be a teenager again for all the fancy dresses in the world.

Discovering Ben

Right from the beginning, mothering involves discovering who this child is.

"What is it like when you give birth and first see your baby?" my daughter, Emily, asked me not long ago. I told her, "Of course you're just thrilled, and then you feel like, 'Oh! So that was you in there all that time! I knew there was somebody but I didn't know it was YOU.'" She thought that was funny. But that is how it was, every time, and I found it doesn't stop at birth but continues constantly as a mom explores who her children really are and then helps them find out the same for themselves.

As part of this process, I take each child on a one- or two-day excursion when they're 12, known in our family vernacular as their "Twelve Trip"; my husband takes them on a longer "Thirteen Trip" the next year. With six children and a swarm of responsibilities, our emphasis is on functioning as a group. These trips help us focus on each child alone, outside the context of a large family.

Ben, our second son and fourth child, didn't mind that his trips were reversed. He and Paul went camping in Yosemite for a week last summer. He and I decided to go to Bend after the snow melted in the mountains.

So while Ben was discovering Bend last weekend, I was busy rediscovering Ben. Of course I already knew that Ben is a likable and brainy young man who enjoys nature and sports and dislikes shopping, which is why I suggested Central Oregon as a destination and not the outlet malls in Lincoln City.

I picked him up after school in Brownsville and we headed east. In Sweet Home, I pulled in at an espresso stand to treat him to a fruit smoothie. Twelve Trips allow indulgences made impractical at other times by voices hollering from the back seats: "Can I have one, too? That's not fair!"

To my surprise, he shrugged. "Naaah, you don't need to."

"Really?"

"Yeah, I don't really want anything."

I thought, "Amazing," and, "How different from his sisters."

It seems things that matter terribly to his siblings don't bother Ben at all—a worrisome trait. What if I have produced a child without much personality? Or, even more troubling, what if he has deep feelings that he doesn't know how to communicate?

Yet he does have his passions, including geography, the outdoors, and facts and figures. Driving through the Cascade Mountains east of Sweet Home, he said, pointing, "That's the Calapooia River. And over that ridge there is the Marcola Valley. And the Santiam is a little ways that way, kind of north."

"How do you know this stuff?" I asked.

"Oh, from observation. And from studying the atlas."

As stunning views of Mount Washington and Three-Fingered Jack appeared through the trees, Ben kept asking me to pull over. Swinging his camera, he trotted back along the guardrail so he could frame the mountain peak between two trees, just right.

His older brother, Matt, I recalled, loved nature as well and stayed awake nights worrying about endangered species. Ben loves nature by going out and enjoying it. Having a less complicated child is not a bad thing, I decided.

I treated him to pizza at Izzy's when we got to Bend. He would have been equally happy with dollar-menu hamburgers at McDonalds, but he let me think I was doing something special for him.

At our motel, he flopped blissfully back onto the four fat pillows on his bed and began to read *Great Moments in Baseball History*. Contented and easy to please—this is a good thing as well.

The next day, I forced myself to bypass tempting fluorescent green garage sale signs and focus on what Ben would enjoy. First, a visit to the top of Pilot Butte in the middle of town, where a circular engraved metal plate pointed us toward the peaks on the horizon. We are both sign-readers and information gatherers. "OK, so that's the North Sister over there, and it's 25.4 miles away. And that perfectly symmetrical mountain there is Black Butte. And that mountain there is actually smaller than the South Sister but it looks bigger because it's 4.6 miles closer."

Why is it, I wondered, that Ben and I get along so well? Our only disagreement of the morning was at the High Desert Museum: Should we hang around to listen to this old-fashioned group sing "Clementine" and other folk songs? We compromised: one song, and then we wandered through the pioneer section and were equally intrigued with realistic displays of a covered wagon and the Oregon Trail. Ben was interested in the statistics of pioneer life; I wanted to weep for the women who wore "dun-colored" sunbonnets so they wouldn't show the dust of the trail and who buried children along the way.

Is it a bad trait for Ben to have so few feelings? I wondered. Back in the car I began to probe. What is he thinking, are there things he wishes he could tell me, what does he hope for the future, is he worried about anything?

Three minutes of this was enough. "Mom, why are you asking me all this stuff anyway?"

I sighed. "Because good moms talk about heavy things when they're alone with their kids." He chuckled, "Hey, did you hear about the guy who could bench-press 2,400 pounds?" I gave up.

Then we hiked for a long time, along an old logging railroad grade to a waterfall on the Deschutes River, and over a huge lava field covered with rough black rocks and ominous gullies where a mountain blew up long ago and where astronauts once practiced for the first moonwalk.

Then, under the hot sun, a light-bulb moment for me: Ben is a replica of his dad. That explains everything—the contentment, the calm, the scarcity of emotions, the abundance of action, the preference for planning and doing over talking and feeling, the barrels of facts in his brain. That also explains why we get along so well. And, a thought to put off for another day: Why do I get along best with the children who are least like me?

Halfway through the lava field I was so tired I thought my knees would collapse, but Ben was eager for more. Up ahead was Lava Butte, a 500-foot-high hump with gravelly sides that sloped upward at what seemed an 89-degree angle.

"I'd like to climb that," he said. "You can wait around here somewhere if you want." I let him go on ahead, guessing correctly that there was no way to get there from the trail. He came jogging back, only mildly disappointed. "We need to come back sometime and figure out how to get up there."

"Yes," I said. "We do. Maybe this summer."

This is my job: to guide and encourage him so he has the tools to do his job, which is this: to discover himself, to discover the world, and possibly to someday repeat this journey of discovery with a child of his own.

Rivers of the Soul

My daughter looked worried. "But Mom, you haven't been in the back of a canoe for – what? Years?"

"It's like riding a bike: You never forget," I said flippantly, too preoccupied with packing marshmallows and matches to wonder if I actually remembered the finer points of J-strokes from our long-ago years of roughing it in northwestern Ontario. In a two-person canoe, the front person's job is straightforward: paddle. The person in the rear bears most of the responsibility for steering the canoe.

I was about to join my husband and children on an overnight canoe trip down the Willamette River. When Paul took the boys two years ago, he didn't realize he was starting a June tradition. The next year, our teenaged daughters joined them. Eight-year-old Jenny wanted to go this year, and Paul preferred not to take her unless I was along as well – which meant that I had a decision to make.

I stayed home the last two years because the greatest treat for a mom of many is not to go away somewhere, but to have the house all to herself. Also, I prefer civilized vacations.

Roughing it is fine for the guys, who like to sit around the campfire, gnaw on meat, and grunt like Neanderthals, unshaven and unshowered. But I appreciate scented soaps and deep mattresses. Yet, previously, even while I sewed without interruption, I often second-guessed myself. Were laziness and inertia and fear keeping me from fun and adventure and making memories?

So I decided: This year, I would go along, not only for Jenny's sake but also to make sure I wasn't missing out on something. Since I was more experienced than the boys, Paul wanted me in the back of Ben's canoe.

We put in at Marshall Island, south of Junction City—seven people, three canoes, and roughly as many supplies as Lewis and Clark took up the Missouri. As soon as we pushed off, I realized three things: The determined current of the Willamette was a whole other category of water than the lakes and rivers of Ontario; I had a well-meaning but oblivious teenager in front; and I had forgotten everything I ever knew about managing a canoe, including which hand was left or right.

The others were soon stroking efficiently up ahead of us as I sweated through the complicated maneuvers—pushing out, pulling in—and shouted at Ben to just paddle and quit trying to steer from up there. Old tree roots stuck out of the water, perilous sieves threatening to pull us in as we zigzagged clumsily by. Strange currents pushed us sideways and dangerous-looking swirls on the water seemed to flaunt their power over me.

Before long my arm throbbed from shoulder to fingertips with an extreme version of the tendonitis that often afflicts my wrists. If a few tears dripped into the Willamette, we will not mention it here, but I kept going, determined to conquer this challenge if it was the last thing I did.

This is the trouble with new adventures: They take you to unexplored territory of the soul as well. You find out things about yourself you'd just as soon not know, things you don't have to face when you stay home and piece quilts.

Why, for instance, do I have this enormous fear of being thought weak and wimpy? Never mind that I actually am weak and wimpy; I just don't want anyone else to think so. And why, I wondered, furiously paddling, would I rather stomp off and quit entirely than admit that this isn't working and ask if we can rearrange?

My thoughts churned on: Why am I just like my mother, who at 87 won't ask for help with anything, including washing windows and cleaning gutters? Desperately pushing on, as pain screeched up and down my arm, I wondered what possessed me to put myself into a situation that exposed my weakest areas and worst faults.

Paul is not one to grasp subtle nuances, but my demeanor must have somehow told him things weren't going too well. We stopped to rest at a gravel bar near the railroad bridges. "How are you doing?" he asked, so kind and concerned that I resented it, because sympathy does me in every time, including this one.

Paul is often amazed at how he has to spell out the obvious. "You actually have the option of saying that this isn't working and could we rearrange," he said, wisely refraining from stating the also-obvious—that I carry bravery and determination to insane extremes.

So I ended up in the front of a canoe, with 17-year-old Emily in the back. My arm and outlook slowly improved as we worked our way north through Harrisburg. Emily is excellent at managing a canoe, but neither of us is very strong, so we were still the last stragglers.

Patiently, Paul rearranged us all again and put me in the front of his canoe, which improved everything. Paul called our oldest son, Matt, on his cell phone, and he met us at the McCartney Park boat landing with the wrist braces that I wear for typing. Then it no longer hurt as much to paddle, and slowly the world righted itself as the smell of the river and calm green of the trees dissolved the tension in my tortured soul.

We ate supper on a poppy-covered bar. Paul grilled burgers while I laid ketchup and plates on the plastic tablecloth that the girls had poked fun at me for bringing along. "Eating is more efficient when Mom's along," Amy observed. Paul told me, generously, "Everything's less chaotic when you're along."

Two hours downriver, we set up our tents on a mysterious island with tall bushes and oversized morning glories. Jenny appointed herself Official Wood Gatherer, and scavenged armloads of driftwood. Then, to my surprise, she expertly arranged the wood in a careful teepee – broken bits of kindling below, larger pieces above, air pockets here and there – as though she had been building campfires all her life. We lit it and it burned, just as a proper campfire ought to.

This is the nice thing about new adventures – they expose skills and talents you never knew you had. Emily, for instance, is far from athletic. Yet when she and Paul first went canoeing on Muddy Creek, about four years ago, they discovered her remarkable knack for handling a canoe. "My strategy," Emily says confidently, "is to avoid the funny-looking water."

Steven grabbed the fishing gear as soon as the canoes were unloaded and precisely cast and reeled in until long after it grew dark and the rest of us were relaxing around Jenny's campfire.

The next day, on a calm stretch of water, we put the two boys in a canoe by themselves and were happily surprised at how soon they caught on to navigating it. The rest of the day was simply fun: alternately drifting with the current and paddling, watching ospreys, listening to the children singing Veggie-Tales songs and "The Star-Spangled Banner," and waving at a farmer on the bank.

Before we knew it, we saw the houses and church steeple of Peoria, where Matt met us and we piled our smoky bags and pillows in the back of the van and loaded the canoes on the trailer.

"So, are you glad now that you went?" Amy asked me a few days later.

"Yes," I said, not only because I knew that's what she wanted to hear, but because I really meant it.

When the next opportunity for adventure comes along, I hope I have the courage to leave my calm familiar backwaters and again launch into the unknown currents of the soul.

Three "Girls" Cross the Country

*W*e were ready to conquer the country, so to speak. Amy's massive suitcase took up most of the trunk; half the back seat was piled high with supplies. We hugged the others goodbye and were on our way.

In the pocket of the passenger-side door, I found a pink-and-green striped notebook titled "The Shotgun Soliloquy." "Anyone who sits there can write in it," Amy explained. I pulled the pale green pen out of the black wire binding and wrote:

"July 30, 2007. Off we go on a girls' adventure—me, Amy, Emily. Off to Ohio, Pennsylvania, and South Carolina—loaded with suitcases, paperwork, iced tea, food, pillows, and expectation."

Amy is 19; Emily two years younger. We have done many things together—going to garage sales, teaching Vacation Bible School, and processing sweet corn for the freezer with efficient teamwork. But we had never considered undertaking anything as extensive as driving across the country.

Amy had accepted a job offer at a church school in South Carolina, and she needed her car there. A nephew was getting married in Pennsylvania in August, the girls wanted to attend a church convention in Ohio, and my publisher was eager to arrange signings in the East for my new book.

My husband, Paul, is the family organizer. "I think the three of you should drive out," he said, "and then the rest of us can fly out for the wedding."

Drive? Three non-mechanical females? For thousands of miles?

"You'll be fine," Paul said, and so I somehow knew we would be, even though for the last 25 years I have gratefully let him be in charge of our road trips.

We left on a Monday afternoon, the last bags nestled around our feet. "Mom is so proud of herself for having only one suitcase, but then she has like *five* purses!" Amy muttered.

We had three-and-one-half days to cover the 2,400 miles to Ohio. Two missed roads put us behind schedule, and our first difference of opinion occurred at Burns. The girls wanted to kick back at a motel. I wanted to push on to Ontario. I gave in, grudgingly, and for the first time understood my husband's irritating conquer-the-miles insistence when we travel.

At a rest stop just after we crossed into Idaho on Tuesday morning, Amy popped the hood and pulled out the dipstick. In the blazing sunlight, it was almost impossible to tell if the little holes had a film of oil over them or not. Amy finally decided they did not, and poured in another half quart of oil.

"Women find a trip with best friends and no menfolk is a relaxing, empowering experience," announced a feature in *The Register-Guard* some time ago. There was, indeed, something empowering about learning the skills we had always left to Paul. Later that day I taught Amy how to pump her own gas, something she had had no chance to learn in Oregon.

We navigated the mountainous northeast corner of Utah in a steady rain and entered the interminable desolation of Wyoming. "Wyoming brings out my inner teenager," I told

Paul on the phone after several hours of cruising at the speed limit of 75 miles per hour. To stay awake as we approached Laramie late that night, we took turns making up verses to "She'll be comin' round the mountain," such as "We'll be comin' into Laramie, but that really doesn't scare me."

The three of us are more different than alike, but we blend well. Amy and I try to motivate Emily, who, like a toy car on cheap batteries, has short-lived bursts of energy that quickly run out. The girls attempt to pull me into the 21st century, telling me to untuck my shirts and tone down the "pouf" in my hair. And Emily and I try to loosen up Amy who is sometimes too sensible and thrifty for her own good.

Somewhere around Nebraska it began to dawn on us that if all went well, this was actually less about grand adventure and more about just plain hard slogging, hour after hour. We stopped to sleep and took brief breaks; otherwise we simply drove, with virtually no drama or memorable events.

Actually, the most dramatic event of the trip was when Emily suddenly screamed and flailed her arms in front of Amy, who was driving. "Emily, stop that! What on Earth?" I said.

"A moth!" she shrieked, swatting at the windshield.

"A moth isn't worth dying for," Amy snapped.

The long mother-daughter talks I had hoped for never materialized, as it seemed that whoever wasn't driving was sleeping or studying the atlas or reading. However, we spent hours listening together to *Chronicles of Narnia* CDs, the fantasy-land of the story contrasting with the cornfields of Nebraska and Iowa.

A steamy heat covered the Midwest. We Oregonians, accustomed to air with oxygen in it, felt half smothered whenever we ventured outside. In Iowa, the air-conditioner fan quit and we drove with the windows open, the moist air whipping across our faces.

By the next day, mercifully, the fan worked again, but Emily wrote in the Shotgun Soliloquy: "Once upon a time a starving monster went to Indiana and realized that there, the people were already cooked. 'Yum Yum,' he said. But soon he, too, was cooked in the insane heat. That was the end of the starving giant. Note to self: If you fall in love with some-one from Indiana, convince him to move to Oregon."

On the fourth day, we finally reached Ohio and the home of Paul's nephew, Kevin, and his wife. Over the supper table, we recounted our journey. Kevin was impressed with our fearless sense of adventure.

The worst driving came after our weekend in Ohio, when we followed Interstate 76, narrow and twisting, to eastern Pennsylvania. Like a rabbit caught in a buffalo stampede, I maneuvered our little Civic among hundreds of huge trucks, through rain and road construction and single-lane bottle-necks, thinking nostalgically of wide-open Wyoming.

We reached my sister's house at last. The other family members joined us, we saw the nephew get married, the books were signed, and the rest flew home. On the final leg of our journey, Amy and I drove to South Carolina, the accents and tea getting thicker and sweeter as we headed south. By the time we reached her new home, we had cov-ered 4,000 miles.

I wrote in the Shotgun Soliloquy: "How to drive across the country: Get in the car. Drive and drive. How to reach big goals: Start. Work and work."

Amy left me at the airport the next day where I cried the sort of tears that only a parent understands.

The real adventure has been the past 19 years; the best thing has been the journey itself. The accomplishment was not so much driving across the country as it was having two daughters who didn't hesitate to get in the car with their 40-something mother to do so, and I count myself blessed and successful.

Romance in Florida

At first glance, it couldn't get more romantic than this: leaving rainy Oregon in the middle of a long winter for a trip to Florida, just my husband and me, and right over Valentine's Day.

However, the rose of anticipation was wilted a bit by the fact that the trip's purpose was actually an "Enrichment Weekend" for Mennonite ministers. We would spend our time not sunbathing on the beach but, with a hundred other couples of the button-down shirt/homemade dress variety, listening to lectures on such dreamy subjects as "The Pastor as Biblical Counselor."

But the fact remained that this still was a trip to Florida, and I was determined to make the most of it. My wise neighbor and friend, Anita, has an enduring philosophy that comes up whenever we discuss marriage or our adult children or life in general. "Be thankful for what is," says Anita, "instead of complaining about what is not."

After 23 years of marriage, I am well aware of both. Daily life is mostly realism and responsibility, and Paul is not a poetry-reciting, roses-in-his-teeth sort of person. He is a steady, practical man who installs a new bathroom sink and hopes desperately that I will say that this counts as my birthday gift so he won't have to buy me anything.

So, while I am grateful that things are good, I also like to make them better. Could a busy, long-married, many-childrened pair of opposites headed for a pastors' seminar still manage to stir up the embers of romance? It was worth a try. And even if that didn't happen, I was determined to extract all the enjoyment the trip could offer.

There are people, I am told, who do not have children and can just pack up and leave on weekend trips. We, on the other hand, had to arrange rides to school, post lists of duties (Feed the cat! Turn off lights! Get the mail!), plan meals, find someone to stay overnight with the children, and sign medical-decision permission slips.

Paul was patient with my last-minute stress and then, driving to Portland, he deliberately chose to talk with me instead of shouting into his cell phone all the way about seed tests and how many loads of rice bran to haul to Kropf Feed while he was gone. I appreciated this.

On the plane, I pulled a *Spirit* magazine out of the seat pocket and read a wonderful article entitled "There Must Be 50 Ways to Woo Your Lover" about a practical, econo-mizing man's attempts to romance his wife—on a trip to Florida, no less.

It was perfect for Paul, who never reads this sort of thing, but ought to.

I poked him. "Hey, there's something on page 64 of this magazine that you might want to read." Then I tucked it back in the pocket without pushing my point further, and went to sleep, snuggled on his shoulder. I have learned a few clever management techniques in 23 years.

Following a long layover in Las Vegas, we boarded the plane, which was shaking so much I started to feel sick. Finally the pilot announced that 84-mile-per-hour winds and lots of debris were flying down the runway, so we couldn't leave.

I rested my head and slept on Paul's lap, one of the many perks of traveling with a husband, until we finally took off, three hours late, which meant that we arrived, exhausted, in Tampa after 3 a.m. Naturally, as a frugal Mennonite minister, Paul had reserved an economy car. However, those were all taken, so we had three choices, all for the economy price: a sedate minivan, an SUV, or a Mitsubishi Spyder convertible. This was a terrible moral dilemma for a Mennonite minister—two large gas guzzlers vs. a worldly sports car.

Stewardship and gas mileage won out, and we sank into the convertible, kayak-like, and took off to find our hotel. Paul had indulged me by reserving a three-star room and satisfied his conscience by getting a fantastic deal on Priceline. There was only one problem: We couldn't find the hotel. Paul had directions and a map, but neither correlated with actual freeway signs, and as we swung past endless road construction and the clock inched toward 5 a.m., the last bubbles of romance popped from our exhausted minds and we stewed in irritation and near-despair.

Paul finally reached the right Hyatt Hotel on the phone and a nice woman talked us in: "Turn right at PetCo, OK, past the Denny's," and there we were at last. She told us we could extend the normal checkout time to 2 p.m., and we fell asleep and woke up many hours later in a beautiful room with brilliant sunshine edging the drapes. I made coffee in the little machine and all was well once again.

Later that afternoon we headed down to Sarasota in our Spyder and Paul, of his own volition, stopped so we could take a romantic walk on the beach. We arrived at the church early, so Paul put the car top down and we leaned back and napped in the sunshine. When I woke up, squinting, a pink envelope was propped on the gearshift beside me. He remembered Valentine's Day! With a card! With extra stuff written in it! "I like to spend time with you," the card said, and I was perfectly happy.

I gushed gratefully, and he grinned. "That ought to be worth two or three points." Hey, he must have actually read that article on the plane while I was asleep! My cup of joy ran over.

Our marriage has resulted in six children whom we love dearly but enjoy getting away from now and then. We found, however, that the tether that joins us stretches clear across the country, thanks to cell phones. Mine buzzed frantically in the middle of an evening service. I checked the caller— "Home"—and sensed that this was something bad—vomiting children, a broken leg, maybe a dead dog. I wanted to rush out to take the call, but our pew had about as much leg room as a coach seat on Southwest Airlines. There were six adults to my right and one very large one to my left, so I was stuck.

As I sweated through the speaker's closing comments, the phone buzzed twice more and I was certain the house was on fire, Jenny was kidnapped, or someone had totaled the van. Immediately after the last "Amen" I wormed out through the crowd and called home in a panic. Fourteen-year-old Ben answered. "Oh, Mom, it's you. Hey, when you're making spaghetti, do you boil the water before you put the spaghetti in?" I yelled at him, I admit, and Ben, a replica of his dad, was completely bewildered at my alarm.

The night before we left Florida, we lowered the car top again and drove out to the beach as the sun was setting and the warm breezes blew. "Maybe people will think that you're really rich and I'm your trophy wife," I told Paul.

And Paul, who I think is predictable but who actually never stops surprising me, replied, "You're my trophy wife whether people think so or not."

And then we flew home, where the daffodils were starting to bloom, which means that winter is officially over no matter what the calendar says, and I am thankful, as my friend Anita advises, for what has been, and for what is, and for what is yet to be.

Visiting my Amish Past

I've noticed that when my husband's relations gather at Kropf reunions, the ones who have strayed furthest from their Mennonite heritage rhapsodize the most about its value. I reflected on this during my recent experience of following eastern Iowa's muddy country roads back into my Amish past.

How much of that unique way of life have I lost? I wondered, as I confidently drove our rented Subaru Outback and gushed like a tourist about those adorable Amish children and the quaint navy-blue dresses on the clothesline. And how much have I kept? I also wondered, surprised at how easily I clicked back into discussing gardens and babies and family trees in Pennsylvania German.

My parents lived in the large Amish community of Kalona, Iowa, for a number of years in the 1950s and '60s. Four of us children were born there; Dad taught in the Amish schools. Mom and Dad now live in Minnesota but still have many relatives and connections in the Kalona area. My brother, Marcus, drives them the seven hours to Kalona now and then for funerals and such, but he seldom has time for the leisurely visiting that Mom and Dad enjoy. So my sister, Rebecca, and I came up with a plan: We would both fly to Minnesota—she from Virginia, I from Oregon—and we would take Mom and Dad to Iowa, wherever they wanted to go, to do all the visiting they wished.

Astonishingly, despite a family on each coast and Mom and Dad's precarious health in the middle, our plan worked out. Stocked with pillows and Mom's bag of homemade snacks, we headed south on Interstate 35. We headquartered at Aunt Vina's house and made meandering forays around town, to the nursing home to see Uncle Mahlon and down A Avenue to see where we used to live, and on out into the countryside, on roads sticky as rubber cement from the recent rains, to one quiet Amish home after another.

Dad's 100-year-old friend, Joe, sat at the dining room table wearing thick black-rimmed glasses, reading his German Bible with light from the window, since the gas lights aren't lit until dusk. Joe's two unmarried daughters care for him, keep the house immaculate, and run a fabric store next door. Rebecca and I browsed its dim interior, among baby bibs and black polyester, while a buggy and a patient horse waited outside. And then a voice said, "Who do I hear out there?" and out from behind a rack of fabric came my sweet cousin, Katie, and her husband, Harley, shopping for suspender clips, and we had a warm reunion right there at the cutting counter.

"Glen Beachys are next," Mom said, referring to their old friends in that Amish and Mennonite way of pluralizing the male head of the household to include the whole family. We pulled in and melted in awww's as we saw a dozen small children—boys in straw hats and homemade pants and shirts; girls in dresses and white organdy head-coverings—playing around the swing set. A small boy in a gray shirt grabbed the cross-bar at the end and swung energetically, knees bent, his bare feet pointing stiffly out behind.

Mrs. Beachy greeted us at the door, and suddenly people appeared on all sides. Women came from the kitchen, teenage girls looked over their mothers' shoulders, children wandered in from outside, men stopped tearing up the dining room linoleum and stood to welcome us. "We all came home to have a work day for Mom and Dad," explained a daughter. And there, suddenly, was Priscilla, now a Beachy daughter-in-law, who was my best friend when I was 4 years old, and who somehow looked just like she did back then, dark-eyed and smiling.

We felt like royalty as we gathered on the deck, their projects abandoned for, they implied, the joy and honor of having us there. There was no rush, no hints of unfinished work waiting, no hidden glances at pocket watches. Dad caught up on news of his former students while out on the lawn a small child held a doll in one hand and played with the dog with the other.

Later, at my cousin Perry's house, his wife, Rebecca, told us about their egg business, their 5,000 chickens, and their teenage son who spends most of the morning gathering eggs. And they also milk cows, she mentioned off-handedly. Forty of them, as I recall. While we talked, their daughter sat in the semi-darkness of the kitchen, cutting up apples to make applesauce.

At another house, a barefooted woman, mother of 12 children, paused in her work of canning meat for her daughter's wedding to take us across the road to visit with her elderly father. I asked about the boxes of onions piled in the shed. "We grow produce for a co-op," she said. "And we also milk 200 goats."

I confess I had expected the trip to be a bit boring, dutifully driving Mom and Dad from one house to the next along corn-lined gravel roads. I had no idea the trip would bless me in return with its warmth and surprising meetings and serene beauty, an unexpected bonus for doing the right thing, and a concept that is ingrained into Amish life. Joy and pleasure, they say, come not from selfish pursuits but as a bonus for obedience to God.

I meet people sometimes who envy the peace and serenity they see among the Amish. So they purchase plain clothing off the Internet and tell me proudly that they just bought a new manual wheat grinder.

My Amish relatives would be the first to insist that they're not perfect, nor is their life a sort of Utopia. And the serenity and contentment on their faces come not from kerosene lanterns or black hats. Rather, they come from the clarity of knowing what's important and what isn't, and then deliberately making choices to live by those priorities. God and their Christian faith come first. New options are evaluated not by whether this would be fun or make money or feel good, but by whether it would be God's will. Faith encompasses all of life.

People are next—primarily family and the local church. Families are large, and the elderly are cared for at home. Personal opinions give way to the larger voice of the church group.

Work is third, serving many purposes—providing for a family, building character, teaching skills to children. Thus, housework is set aside in order to entertain visitors, the efficiency of rubber tractor tires is subject to the church's decision, and the old man reading his Bible is not more holy than his daughters who work hard to care for him.

It would not occur to most Amish to pursue, for their own sake, what many of us consider ends in themselves—fun, entertainment, personal fulfillment, physical fitness, money, influence, creativity. And yet, few of these benefits are missing from their lives, the result of first pursuing what's most important. Fun is sitting under a shade tree with the rest of the family and shelling peas; entertainment is watching two toddlers playing together; staying in shape comes from hoeing the garden and cleaning out the barn; influence and finances from striving for excellence.

Peace and harmony in my own life are not going to come from a vegetable garden and speaking Pennsylvania German. The lingering lesson from this visit to my Amish past is that I need to daily clarify my priorities and actually live by them. Even with my cell phone and store-bought clothes and Kia Optima, I can choose to do that just as thoroughly as my smiling cousin, Katie, in her plain blue dress, climbing into the buggy with her pleasant husband, Harley, and a small package of suspender clips.

Grief and Grace

Carolyn's Miraculous Faith

A hundred different things remind me of my friend Carolyn Schrock's loss, and I have grieved for her in a hundred different ways. Today, again, I thought of her, and of how she was denied a simple reward that every mom ought to enjoy: to have her children grow up to bring her tea and Tylenol when she's sick.

This past week I was knocked off my feet with a vicious virus that began with a sore throat and turned into a strangled cough and what felt like a head full of hot cement. It reminded me of that difficult winter back when my daughter, Emily, was a baby. I seemed to be sick all the time with everything from strep throat to a viral pneumonia. With three small children, I forced myself to keep going, changing diapers and washing little faces in a feverish daze. I remember how desperately I wanted to go to bed, how I thought I would give almost anything to go lie down with a cup of tea.

Parenting at that stage is an act of faith, of giving, investing and sacrificing while believing that someday it will all pay off in mature, generous young adults. It is like planting and watering a garden but waiting many years for the harvest.

How gloriously different my recent sickness was from the old days. Seventeen-year-old Amy made lists of jobs to do around the house and somehow persuaded her little brothers to fall in line and work. Fifteen-year-old Emily did laundry. Both girls brought me pots of tea on pretty little trays, gently closing the bedroom door so I could sleep in peace.

"I've never had this much fun being sick," I croaked, remembering that awful winter 15 years ago and basking in the accomplishment of having turned those dependent babies into young adults with the sympathy and skills to take care of me in return. I was reaping the fruit of my labors, and it was delicious.

And after a hundred ways of grieving for Carolyn, I find a new one today: She had only the investing and giving but was denied the joy of seeing her hard work come to fruition. Her daughters would never be teenagers, bringing her tea when she was sick.

Carolyn was a dark-haired fifth-grader, efficient and hardworking, when I first came to Oregon to teach school. Jeff was the nerdy 14-year-old son of the family I boarded with who discussed electricity and radio waves at the supper table. The two of them married some years later, moved to Washington, and started a family, beginning with three little girls in dark pigtails, and then two boys. I saw them occasionally when they came back to this area to visit.

The phone call came last November with news so shattering, so beyond-words heartbreaking that I couldn't comprehend it: A pickup truck had crossed the median and crashed into the vehicle that Jeff was driving. All five of their children were dead. Jeff was badly injured.

There are no precedents for such grief, no directions through such a jungle of pain. The entire Mennonite community in Oregon wept with them. The city of Spokane, where the accident happened, erupted in gifts, memorials, and sympathetic gas-station readerboards. My friends and I were almost too stunned to function. We called each other on the phone and cried so hard we couldn't talk.

And our faith was tested in ways it had never been tested before.

Faith is easy and seems almost unnecessary when everything is going well, and philosophical arguments on such matters as Calvinism vs. Arminianism seem deep and important. But devastating loss peels away the surface issues and exposes the bare rock: Is there a God? Does he care?

There are, at these times, three theological options: There is no God. There is a God, but he is cold and uncaring. There is a God, and he is loving and involved. None of these options make the grief and pain disappear, but only with the third, we found, could we avoid a dark and utter despair, even if it made no logical sense from our perspective.

The Bible speaks of a mysterious gift called grace, something that makes the weak strong and enables ordinary people to do the impossible. As believers, we are promised that we will not be tested beyond what we can endure, that there will always be enough grace. I have experienced this myself in difficult times, when an unexpected strength held and suspended me above a catastrophe and helped me to do what needed to be done. But surely this was too much. "There can't possibly be enough grace for this," I thought, expecting to hear that Carolyn was curled in a fetal position, sedated and catatonic.

I was wrong. Amazingly, it was Carolyn herself who showed the way for the rest of us. When the police spokeswoman told her there were five fatalities in the accident, she stayed calm and responded, "Thank you for telling me." She made decisions. She helped plan the funeral. She encouraged her husband as he moved from near-death to a long recovery.

And, while others spoke of revenge, lawsuits, and criminal charges, Carolyn was concerned about the driver of the other vehicle, a 55-year-old man named Clifford Helm, who suffered less severe injuries and, according to the Schrock family, did not know why he crossed the median.

Several days after the accident, Carolyn visited Helm in his hospital room. She shook his hand and told him that she and Jeff forgave him. Soon after, he and his family attended the funeral, where five white caskets were placed at the front of the church and 1,500 people came to say goodbye and offer their support.

Six weeks later, Carolyn gave birth to a beautiful, dark-haired daughter, a miracle of new beginnings.

Carolyn, along with her baby and her mother, stopped in at our house recently. "How is it now?" I said, a bumbling way of asking, "Does life go on? Is your soul scarred forever? Is there any beauty in that land of grief in which you now live?"

"There is grace," she said simply, and added, "I feel like Job," referring to the biblical character who lost all his possessions and children in one day, yet did not lose his faith. "He said, 'My ears had heard of you, but now my eyes have seen you.' I feel like I have experienced God for myself instead of just hearing about him." Thoughtfully, she rocked the baby in her carseat, a somewhat worn apparatus with a loose handle that had obviously been used for two or three babies before. She left that day, a woman with her life forever divided into "before" and "after."

I think of her often. I have grieved for her in a hundred ways; she has no doubt grieved in thousands. I have teenage daughters to bring me tea when I'm sick. She lost all her children when the oldest was only 12. And yet, in an amazing and miraculous way, Carolyn continues to lead the rest of us to wholeness and a strong and undiminished faith.

A Journey of Grief

It has been a month of journeys: a sudden trip to the Midwest, a Frodo-like quest, and a pilgrimage into the alien world of grief, with no map or directions and no idea when I would come back home.

On a recent Sunday, I made a list of things to do that week—pick blueberries, weed the garden, and sew pajamas for the boys.

On Monday, my brother, Marcus, phoned at 5:30 a.m. and told me that his 23-year-old son, Leonard, my oldest nephew, had taken his own life the day before. My to-do list and everything else forgotten, I wandered numbly around the house and tried to muster the strength to brew a pot of tea and take a shower while my husband scrambled to find plane tickets and my daughter packed my suitcase.

The next morning, I flew to Minnesota with two of my children, Matt and Emily. It was one of the hardest things we have ever done. In Minneapolis, the three of us would have liked nothing better than to turn and run. Yet we somehow found our way to the rental-car counter and drove west toward the farm.

"We are taking the Ring to the mountain," Matt said, "and it grows heavier the closer we get." All day my feverish, stunned mind had been searching for an analogy, for words to explain what this was like. Then my insightful son provided just what I needed.

He referred, of course, to the *Lord of the Rings*, in which Frodo the Hobbit is chosen to take the One Ring to Mount Doom to throw it back in and destroy it. The closer he gets to the mountain, the heavier the ring becomes. Yet this is Frodo's destiny and his calling, and with the help of his friend, he accomplishes it. That story gave me an odd stability all week. "I am taking the Ring to the mountain," I kept telling myself, before pulling into my brother's driveway, before each visitation, and before the funeral and burial.

It was the longest week of my life. To imagine Leonard's mental suffering was terrible, to see his parents' was much worse—his mother like a little broken sparrow; his dad, with a world of pain in his eyes, gently washing the family van that would bring his son's body home from South Dakota. Since Leonard had lived in South Dakota for the past four years, a visitation was held there before the funeral and burial in Minnesota.

In a surreal side trip, I found myself in a funeral home in a small South Dakota town on a Wednesday evening. As I watched, dozens of clean-cut young cowboys set their black hats on a shelf in the entrance, said a few words to the family, walked respectfully by the casket, then clustered in silence in a small anteroom. Farmers followed them, along with warm, down-home families with pronounced South Dakota accents.

I forced myself to talk to a few people. "How did you know Lenny?" I asked, and out poured their stories. "Lenny took me hunting. I didn't have a big brother, so he said he would be my big brother."

"Lenny was my friend."

"Lenny and I baled hay together."

"Lenny was in my Bible study."

"Lenny was like a son to me."

I thought, over and over, "Oh, Leonard, how could you not know how much you were loved?"

Grieving a suicide means living with a hundred unanswered questions that whine like sirens when I try to sleep. Why would a fun-loving, hardworking young man with truckloads of friends want to die? Were there signs we should have seen? Was there something we should have done? Didn't he know I would have moved heaven and Earth to help him? Why didn't one of his friends knock on the door at the right moment?

Drugs and alcohol are often implicated in suicide, the books say. Leonard used neither. Nor, beyond snowmobiling and bullriding, did he engage in high-risk or self-destructive behavior. But he had admitted, earlier in the year, that he was struggling with depression. Obviously, it was much worse than anyone realized, and I found my anger focusing not on God or Leonard or anyone else but on the thread of depression and mental illness that has afflicted our family tree ever since my great-grandfather took his own life many years ago.

Beyond the questions and the pain, this journey of grief has been full of surprises. The first day's numbness gave way to what seemed like a hot water bottle in my chest, with tubes leading to my eyes. At the oddest times and places, such as the middle of the Denver airport, something punched the water bottle and the tears flowed. At other times, I wanted to cry and couldn't. I had always thought I wouldn't laugh for a month if something like this happened, yet my sister-in-law and I found ourselves laughing hysterically at nothing.

Underneath all the anguish, I was amazed to find something I would never have expected in such a circumstance: a strange, solid sense of peace.

There were touches of grace. The muggy heat gave way to a pleasant breeze on the day of the burial. Emily's 16th birthday fell, unfortunately, on the day before the funeral. Three strangers, friends of my niece, made a special effort to hug Emily and wish her a happy birthday.

Now, we are safely back in the Shire, having taken the Ring to the mountain and shoveled the sandy Minnesota soil into my nephew's grave. I have been sewing pajamas, picking blueberries, and weeding the garden. But the journey continues. I see an advertisement for Western wear in a farm paper, and a rogue wave of grief drenches me. Paul's nephew and his girlfriend sing together at church, I realize I will never attend Leonard's wedding, and the "water bottle" gets a violent punch. When cheerful cashiers say, "How are you?" I flounder for an answer. I am still dazed: Last Sunday, I wore both glasses and contacts to church and wondered why my husband looked so smudged up there in the pulpit.

Touches of grace and surprises continue as well. The most unlikely people say the most comforting words. They tell me they have also taken this journey, and that I will make it—like Frodo—with help from my friends.

"I continue to have a deep sense of peace," my brother says. And so do I. This is surely the biggest surprise of all, a gift to guide us on the long road back home.

Processing the Gifts of Fall

Summer is my favorite season. The sun shines dependably every day, and the air smells of dust from the grass seed harvest, one of the best scents on Earth. Summer is sprinklers, sandals, fuchsias and fresh strawberries. It's cookouts and sleepovers and tea on the porch.

Sometimes I think I'd like it to be summer forever, all warmth and light. No early darkness, no rain, no winter blues to fight, no shivering on cold mornings. Yet the seasons change whether I want them to or not, and each one brings its gifts. Fall's offerings are more subtle than summer's, less visible, more of the soul.

In July, I wake up early as the sun shines through the trees across the creek. Now, I wake to a filtered light through the bedroom window. Fog hides the field across the road, and the oak trees stand out against it in sharp outlines.

A sunny day in September has a charm not found in June. In summer, I expect sunshine. In the fall, I know it could very easily be raining instead. When the light angles onto the front porch and forms a golden square on the floor, I smile like Pigga the cat, who is stretched out in the sun's warmth, happily asleep.

Fall, in many ways, is a time for processing. There are apples and tomatoes to cook and preserve, and there are goals and grief and memories to examine and dissect and put where they belong.

I once took a class in early childhood education in which the instructor introduced me to the idea of what she called "process vs. product." The process of handling a paintbrush and experimenting with colors, she said, is much more important to a child's development than the product of a finished painting; shaping and squeezing clay is more important than a final sculpture. Her theories tickle the back of my mind when I'm processing fruit because, frankly, I hate the process and love the product.

Summer fruits are often picked in gallon buckets and frozen in pint containers—strawberries, blueberries, blackberries. Fall's bounty, in contrast, comes in astonishing quantities—wagons, bushels, tubs, and five-gallon buckets of corn, tomatoes, grapes, and apples. Many Mennonite women love to "put up" fruit and will do a thousand quarts a summer. I, too, love to see dozens of sturdy jars of applesauce lined up in the pantry in military rows, and stacks of plastic bags full of corn in the freezer. But I somehow missed the knack for enjoying the work involved, a mutation in the Mennonite genes, perhaps.

I don't enjoy water dripping off my elbows or having every surface in the kitchen covered with jars, bowls, and kettles. Worms in apples or corn give me chills. Carrying a vat of boiling tomatoes from stove to counter is terrifying, and whenever I pull steaming jars out of a kettle, I fear a stray breeze will shatter them in my hand. Cleanup is the worst part—washing huge canners that don't fit in the sink, chiseling dried bits of corn off the floor, and scrubbing a thousand bits of apple peel out of the Victorio-strainer screen. Yet there is really no way around the work, no Candy-Land slides to whisk us from boxes of apples to jars of fresh sauce.

I try to see the value of the process, however tedious and messy it may be: Paul and the children sitting in a circle in the yard, husking corn. Amy and Emily cutting apples and talking girl stuff. Seeing a box of fruit become dessert for my family in January. Teaching the children that food does not show up in a can at WinCo through some kind of spontaneous generation.

Produce is not the only thing that is washed, cut, and preserved at this time of year. My favorite gift of this season is its gentler, quieter pace and the chance to process matters of the heart. This is nearly impossible in summer, which, at our place, is noisy and constantly busy. Sprinklers tick in the garden, creek-wet children hang their towels on the porch rail and run upstairs to change, Jenny leaves her paints and crayons all over the table, balls and other objects fly through the air, and the younger children have loud arguments on, for example, whether or not Emily was winking with both eyes at the same time. Paul, preoccupied with harvest, pops in the back door at odd times, shouting on his cell phone about seed samples and lot numbers.

In autumn, life slows down, beginning with the flies. In summer, houseflies dart in when the kitchen door opens and spring out of reach when I sneak up with the fly swatter. But every September, for reasons I have never understood, the flies migrate to the living room and fly in slow loops at the center of the room while I flail with the flyswatter like a badminton player gone mad. Unaffected, they fly lazily on. The flies, it seems, signal the rest of life to slow its pace as well. When the children disappeared out the door on the day after Labor Day, I was handed a gift of solitude.

This year, for the first time, everyone in the family but me is in school full time. Paul has returned to teaching all day,

Matt and Amy are in college, the younger ones attend our church school. In this blessing of uninterrupted time, I list my goals for the next year, read the waiting stack of books, and work on writing and sewing projects. And I grieve.

My 23-year-old nephew's suicide a few months earlier was a shattering experience for us all. In the weeks that followed, I found that I had almost no tolerance for the normal distractions and noise of family life. So the solitude that fall brought has been a gift, a chance to work through this loss, to dissect and stir and examine. I can pray, go on a bike ride, or sit on the porch swing and cry.

I sometimes wish I could skip the process of grief and jump to the final product of healing and greater maturity and compassion. Yet I know that without deliberately going through this pain, washing and cutting and stirring, I will never move beyond it.

"To everything," the Bible says in Ecclesiastes, "there is a season, and a time to every purpose under the heaven ... A time to plant, and a time to pluck up that which is planted ... A time to weep, and a time to laugh; a time to mourn, and a time to dance."

The gifts of fall are precious and the work they bring is difficult, but I believe I will come to agree with the biblical writer who concluded, after writing of harvest and work and tears and laughter, "He hath made everything beautiful in his time."

Connecting to the Amish

The school shooting in Pennsylvania in October 2006 pushed the Amish community reluctantly on stage before the entire world. Their loss overwhelmed us, their strength and forgiveness astounded us, and their lifestyle fascinated us more than ever.

"Who are they, really?" people wondered. "Are they like us?" "Is their pain as intense as ours would be?" "Do they want the sympathy we long to extend?"

For me, the most haunting part of the tragedy was the little 7- and 8-year-old sisters who were killed. When my sister, Becky, and I were that age, we were, like them, little Amish girls in an Amish school. The thought of a man coming into our school with both sexual abuse and murder on his mind is incomprehensible. We would have had no concept of such things, no context, no words, no compartment in our little worlds for such evil.

My oldest brother, I was told, heard the news and wept, thinking of his little sisters at that age, with their big innocent brown eyes.

We were Amish before Amish was cool, back when my brother's teacher in public school referred to him derisively as "Dutchy." That was before one could buy dreamy paintings of little Amish girls with kittens in their laps, and long before insurance companies and wineries in Lancaster County painted pictures of buggies on their signs.

My own response to the shootings was to plunge unexpectedly into a sea of Amish memories. I remembered details I hadn't thought of in years, such as how the buggy wheels rasped on the road, how the sound of the horse's hooves changed to a steady clip-clop when we turned off a gravel road onto pavement, and how the sounds seemed to amplify inside the stiff navy-blue bonnet I wore over my white organdy cap. I remembered being in one of a long line of buggies, and how Becky and I giggled when the horse behind us seemed to be peering into the little window in the back of the buggy. I recalled Pennsylvania-German words I thought I had forgotten: *die Laut*, the casket, *die Engel*, the angels.

Especially, I remembered details of my grandparents' funerals—first the wake, when the body lay in a bedroom, which didn't seem repugnant at all, and we all sat on benches and sang for hours while people came to pay their respects. Then, the funeral, when an astonishing number of people sat on backless benches all over the house and the preaching went on and on. People filed by the casket at the end of the service—they came and came and came, men in black suits, women in black dresses. I knew they had all been in the house somewhere, but where? We joined the procession to the country cemetery and, at Grandma Miller's burial, a group of perhaps 10 young people sang a song about *die Engel* while the girls' black shawls flapped in the cold wind.

My parents' leaving of the Old Order and joining the "Beachy" Amish (named for a leader, Moses Beachy), was a gradual process. They didn't want us involved in the self-destructive activities that many Old Order Amish young people engaged in during their *rumspringa* (running around) years before they joined the church.

So by the time I was 10 years old, we had a car, electricity, and a phone, although we still wore plain solid-color dresses and white caps. Few of our Amish relatives condemned us for leaving, recognizing that faith in God mattered more than buggies or cars.

It seems the more our society has moved away from the Amish values of farming, family, simplicity, and community, the more the Amish lifestyle has been idealized, leading to best-selling Beverly Lewis novels about the Amish, and cross-stitch patterns of little boys in broad black hats. When my computer refuses to cooperate, or when I run into Amish relatives at family events, I sometimes have a strange longing to be part of that world again. It looks simple, warm, and defined.

But the truth is that I could never belong again; that door has closed. This, perhaps, is part of the Amish appeal—knowing that even though we can stand at the gate and look wistfully inside, we can never be part of that world. I sometimes meet people who try. The women wear long, full dresses, the men beards and big hats. "We're becoming Amish," they say, and brag about their new treadle sewing machine. How do I tell them that they have a hundred details wrong, from the wrinkled cap to the much-too-confident look on their faces? Worse, they do it alone, when the very essence of Amish life is community.

As a Beachy Amish teenager, I tried to define our lives for my Lutheran friends. "We're just people like everyone else," I would say, mystified at their curiosity. A Granny Smith apple tastes the same to an Amishman as to anyone else. Amish eyes become farsighted after age 40, a ham in the oven smells the same, a stubbed toe hurts equally.

And yet, it is equally true that the Amish are very different. For us, there was first of all a language barrier. English was for the world out there, formal and stilted. Pennsylvania German, or "Dutch" as we called it, was for home and warmth and belonging. We went to the door and spoke English to the salesman on the porch, then shut the door and reverted to Dutch, laughing, recounting the conversation with, perhaps, a snide comment about the salesman's persistence.

There was usually a distinct sense of us and them. "They" talked about sports and TV shows and getting their hair done, things we knew little about. One put on a proper face for public, where people were often patronizing, reverent, curious, or at times hostile. At home, the formality dropped and we ran around barefooted and laughed and had water fights. Looking at news photos of a long line of buggies driving past aggressive photographers, I thought again of this dichotomy. Essentially, at heart, the two groups of people were the same. And yet, at the same time, they were completely different in language, goals, employment, recreation, clothing, and much more.

I saw this stark difference when my Grandma Yoder died 18 years ago. After the funeral, we ate at my cousin Edna's house. It was packed with hundreds of people standing shoulder to shoulder, all of them dressed in black. For three hours, a line of people inched down to the basement for the meal; a similar line inched its way back up. My sisters and I had a wonderful time catching up with relatives, but the day was less enjoyable for our husbands, who escaped outside and sat in the van, and who felt, as many Americans probably would, that they had almost nothing in common with these people.

A tragedy such as the Amish school shooting in Pennsylvania, makes us reach across our differences and seek for connections. Perhaps we are trying to justify our deep feelings or prove that our grief is valid, and so we grope for points of contact. In this case, those of us with Amish in our background or distant relatives among the bereaved felt compelled to tell everyone. Every mother of young children saw her daughters lined up along that blackboard, her sons forced to leave their sisters behind.

On a Lancaster Online page of condolences, people from around the world shared their slightest connections to the Amish. "The Amish Community is very special to us," wrote one. "We have visited many times and always come away with peaceful hearts." On the Internet, bloggers recalled how they once drove through Lancaster County and waved at little Amish children on scooters on their way to school.

The truth is, at a time like this, there is no need to prove a connection. Nothing unites us in a common humanity like a child's death. It's not "us" modern people and "them" folks in their buggies; it's all "us," Amish, Muslim, Catholic, or anything else. Losing a child is losing a child, and we are all justified in reading the news and weeping.

As John Donne wrote, "No man is an island, entire of itself; every man is a piece of the continent; a part of the main. ... Any man's death diminishes me, because I am involved in mankind; and therefore never send to know for whom the bell tolls; it tolls for thee."

Pruning's Purpose

No one has ever taught me to properly prune the grapevines south of the house, so I always cut enthusiastically and hope for the best, which has never seemed to bother the vines. Each year they send 15-foot tendrils all over the arbor and even far up into the nearby pine trees, and then produce a solid crop of grapes.

This year's pruning began on a rare pleasant day in February, inspired less by the grapevine's needs than by the emerging flock of daffodils on the ground below—I wanted to enjoy their yellow beauty without the interference of a tangle of drooping vines. When I finished, the discarded vines lay on the grass and the arbor and daffodils made a neat, uncluttered picture in the yard.

Cleaning out the oak grove was a much bigger project.

My brother-in-law, Kenneth, owns the fescue field north of our house and also the band of oak trees just across the road. Until recently, the trees stood knee-deep in a tangled undergrowth of blackberries and saplings and unnamed bushes. Then Kenneth and a few friends moved in with a chainsaw and heavy equipment. I watched, worried that the entire site was being turned into more fescue field. But when all the branches and brambles were cleared away, the oak trees remained, clean and clearly outlined, from exposed roots on the ground to long crooked branches against the sky.

These pruning endeavors were soon followed, coincidentally, by a Sunday school lesson from the Gospel of John that likens Jesus to the main grapevine and we followers to the branches. God is the gardener who prunes the vines to make them more fruitful, the verses say, implying that God is not an indiscriminate whacker like me but knows exactly where to cut, and when. Such trimming also implies suffering, that worrisome experience we all try to avoid, from inconvenience and irritations to debilitating pain and loss.

Trusting that there is a gardener and that he knows what he is doing is a fine theory, easily assented to in a theoretical Sunday school discussion, or when the cuts are not too painful and it seems they might actually be for some purpose. I think, for example, of our 18-year-old daughter, Amy, who recently returned home after six weeks away and found that she is now shorter than all but one of her five siblings. She has no hope of ever being taller, which is not a huge handicap, to be sure, and yet she has had to accept that people will never take her seriously at first glance and she will never be able to reach top cupboards unassisted by stepstools.

Yet it is not too hard to believe that there may be something redemptive in this. "Aunt Amy" will no doubt be known to all her nieces and nephews as the first adult they equal in height when they hit their growth spurt. Perhaps she will be able to influence them at eye level in a way that larger adults cannot.

But there are also times when it is much harder to believe in a divine purpose, when the cutting is done with chainsaws instead of shears, and the underbrush is cleared out ruthlessly with heavy equipment.

My niece, Annette, flew out from Pennsylvania recently to spend a week with us. A beautiful 27-year-old, she is in many ways defined by the losses in her life. Other young couples, she says wistfully, seem to float through their first years of marriage with only a wave or two of financial struggles or in-law issues rocking their boat. In contrast, Annette and her husband, Jay, have faced storms far worse than any of their friends have experienced.

Four days after they were engaged to be married, Annette had surgery on a detached retina in her eye. She recovered at her future in-laws' house, and Jay had his first taste of what "In sickness and health" involved when Annette reacted violently to her medication. Her face was swollen and oozing and discolored, and she kept throwing up over and over. Unfazed, Jay took care of her, confirming that she had indeed chosen the right man.

Her eye has continued to be troublesome, both with medical bills and complications that limit her life in unexpected ways. Eyestrain keeps her from doing much work on the computer or reading newspapers, and she worries about how a future pregnancy might be affected by the powerful medications she has to take.

If Annette's eye was a sneaker wave upsetting their lives, her brother's suicide the following summer was a tsunami that changed the entire landscape. Annette was three years older than Leonard and, despite the two of them being very close, she had no idea this tragedy was coming. Then, six weeks after Leonard's death, their only sister was in the hospital having a just-in-time appendectomy.

Annette came to Oregon in search of some "aunt time," as she put it. The two of us sat at the kitchen table for hours, stirring our coffee and talking about changes and grief and loss. She talked about what she calls "The Journey." It encompasses the months past and the years yet to come—the cutting, the growing, the endless questions. If she had called Leonard the night before, would things have turned out differently? If she had been first on the scene, would she have seen a clue the investigators missed?

I longed to do the impossible and dispense answers that would make everything make sense. But she was adamant: She doesn't need pat religious-formula answers, nor does she want to be told that life is all random and there is no purpose or hope. What she needs is people to come along-side her in the journey, to acknowledge her daily struggle, to support her, to listen, to hear the hard questions, to give her time to find the answers herself.

Our conversation wandered to people we know who have been transformed by suffering, changed from cold and some-what judgmental to warm and empathetic. "Was there no other way to do this?" we asked each other. "Did it have to take that?" And, a dangerous question: "Are we supposed to think it was actually better this way, that it was worth the sacrifice?" Annette is honest about her struggles with faith. She told of how she went to get groceries the night her sister was in the hospital. "Oh, I was so mad," she said. "I stomped around that grocery store and I kept thinking, 'Can I trust you, God? Can I really trust you? With my fam-ily? With anything?'"

Then she laughed and continued. "This is Lancaster County, Pennsylvania, you know, and they play hymns on my grocery-store's PA system. And while I was stomping around pushing that grocery cart, the song 'All to Jesus I Surrender' started playing. I said, 'OK, God, I get the mes-sage.'" I chuckled with her, imagining the scene and relieved to see that for all the difficulty in her life, her quirky sense of humor remains.

Actually, I can tell that, like the oak trees across the road, the person Annette really is has been outlined and clarified more clearly than ever before. She has always been funny, loving, strong, and wise; she still is. "I make it," she said, "by the grace of God and my stubborn will."

For all the things I do not know, I do know this: What remains after the pruning is firm and solid, spring will eventually come, and new growth will appear, determined and green.

$\mathcal{F}inding\ the$
$\mathcal{H}owevers$

We sat at the kitchen table last week, my 17-year-old daughter, Emily, and I, discussing how someone who missed almost her entire senior year of high school could write a graduation speech. "There's nothing to say," she insisted.

And I said, "Pretend I don't know a thing, and tell me what you've been through." So she talked and I took notes, and when she finished telling about the complicated anguish of being sick for so long, she stopped.

"However..." I prodded, like a too-typical, kiss-it-and-make-it-all-better mom.

"There are no howevers!" she burst out. "I feel like everybody will expect me to say, '*However*, all these wonderful character-building things came out of this so it was all worthwhile and now I'm so patient and compassionate and everything.' But in my mind there are no howevers yet! I still feel sick, and I don't think I've changed into some sort of wonderful patient person. And I don't understand why I had to go through this!"

"Then say exactly that," I said, and she did, the following Thursday, in her new elfin-silver dress with the green jacket, and in the audience people who love her listened and wiped their eyes.

Emily has had vague health issues for years—food allergies and migraine headaches and prolonged bouts of the flu. But by the time she was 16 she seemed to have outgrown much of this and reveled in the activities of a normal junior year of high school. She had endless plans for her senior year. "I was going to be editor of the yearbook," she said, "and I was all excited about making it interesting and unique. I wanted to get a job on the side and take college algebra at a community college, because this was the first year I could drive myself around. And I was going to write and direct a play for the youth group to act out for a fundraiser."

A week into the school year she got sick.

"No big deal," we thought, and after a week she was better again. But the aches and fever returned, and by October she was constantly ill and had been examined, tested, poked, and re-examined, and the medical experts seemed to have no more answers than we did.

I Googled "teenager fever aches fatigue" and wanted to throw the mouse at the computer and run screaming from the room as an ominous list popped up, from leukemia on down through mononucleosis and fibromyalgia. Only one test result was positive and that only slightly: West Nile Fever, a virus spread by mosquitoes. One doctor said, "No, it's not West Nile"; another said, "Yes, of course it is." We chose to believe that it was, a conclusion affirmed by other victims whose experiences paralleled Emily's. There is no cure, we were told, and recovery can take from two weeks to two years.

In her speech, Emily described the moment when she realized she would probably be sick for a long time. "I sat in the darkness and cried, thinking about all my wonderful plans. I had to finally accept the fact that I wouldn't be able to do them."

"Surely by Thanksgiving she'll be well," we said in the fall. "Well, then, surely by Christmas, by spring, by summer."

By January, she was so weak she asked me to buy her a cane.

I have learned that for every sick child there is a care-giver parent in the background, enduring not fevers and aches and accumulating losses, but the quiet grief of watching. When she asked for a cane I thought, "OK, this is it, end of the road, I cannot buy my beautiful, elegant, 17-year-old a cane." But of course I did anyhow, because that is what parents do.

The sickness had not destroyed Emily's sense of fun, an important "however." She decorated the cane with stickers and pink ribbons, and named it John McCane. As she felt able, which wasn't often, Emily did her schoolwork at home. Mercifully, the school board of our small church school told her she could go ahead with graduation exercises, and her principal dad promised to make sure she eventually finished the required courses so she could get her diploma.

With characteristic honesty, Emily described how the sickness tested her faith. "I always believed before this sickness came that God would never give me more than I could handle. But I realized during this time that the big flaw in that is we can handle anything if we're not given a choice. We think there are things we can't handle ... we'd just go crazy ... but if something is handed to you, you just get through it if you think you can or not, because going crazy is a lot harder than it sounds. I can't say I ever got mad at God, or that I ever felt like he deserted me, I just don't understand so many things."

And then she told the audience that they are no doubt waiting for her to list the "howevers," but that there are no howevers yet. She ended the speech with gratitude to every-one who had been there for her during this time, and added,

"My mom has done the most of everyone. I have been sick for nine months, and she still brings me tea in bed. I cannot thank her enough."

Listening teary-eyed to this tribute, I had to disagree with Emily. I think there are many howevers in her story, like seedlings pushing out of the dark garden soil, unseen at first glance and then suddenly there, all in a line, tiny and green. She just can't see them yet—the grace, the growth, the hidden gifts of empathy and gratitude. Emily still doesn't feel well, but she is strong enough that John McCane hangs unused behind her bedroom door.

She has new determination, goals, and creativity, gradually redecorating her brother's old bedroom for herself in an eye-popping "Shimmering Lime" color and asking for a dress form for a graduation gift so she can design clothes and costumes. "She will not be the same Emily coming out of this as she was going into it," a wise friend told me.

I would not for a second calculate whether the hard times have been worth the howevers, but I do know that I like the emerging Emily, this newly mature young woman who waters my life with laughter dipped from sickness and gentleness wrung from suffering.

Sloshing Emotions and New Pursuits

Lately I seem to be crying more than normal, not because of depression or trauma, but because I am a sentimental 40-something mom brimful of liquid emotions that easily slosh over the edge. Especially at Christmas, with its music and celebration and family times, a slight jar brings the tissues out of my pocket.

So I cried happily when my two handsome teenage sons sang in their choir's Christmas concert, Ben's newly deep voice vibrating out confidently on the bass notes of the jubilant, "All the Trees of the Field Shall Clap Their Hands." This child spent too much of his life thinking he hated to sing, and yet there he was, miraculously singing out and enjoying it—and what could I do but cry?

My brother sent me a picture of his family, with everyone cheerfully smiling. But I looked at it and wept at what was missing—my nephew who died tragically a year and a half ago.

We went to hear the African Children's Choir in Harrisburg one evening. Bright-eyed little children the age of my youngest daughter took the microphone and introduced themselves as Joshua or Esther or Enoch and said they want to be a pilot or nurse or plumber when they grew up.

And then I thought about Kenya going up in flames after the recent election, and innocent people suffering even more, and our son Steven coming from that life to this one, and it all bubbled out in hot tears. "Tears are significant,"

423

our Kenyan friend, Vincent, told me once. "It shows you a lot about a person's character, what they cry about."

So, I wonder, what does it say about me when I get the most emotional of all about my children leaving home? At our large Smucker family Christmas, someone asked me how I was doing, and I unexpectedly burst into tears because, I sputtered, I have all these conflicting feelings about my kids growing up.

Matt, our oldest, finished his finals at Oregon State University in early December and came home for a month, and then Amy flew in from South Carolina for the holidays. I felt and behaved like a contented, clucking hen with all her chicks safely back in the nest. The feeling of utter fulfillment I got from having everyone home, especially when we lingered around the supper table for long, rambling discussions, was just what I had hoped for and expected.

What took me by surprise was the paradox of feeling such joy yet at the same time being plagued by a vague hunger, a longing for something from my children that I could not define and that they seemed unable to give. Both Matt and Amy enjoyed being at home, high-fiving wildly while listening to Ducks games in the boys' bedroom, opening gifts on Christmas morning, and cleaning the kitchen together. But they seemed equally eager to dash off to hang out with their friends or go shopping or take in a church youth activity. I found myself watching them go, perplexed by this strange, dissatisfied wanting.

My husband's sister, Lois, whose three oldest, as she says, "are marrying faster than they came," had this explanation after my little meltdown at the family gathering: "You want them to need you like they used to," she told me sympathetically. "It's this paradox," she went on, "you've worked for this all their lives, to get them to where they can make it on their own, and then when they do, you want them to need you again just like they did when they were little, and they don't, and it hurts."

The more I thought about this, the more sense it made, especially since I had chosen to invest more of my life into my children than in any other pursuit. It also made me suddenly understand my mom a lot better. So many times I have gone home and spent time with her, yet when I left I felt like there was a vague disappointment in her soul that I could not fix, a hunger I could not satisfy.

"Sometimes I wish I just had one day with all of you little again," she would say wistfully. "Just one day, all at home and around me again."

Why? I wondered at the time. As poor as we were then, as hard as she had to work, as difficult as I was, why would she want to go back?

Now, I'm starting to understand.

When three of us siblings all left home in a single summer, Mom coped not with my sort of dripping waterworks but by throwing herself into a frenzy of quilting and crafts. In the following years she produced quilts, pillows, dolls, rugs, and much more, coming out on the other side of that transition with polished skills and a large, colorful collection of useful artwork.

A gentle inner nudging has been telling me that, busy as I am, I should do a bit of the same. In fact, I turned impulsively to my 17-year-old daughter, Emily, the other day and announced, "I think God might be telling me to make a quilt instead of obsessing about my kids." She looked a bit stunned and then said, in teenage lingo, "Well! That was random!"

Thankfully Emily, like the rest of the family, is kind and indulgent with me, recognizing that this is not an easy transition, and tolerating my tears and outbursts with gentle amusement.

Then came a sweet little confirmation that quilting was the right pursuit. On the very day that I had told Emily I was thinking I should make a quilt, Lois pulled her sisters-in-law together at our family supper and announced, "I've decided that for your Christmas gift I'm going to pay for all of us to take a quilting class together. Depending on which class we decide to take, and if we do our homework, we can all have a king-sized quilt pieced by the end."

Surprisingly, for all my delight and gratitude at this news, I didn't cry. I just knew, deep down, that someone was watching out for me, life would go on, I was going to find new worlds to conquer, and everything was actually, eventually going to be all right.

Gathering In

Swatting Flies Like Grandma

*F*all is the season of crane flies, skinny awkward insects that my 17-year-old daughter, Emily, describes as "a little bit like an overgrown mosquito and a little bit like a daddy-long-legs with wings." The lights on the porch attract most of the crane flies around here, but a few slipped inside one evening, resting delicately on the kitchen walls. Emily, who hates bugs, couldn't leave them alone. She rolled up a newspaper and went to battle.

Watching her, I had a sudden memory of my mom, in recent summers, and my grandma, many years ago, marching around the kitchen with a flyswatter in hand and murderous determination in their eyes. These were kind-hearted women who crooned in German to newborn piglets and spoiled the cats, but they had no patience with flies in the kitchen. After she killed one, my grandma often told us, in her German dialect, "Every time you 'schwat' a fly, seven more come to the funeral."

As I watched Emily stalk the crane flies I thought to myself, "OK, this will be the big test: If she leaps up on a chair to reach a crane fly, I will know for sure that she is officially carrying the torch of her grandma and great-grandma." Sure enough, Emily boosted herself onto a green stool in the corner and smacked a bug high on the wall, then jumped down, looking satisfied, and took off after the next one.

Seeing this remarkable similarity to Emily's foremothers made me wonder again about the intricate threads that bind generations of women. How much are we tied into family patterns without even knowing it, and how much power do we have to carry on the good and meaningful and to break free from the unhealthy and unhappy?

When Emily and her older sister, Amy, were little, we lived in a cabin in Canada and I heated water on the stove for their baths. As I bathed them in the galvanized-tin bathtub, I imagined us as part of a long chain of mothers and daughters—my mom scrubbing me like this in the little house in Kalona, Iowa; Mom's mother washing her in a farmhouse in Indiana; and my great-grandma, "Mommie Schlabach," washing Grandma in a makeshift tub wherever their family had most recently moved. And I wondered: Did each generation before me have the hopes for their daughters that I had for mine?

I come from a long line of strong, determined women. Deep in the Amish subculture, the ebbs and flows of the women's movement in the larger society completely passed them by. They never got the message that housewives should be all dainty in lipstick and heels, or the later one that they should be liberated and find fulfillment through employment or education or positions of power.

Instead, these women raised large families and hoed their huge gardens and sold produce in town. They hitched up the temperamental horse to the wagon and picked huckleberries in the back 40 all day and then came home to do a day's worth of housework in the evening. They built closets in the bedrooms and sewed denim trousers for the men and chopped the chickens' heads off on butchering days.

And they seemed to love every minute of it.

"We wouldn't have had to work so hard," my Aunt Vina told me once, chuckling, "but I guess we used to think we were half horse."

I am in many ways as traditional as my great-grand-mother. I like children, stories, cats, making something out of nothing, and growing a vegetable garden. Somehow, though, I missed out on the endless energy of previous generations, and I envy their stamina and courage.

I can think of only one area where I actually try to be different, and that is in the hidden thread of silence that connects these women. They had plenty to say on almost every subject, but there were times and situations when they should have spoken, and, for reasons I don't fully understand, did not. My great-grandmother had a child at the age of 15, and I am told that she did not talk about this. In later generations, there was abuse that no one exposed, and an unwillingness to ask for badly needed help or to talk about personal things, or even to verbally express affection.

My mother, in her own way, was determined to be different. When I was a child, she courageously told us what her mother had been unable to tell her—the things we needed to know when our bodies started changing.

While my great-grandmother's silence seems incomprehensible to me—and I am far more likely than my mom to call a friend when I have a bad day—it still has not been easy to find and speak the words for both affection and anger, to ask for help when I need it, to speak out, to realize that secrets lose their power when exposed to light. For all the mistakes we and our mothers made, we keep believing that our daughters will somehow get it all right, that they will keep the healthy and humorous legacies in one hand while releasing the regrettable and sad with the other.

I see this in Jenny, my fearless, red-headed 8-year-old, who likes to climb and jump and play kickball with the boys. "It makes me feel tough when I'm all banged up," she told me the other day, proudly examining the bruises on her shins. Another day she announced, "It makes me feel so good when people cheer for me. Like when I'm playing soccer and Kyle says, 'Go Jenny!'" Jenny's energy and determination come straight from her grandmothers, I'm convinced, and that makes me smile. But what really makes me happy is to see how easily she identifies both her feelings and the words to express them, freely and confidently.

I am immensely proud of my daughters and wish only good things for them. Realistically, though, I know that they will make their own choices and their own mistakes. But when I see them roll up a newspaper and stalk through the kitchen with a determined glint in their eyes, I am confident of this: They come from good stock, and it would take an awful lot to defeat them.

Pondering in My Heart

I memorized the Christmas story in the first grade, in preparation for the program at our little Amish school. I still have the dress I wore that night, a maroon corduroy dress with a pocket on the front, that Mom had sewn for me.

As I recall, the dress was much more exciting to me than the lines I recited. We younger ones quoted from the second chapter of Luke, with its descriptions of startled shepherds and rejoicing angels. The older children repeated prophecies from the Old Testament, rattling through "Behold, a virgin shall conceive, and bear a son, and shall call his name Immanuel," and stumbling over "But thou, Bethlehem Ephratah, though thou be little among the thousands of Judah, yet out of thee shall he come forth unto me that is to be ruler in Israel."

By the time I was an adult I could recite large swaths of the Christmas scriptures and had heard and read the story of Christ's birth hundreds of times, a familiarity that unfortunately dulled the wonder of the essential kernel at the heart of it all: Jesus coming as a baby in a poor family to rescue a lost world. I always believed the story, and loved it, but I remember the moment when it actually became real to me, bursting out of the familiar poetic narrative like a sudden bright light from a dark window.

Paul and I had been married for nearly a year and a half, and we were consumed with the wondrous fact that we were going to have a child. I had survived months of relentless nausea and was just getting back on my feet when a friend invited me to see the Christmas pageant in Rickreall with her. Rickreall is a small town north of Corvallis that has put on an elaborate dramatization of the Christmas story for more than 60 years. All dialogue and narration are strictly quotations from the Bible, but the actors include plenty of dramatic fill-ins and pantomime. A large choir sings between scenes.

I sat there enthralled as a richly costumed angel brought good news and the choir sang like the original heavenly chorus. Then a live donkey emerged from the side of the stage, and a young woman, playing Mary, sat on his back. Mary looked tired, and her hand rested on a gentle bulge on her stomach. That was when it struck me, and I wept at the astounding realization: Mary was... why she actually was... *pregnant!* Pregnant with her first child like I was with mine, full of the same newness and wonder, facing the same enormous changes and fears. I did not analyze our differences then, such as the prospect of laying her baby in a manger vs. a clean bassinet at the Silverton Hospital. I only saw with astonishing clarity that Mary was not just a sweet character in a familiar story. She had been a real woman with a real pregnancy.

In the classic children's book, *The Best Christmas Pageant Ever*, the narrator says of Imogene Herdman, the wild, uncombed girl who usurped the role of Mary in the Sunday school play: "Christmas just came over her all at once, like a case of chills and fever. And so she was crying, and walking into the furniture." As it did for Imogene, Christmas came over me all at once at that old-fashioned pageant in Rickreall.

I am older now, and while I chuckle at the hyper-sensitive emotions that accompanied that first pregnancy, I still find Christmas coming over me, cutting through 40 years of repetition to become glowing and vivid. Some years it hits me when I hear "Silent Night" playing above overdone decorations in a crowded department store, sometimes in the music of *The Messiah*, sometimes in my own children, innocent in new homemade dresses or awkward costumes, reciting Luke 2 in a school Christmas program.

This year, I find myself drawn once again to Mary, her life, her motherhood. An obscure little phrase jumps out of the story and stays in my mind as I wrap gifts and prepare shepherd robes. We are told that as Mary became aware of her son's purpose, through shepherds showing up unexpectedly and an old man's sudden mysterious blessing, she "marvelled at those things." And she "kept all these things, and pondered them in her heart."

It seems, in a way, an odd response to the drama of rich strangers bringing frankincense or a special star in the sky. Why didn't she tell all her friends or broadcast it to the neighborhood? Instead, she pondered.

I think of this phrase because I am in a pondering season myself as I observe my three young-adult children. I am not much like Mary and my children's destiny is not like Jesus', yet I find myself watching and marvelling as their own callings unfold.

I've had my years of talking to them, repeating phrases that I picture engraved on permanent cassette tapes in their heads, whirring to life when needed. "Think about how your behavior affects other people." "Don't interrupt." And "Eat what is set before you with a thankful heart," which I always insisted was in the Bible somewhere, but I couldn't find it just then. (My oldest son, Matt, told me recently that, as a modern young man, the phrases in his head are actually on CDs instead of cassettes. But, he assured me, they are there all the same.)

But now, it's time to be quiet.

Two children have left the nest, one to a job in South Carolina and one to college in Corvallis. This year, for the first time, I am in the role of having someone come home to me for Christmas. I am the one fluttering and feathering, putting clean sheets on the beds, jotting down their favorite foods.

And, like Mary, I watch, pray, and wonder.

Is Amy fitting in? Is she happy? Matt is having a hard time with his first engineering classes and has wondered at times if this is really the right major for him. I wish I could tell him what to do, but I can't. And how, I wonder, can Emily best channel her unusual talents after she graduates from high school?

When my big kids are together, they speak in code, exchanging looks or short phrases that communicate in a language I don't know. I sense that they tell each other things and then add, "Don't tell Mom," just like my sister used to tell me when she had to drive through gang territory to commute to her new job in Los Angeles.

But I also sense that this is the time to listen and love and ponder and cook more food, but not to talk. I rest in the fact that, as Jesus' calling unfolded with time, so will theirs. So Christmas has come over me gently this year. I read the familiar story and know that for all the mysteries and unknowns in our family's lives, the goodwill is toward all of us, and ours is again the wonder and hope and joy.

Apple Dumplings

Our neighbor, Leroy, who is my husband Paul's second cousin if you go through Paul's grandma, and his half-first cousin once removed if you route it through his grandpa, gives us apples every year that he grows on land that once belonged to my husband's grandpa, Orval.

The apples are wonderful and the eight of us eat them recklessly, but even then I noticed last week that they were starting to get a bit dried and wrinkled. Since my mother taught me thoroughly that throwing away food was one of the worst sins, I determined to use up these apples rather then toss them on the compost pile. I regularly make apple crisp and sometimes pies, but I wanted to try something I vaguely remembered Mom making. It involved dough wrapped around apple halves, with a bit of syrup at the bottom of the pan.

I hunted through a cookbook from a neighboring church, knowing that church cookbooks have the best tried-and-true recipes anywhere, and there I found what I wanted: apple dumplings. And the contributor was Elsie Knox.

As I mixed up the dough, I thought about heritage and generations and life coming full circle. Twenty-two years ago I married into a large, noisy, generous, opinionated clan whose genealogy was forever complicated by the fact that two of the patriarchs had married their stepfather's younger sisters, giving the family tree a violent twist that we are still untangling today.

Paul and I spent eight years in mission work in northwestern Ontario, far from his Oregon roots. Then, twelve years ago, we moved back to this area and immersed our children in the joys of playing in the creek with cousins, large Christmas dinners with the extended family, and Grandma stopping by with a loaf of fresh cracked-wheat bread.

We live in a 95-year-old farmhouse that was built in 1911 by my husband's great-grandfather. He and his wife raised 10 children here, then the house passed on to my husband's half-great-aunt—well, if you figure it that way. The other way she was his first cousin once removed. And her name was Elsie Knox, the contributor of the apple dumpling recipe.

So it is a strange thing to be making Elsie's recipe to feed my six children in the same kitchen in which Elsie no doubt made the same recipe to feed her six. Only hers were all boys, and they grew up to become the Knox Brothers, a singing group familiar to many Southern Gospel music fans.

There are those who are called to live far from their families and roots. The day will no doubt come for our children when they will move from this comfortable nest to a place where faces are unfamiliar and all the apples are tasteless and store-bought.

So now, while I still have the opportunity, I bake dumplings from a family recipe with apples from a generous neighbor, filling my children with solid roots and values to give them strength for whatever their futures hold.

Blackberries for an Addled Mind

I wonder sometimes why blackberries ripen at the time of year when I am least able to enjoy them. I would prefer them six months later, in February, a juicy boost in the middle of winter when I could make a daily pilgrimage to the berry patch. Instead, the wild blackberries around here ripen at the end of August, right at the time when the demands and obligations of late summer seem overwhelming.

In July, I just manage to stay on top of the weeding, watering, schedules, canning, cooking, and social activities. But by the last week or two of August the flowerbeds are drying up, the weeds on the far end of the garden are out of control, and the green beans should have been picked yesterday. All the windows look dusty and cobwebby, the dog is scratching miserably, Gravenstein apples are dropping off the tree, and the boys still need school clothes—a job I put off as long as possible in hopes that the new jeans won't be outgrown before the first report cards come home.

Some moms I know respond by cutting their losses with the petunias and pinning their hopes for relief on the first day of school and the fall rains. I respond by questioning my sanity, first with an exasperated, "What was I thinking—to plant all these beans and say I'd help with Bible Memory Camp?" but mostly because of the disconcerting evidence that my brain has stopped working. I am absentminded at the best of times, but late summer is when I stand lost and confused in the middle of the WinCo parking lot trying to locate my car—or wait, did I drive the van today?—right after I fed a cartful of sticky pop cans into the machine, forgot to redeem the refund coupon, forgot to return the important phone call, and left my clipboard with all my careful lists lying on the counter at OfficeMax.

I get to the middle of a sentence and forget where I began and where I was going. Normally, I at least make it close to the end of the sentence before I do this. I yell at the dog to quit barking at the sheep, but I call him Steven instead of Hansie.

My seed-sacking nephew, Zack, I was told, texted his mom one day and said, "Is Aunt Dorcas OK? She seems kind of spacey."

And I wonder if I really am accomplishing anything or only frantically twirling a hamster wheel.

In the middle of all this, calmly ignoring the hustle of our lives, the blackberries steadily ripen. The closest ones grow along Powerline Road, beginning at the end of our little orchard and proceeding south, long determined vines twining high into the trees along the fencerow and snaking across the ditch and toward the road. Unlike the roses and corn, they ask nothing of us—no pruning, watering, or weeding. They simply produce countless rich purple berries, free for the taking.

I had sent the younger children out to pick a number of times this summer. They prefer the adventure of crossing the neighbor's field and picking in another patch along the railroad tracks, where they just might have the added excitement of seeing a fox or rabbit or even, one evening, the Barnum and Bailey circus train going by. They return with ice cream buckets full of blackberries that we turn into cobblers and pies or scoop into bags for the freezer.

But I had not yet gone picking myself, and a small prodding voice inside kept telling me I needed to, that this was important, that it wasn't about production and accomplishment, but that I needed the experience itself. So, finally, one evening after a day of canning green beans, I did. Nine-year-old Jenny was happy to go with me. We pulled on the boys' tall rubber boots and squelched out to the bushes just by the orchard.

Blackberry vines are nasty obstacles, studded with thorns that will snag a shirt or an arm and rip painfully. So picking requires patience and finesse, carefully threading a hand behind this vine, up over that one, and then yes!—there it is, the perfect berry dropped into the hand—and then slowly threading a cupped hand back out the way it came in. Despite my precautions, I kept snagging my hands and yelping.

"You don't have to say 'ouch' every time you get poked, you know," Jenny told me.

Of course she was right, this tomboy-princess daughter of mine, who seems to have far more stoic bravery than her mother ever did. Jenny and her blue bucket disappeared around the next bush. I kept picking, carefully, my amateur efforts nonetheless rewarded with a steady increase in the purple pile in my bucket.

A sense of restfulness and peace that I hadn't felt in weeks, maybe all summer, stole into my addled mind. I pulled leaves aside and admired the clusters of berries hiding behind them, beautiful and rich. I pushed vines aside with my rubber boots so I could reach deeper into the bush, and slowly I picked the berries that seemed to be waiting there, just for me, generous and free.

"I want to make my own pie this time," Jenny announced from farther down the ditch. My first response was a sigh— I really didn't have time to help her. But I knew I would anyhow; this was something I needed to do. We tallied our haul—plenty for a couple of pies at least—and went home, first picking a few more tantalizing berries that called to us and couldn't be ignored.

Back in the kitchen, I mixed the flour and shortening in a bowl and handed it to Jenny. She stirred in the cold water and squeezed the dough into a ball. Then she sprinkled flour on the table, rolled out a perfect piecrust, folded it in half, and settled it into the pie pan like she'd done this all her life.

Next she sliced off the edges with a butter knife and then pressed them into a pretty pattern with a fork. She measured and mixed the berry filling, poured it in, and cut decorative shapes from the leftover dough to place on top.

"Where in the world did you learn to do all that?" I asked, astonished.

"From watching you," she answered.

That was my blackberry moment, sweet and succulent. Good things are happening here, I realized, slowly ripening when I'm not looking, patiently developing among the grasping vines of busyness and demands, the thorns of mental lapses and my constant inability to catch up. Blackberries and children and the sweet things of life will not be rushed, and they will ripen in their own time, tasting of serenity and joy.

Slug Bugs and Family Traditions

"*B*eep Jeep!" my son Steven shouts from the back seat as he punches his brother, Ben, in the arm. "Ow!" Ben yells, then responds with a loud, "Hey! Slug bug!" and slugs Steven back.

The boys are 13 and 14, with long arms and legs sprawling all over the back seat. They see no need to corral their limbs, and 9-year-old Jenny, who is a third their size, often gets caught in the crossfire of their strange games.

Given the choice, this is not what I would have chosen as a family tradition. Perhaps a little song that we all sing in four-part harmony as we get into the car, that would be nice, or a ritual of identifying trees and cloud formations on the way to choir practice.

Instead, our family-in-the-car tradition is boys yelling and punching whenever they see a Jeep or Volkswagen Beetle. Often they add the disclaimer, "No take back!" to supposedly make them immune to revenge, but it doesn't work because the other brother mysteriously never hears it. Adding the color of a car adds an extra dimension to the experience, as in "Slug Bug yellow!" or "Beep Jeep blue!"

Then there's also the Smucker ritual of the digital Pioneer Villa sign, when we cross Interstate 5 on Highway 228, headed to Brownsville. Jenny gets involved just as enthusiastically as the boys, and they all elbow each other to get the best view, even going so far as to put their hands over their siblings' eyes to improve their own chances. Then they wait with bated breath through diesel prices and the little pitcher pouring coffee, so eagerly you'd think it was an oracle from the prophet Elijah himself that they were watching for, but actually, it's only the current temperature: "55 degrees! I saw it first!" "Nuh-uh! I did!" "No you did not!" "No fair, you pushed me!"

Back when I had just started out as a mom I would probably have tried to put a stop to these things before they ever became habitual—such violence and sheer foolishness. But now I tolerate the noisy games with patient amusement because I know I'm going to miss them when they're gone.

In the old days, really not that long ago, when the back seats were full of my older daughters and their friends in cotton school-uniform jumpers and long braids, the van would suddenly erupt in what sounded like noisy spitting whenever we passed a field with horses. "Slip slip slopsky!" "Slip slip slip!" A white horse was a "slopsky" and worth five points; anything else was "slip" and worth one. Whoever had the most points by the time we got to school won. A very odd game, I thought at the time, but now, whenever I pass the stables at the corner of Highway 228 and Falk Road, I brace just a bit for an eruption of slips and slopskys from the back seat that never comes. And I miss it.

The older I get, the more fond I am of tradition. Community traditions like the Fourth of July parade, church traditions like singing a capella hymns, family traditions in all their odd manifestations—these are good things. Traditions provide solid footing when life gets muddy and tell us who we are when we're no longer sure.

As a church, we Mennonites are good at tradition. The famous "Tradition!" song in *Fiddler on the Roof* was written of the Jewish community in Russia, but we're pretty sure we could offer them some stiff competition. Most of us chafe at this when we're about 17, including my daughter, Emily, who recently snorted that tradition is only a sign that people are afraid to change.

That was the age when I agitated about it as well, cramped by the rules of our Amish church. Plain, solid-color dresses, for instance, with no scope for personal expression. How stupid was that? There was nothing scriptural about it, I would fuss. "I mean, the Bible says, 'Consider the lilies, yet Solomon in all his glory was not arrayed like one of these,'" which was proof we should toss tradition aside and wear something pretty.

The world has spun around a few times and I have found that once you've survived financial difficulties and deathly ill children and deep disappointments, solid-color dresses are a non-issue and I could go back to them if that were the setting where I found purpose and belonging. After all, this is what tradition offers—something familiar and solid to fall back on, decided on by a group rather than one confused individual, a message that this is where I belong, this is what we do here, this is who we are.

I've found that church customs, while they serve a similar purpose as family traditions, evolve more slowly and are far more entrenched. Families are much more fluid, moving, in only 25 years or so, from a newly established home to having the oldest children grown up and gone.

Family traditions, I have found, often spring out of the moment, an impulsive decision that inadvertently becomes what we "always" do. And then, all too quickly, the children outgrow the custom and look back nostalgically, saying, "Remember how we always...?"

My husband, Paul, has read bedtime stories to the children ever since they were little. With three fiercely competitive children born in four years' time, the bedtime ritual turned into a complicated series of rules and turns: who got to sit on Dad's lap, who sat on either side, who could go hug Mom goodnight first, who got to stand on the orange chair to brush their teeth.

By now, of course, the need for such regulation is long gone. The three youngest still lounge on the couch to listen to a nightly story, the latest being *The Marvelous Inventions of Alvin Fernald*, and the older ones chuckle and recall, "Remember how Dad had to make all these rules so we wouldn't fight during the story, and the last one to hug Mom goodnight got to sit on Dad's lap the longest?"

In an effort to accustom our children to speaking in public, we used to take a bag of treats along to prayer meeting and afterward give them to any child who had quoted a Bible verse during "testimony" time. This led to one prayer-meeting leader rapturously praising our children, who had just burst out popcorn-like with Bible verses. I thought, but did not say, "Brother, don't be too impressed; we have chocolate waiting in the van."

When our finances improved, this custom slowly changed into ice cream bars at the Shell station on the way home for anyone who either said a verse or led in prayer. Changing it now would be unthinkable. It's a family tradition, it's what we do, and the clerks at the Shell station have been known to watch for us on Wednesday nights. And it has served its purpose: Our children aren't afraid to speak up in public. This is part of who they are, thanks to a seemingly insignificant family tradition.

I have a hard time imagining anything profoundly redemptive ever coming out of my children watching for the temperature on the Pioneer Villa sign or hollering when they see a Jeep. But I am certain that when they're all grown up they will cross the overpass at Interstate 5 and remember, laughing, how they were long-legged kids in the back seat, punching each other. We were a family, and this is who we were, and this is what we did, and it all had a part in who they eventually became.

Making Peace With Change

I wish a bell would ring to warn me whenever my life is about to change. Not only before big calamities, but also when I've settled into a nice routine and am about to be jolted out of it.

There was no indication that anything would be different that morning last week when I put the three youngest children and a pile of buckets in the van and we headed out to a strawberry patch, just as we have done every June for the last 14 years. I wore my old denim skirt and stained shirt that I always wear, happy in the knowledge that I've finally learned how to do this well—when to go, how many to pick, how to motivate the children.

We drove the country roads to a farm near the west end of Cartney Drive. There, the children reluctantly emerged from the van, nearly locking the keys inside, as always, and we weighed our buckets under a canopy cluttered with berry-stained buckets and boxes. Shivering in the chilly morning air, we followed the rows down to the little orange flags, pushed the dewy leaves aside, admired the wealth of shiny red berries, and began to pick. Then, knowing how quickly children tire of berry-picking, I reminded them, in my oh-won't-this-be-fun voice, of the incentive that I have used successfully for years. "Remember, every time you pick 50 berries, you get to throw one at me."

"Yeah, Mom, we know."

After a quarter-bucket, I looked around. No berries had yet come flying my way. Hmmm, strange.

Five minutes later Jenny, age 9, gleefully threw a squashed berry in my direction and groaned when it missed me by five feet. Steven and Ben, aged 13 and 14, quietly kept picking. A few minutes later a berry hit my back and Jenny shrieked with joy, but the boys showed no reaction.

Impossibly soon, the boys and I had each filled a bucket. We helped Jenny finish hers and then quickly filled a fifth bucket and carried them to the canopy to weigh and pay. Chitchat with the farmer, pull out the cash with red-stained fingers—all was as it ought to be. We started for home. "So," I said to the boys, "I noticed you didn't throw any berries at me."

They shrugged.

"So what's with that?" I pressed.

"I dunno." They stared out the window, bored. "Do you know what time Dad wants us at the warehouse today?"

I drove on past fields heavy with the reliable green-gold of late June, feeling like an era was coming to an end and a clever-mom idea, of which I had had so few, had turned into something silly, useful only with Jenny now, but probably not for long. Why, I wondered, do things have to keep changing on me just as I finally get them figured out?

Our family e-mail account, for instance. There was no warning about this, either, or else I would have made a backup as everyone ought to but most of us find out the hard way. Ten years ago my husband was all excited about the amazing possibilities of hooking our computer to the phone, which would open up something called the Internet. It all sounded vaguely dangerous to me, so he said he would wait until I felt comfortable with it. Finally, my gift to him one

449

Christmas, probably one of his favorite ever, was permission to buy a modem. My motive was partially selfish, as I vaguely understood that this might make it easier to communicate with my sister in Yemen.

First we had a primitive fax program, and not long after, we advanced to Juno, an efficient and easy-to-use program that let me send and receive e-mails. It wasn't difficult to master, and at last I could communicate quickly and inexpensively with my sister. The days of two-week delays with letters and $1.50-a-minute phone calls were over. At first it seemed everyone had Juno, but then others in my life advanced to fancier programs. Later, for my teenagers, e-mail became passé and they communicated via Xanga messages and texting on their cell phones.

But I stuck with my old, basic version of Juno. I liked it, it worked, it didn't come up with new options, and I had all the messages stored on our computer instead of, as I imagined, some damp warehouse in Seattle, all of which came back to bite me when it suddenly overloaded its capacity and locked up tight.

Our son, Matt, calmly rescued what he could, which wasn't much, and I knew the time had come for something different.

"Gmail, definitely Gmail," said helpful young friends. "Yahoo, with Outlook or Thunderbird" said others.

Reluctantly, I checked them out. It was overwhelming. Click here for weather in Harrisburg, there for world news, over here for entertainment. Faces popped up on the sidebar to tell me what to take for asthma or heartburn. Did I want to chat? asked this button. Or invite a friend? offered that one.

Like a frightened kindergartener on her first day of school, I didn't want any of it. "Just take me home," I wanted to wail, "back to how it's always been."

Maybe my resistance to change is cultural, like the joke my brother likes to tell: "How many Mennonites does it take to change a light bulb?" Answer: "Change?"

Or perhaps it's a normal feature of the post-40 landscape.

For whatever reason, I find myself fighting change, unable to reconcile myself to it, and having to be yanked or shoved into the future. Sometimes, however, I am reminded that what is familiar to me now was once unfamiliar, and that my life is what it is today because of a long series of mostly unwelcome changes. I was invited last winter to speak to a group of third-graders in Santa Clara about being an author. I told them about my Amish background, and how, when I was their age, I learned to write letters to Grandma because you can't pick up the phone and call Grandma when you're Amish.

I also told them about my current writing projects, including the fact that I have a blog that they can look up on the Internet and read a new entry every few days. I started this at the insistence of a nephew who had one before anyone else did, it seemed, and who kept saying, "Aunt Dorcas, you need a blog," and showed me how to get started.

Afterward, one of the teachers remarked, "Isn't it amazing—how far you've come, and how your life has changed?"

"Changed?"

"Yes. Think about it. You went from being this Amish girl who didn't know how to use a phone, to having a computer and a–what's it called? A blog?–I hardly even know what that is."

Of course she was right. Many of the things I enjoy today–laughing with my young-adult children, talking on my cell phone, new messages in my inbox–came about because of change, most of which I resisted.

If nothing ever changed, my old e-mail program would still work when I'm 70, and my sons would be middle-aged men, meekly following me to the berry patch and tossing a strawberry my way every time they picked 50.

I know that life will keep changing and no bells will ring to warn me ahead of time. My family will keep dragging me into the future. And long after the fact I will finally make peace with change and recognize that perhaps it was really for the best after all.

Passing On the Story Heirlooms

A few days after Christmas, I gave my daughter a precious family heirloom disguised as a simple story.

Seven-year-old Jenny was sick with the flu but improving just enough to be grumpy and bored. "Adventures in Odyssey," hot chocolate, and Ramona Quimby had exhausted their appeal, and only one thing would do: a story from Mom. So I left the dishes, snuggled on the couch with her, and told her the story of my grandma and the windmill. Grandma always told us the story in Pennsylvania German, so I used some of the same phrases.

Grandma was probably 5 years old, I told Jenny, and her family lived out in the country but I'm not sure where, since they moved around so much. She had an older brother, Noah, who was like many big brothers, and he told Grandma that if she climbed up to the top of the windmill, or the *vint-boomp*, she would see a wolf! Except that Grandma always stretched out the German word—*voollllllffff*.

Grandma knew better, of course, but she really wanted to see a wolf, so up she went. There was no wolf to be seen anywhere, but suddenly the wind whipped her dress forward and it caught on the center of the turning blades. The windmill turned around and around, and Grandma couldn't get away. It twisted her skirt, tighter and tighter, and she was scared half to death, or as she put it, *halp-doat faschruka*. Finally, the fabric gave way and a large piece ripped

453

out of her dress. Grandma climbed down the windmill, shaking, and there her mother spanked her half to death, *halp-doat*, she claimed. And then they somehow retrieved the torn piece of fabric and her mother mended the dress so Grandma could wear it again.

And then, of course, I had to tell Jenny the rest of the story—how my sister and I reacted to Grandma's story when we were little girls.

"But Grandma," we always protested at this point. "That couldn't be! If you were scared half to death, and then your mother spanked you half to death, you'd be all dead!"

But Grandma never wavered in her story. No, she insisted, that's how it was—first she was *halp-doat faschrucka*, and then her mother spanked her *halp-doat*.

I finished the story and Jenny grinned despite her sore throat and miserable cough. "A *vint-boomp*?" she croaked, trying out the new word. "And a *volf*?" She giggled, working her mind around the idea of her mom and Aunt Becky trying to get their old Amish grandma to see the logic of half-dead plus half-dead equalling all-dead.

Emily, who is 16, was also listening. "I think that would be cool to tell your grandchildren stories that your grandma told you," she said.

"I think so, too," I said, realizing that I was actually looking forward to this.

The truth has been slowly dawning, lately, that I may soon be entering a new phase of my life. I do not enjoy change and am usually the last one to acknowledge that the wind is shifting. My youngest child is barely in school, I feel like I have only just now figured out how to be a mom, but I can no longer ignore the signs that new experiences are inevitably ahead.

For one thing, a sudden swarm of my children's friends are dating, and three different cousins announced their engagements in the past few weeks. Courtship, among conservative Mennonites, is generally not undertaken for its own sake but as the means to an end. So teens tend to begin dating at an older age than the average (at least 18) and marry younger, often in their early 20s, a system that seems to result in a remarkably large percentage of long-term, successful marriages. This means that, since my older children are 20 and 18, the topic is on their minds. But it was something I conveniently told myself was still far off in a hazy future for us, Matt and Amy thankfully being busy with other pursuits.

But at our Christmas dinner I was drawn up short with just how close this possibility might be. After the pumpkin pie, we talked about what our family would be like 10 years from now and wrote down our predictions, to be read at our Christmas dinner in 2016. "This table will need to be bigger," Matt said. Amy added, "There will definitely be a few kids running around." Paul guessed that he and I would have three in-laws and three grandchildren.

None of the others seemed to think this remarkable, but I, as usual, was the one "freaking out," as my children say. "I could be a mother-in-law and a grandma in the next 10 years? Ten years is nothing!" I bleated. "But ... but I don't know how to be a grandma!"

"Oh, Mom, you'll be a good grandma," Amy assured me. "You'll tell lots of stories."

How sweet of my daughter to zero in on the one thing that I have in abundance and do as naturally as breathing, and to reassure me of its value. Heaven knows, I probably will never pass along land, like my husband's grandpa did, or quilts and rag rugs like my mom, or money or silver tea sets or recipes or prize-winning roses. But I have hundreds of stories filed away, and in this area, more than any other, I trust my skills and ability.

Telling Jenny about my grandma and the windmill is much more than a moment's distraction from the flu. It is telling her, subtly, that she is connected to people of long ago who were once children just like her, that behavior has consequences, that even a sad story can become funny in its own way many years later. A story is much more than just a story; it is a connection, a reassurance, a lesson, a door opening. It can last for years and stay fresh and fascinating. It is a mystery—why do I gravitate to tell this story and not that one?

Through stories, I hope to pass on what's most important—faith in God, love, hope for the future. When I tell of how our lives were spared when we hit a moose and our van burned up, I am saying, without actually saying, "God is real. He still does miracles."

One of the most remarkable characteristics of a story is how it gathers layers, snowball-like, as it rolls along. My older children loved the story of when I was a child and Alexander, our cat, died, and my sisters and I had a funeral, with Becky wearing a filmy black scarf over her face like Jackie Kennedy and Margaret carrying the sad little box. I had made up a song for the occasion, to the tune of "Father I Stretch My Hands to Thee": "To you dear Alexander cat, we sing our lonely song. But we are also thankful that we had you for this long," and so on.

But my younger children equally love the next layer of the story: how their tough older brother, Matt, when he was about 6 years old, would beg me to tell this story even though he always broke down and cried when I sang the funeral dirge. "Why did he keep wanting to hear it?" they say, and I don't know. And they smile, the sadness of it all somehow turning into something special.

And Grandma's story of the windmill now includes my reaction to it as a child, trying to teach Grandma math and logic. I hope that someday, years from now, Jenny adds another layer to it, snuggling with her grandchildren. "Many years ago when I was sick with the flu, my mom sat with me on a blue plaid couch, and she told me a story about her grandma and a *vint-boomp*."

To Each, Her Own Snow Memories

For some reason my children have never been as impressed as I think they ought to be that I survived Minnesota's "Blizzard of the Century" in January 1975. At least once per winter, when we get just enough snow to cover the sidewalk, I lapse into rambling memories of that adventure.

"Mom and Becky and Margaret and I were home alone for most of it," I say, "in that old house we were renting, you know, down the road from where Grandpa and Grandma live now. Dad and Marcus stayed over at the new house to take care of the animals. Nobody knew it was coming, and they sent us home from school an hour after we got there, and it was snowing like crazy already.

"The wind blew so hard that this gritty snow blew in around the storm windows and the plastic over the outside and everything, and when we got up in the morning there were little piles of snow on the windowsills. We all slept downstairs to stay warm. Margaret remembers that the cylinders in the oil stove glowed red-hot and Mom was worried about the house burning down.

"When the storm was finally over there were drifts outside 10 and 15 feet high, and we could walk right on top of them without sinking down. It was like this bizarre world out there. We walked up on a drift higher than the top of the chicken house, and out by the field you could see a row of fence posts sticking up three inches out of the snow."

At this point I am lost in vivid memories—seeing that strange landscape, feeling the cold wind—but their eyes are glazing over. "Yes, Mom, and you and Aunt Becky got so bored in the middle of the storm you decided to bake something," they say, no doubt thinking to themselves, "and then, Grandma, you walked 5 miles to school, uphill both ways."

No matter how often I try or how many adjectives I use, I seem unable to convey to my Oregon-grown children the intensity of that storm, the dangers, the isolation, the cold, the family bonding around the stove, and the sense, afterwards, that we had survived something terrible together. Online resources confirm my memories, thankfully, so I know it wasn't just an exaggerated perception in my 12-year-old mind. The wind gusts reached 70 to 90 miles per hour and produced snowdrifts up to 20 feet high, Wikipedia tells me. "The combination of snowfall totals, wind velocities, and cold temperatures made this one of the worst blizzards the upper Midwest has experienced."

Why is it that, much as they enjoy stories from when I was young, the children yawn through this one? Maybe snow is something that you can't explain: You simply have to experience it for yourself.

When an unusual snowstorm hit the Willamette Valley recently, it wasn't anything like that famous blizzard. However, as I compared the two, I discovered a few similarities, and came to the surprising conclusion that my children found the recent storm as impressive and full of adventure—and would probably remember it as vividly—as I do that long-ago event.

This storm, for example, was just as unexpected as that one, with no indication that Saturday night's rain would turn to snow. We woke up expecting our normal Sunday-morning bustle to get ready for church, and were surprised to see a thick, steady snow falling, with everything but a few green circles under the pine trees already turned white.

How quickly a normal morning can be turned upside-down, the rain turned to snow, the green to white, and—impossible thought—would we stay home from church? Sunday morning services for our family are as dependable as the tides. They always are. And, barring sickness, we always attend.

The boys dressed in khaki pants and buttoned shirts. My husband, Paul, and I watched the snow accumulate. Finally, after a flurry of phone calls, the decision was made: Church was canceled, the only time in my kids' memory that this had ever happened. Gleefully, they hauled winter supplies from the attic, traded dress clothes for snowsuits, and stomped outside to pound each other with snowballs and build large snowmen with stick arms and billed Trailblazer caps.

Canceling services because of the weather wasn't that unusual in Minnesota, but I remember that the difference during that blizzard was this: It was the only time in my life that church was canceled and no one phoned to say so. Everyone just knew.

A strange sort of boredom sets in when the weather confines you at home. Blizzard syndrome, I call it, remembering how antsy we got by the second day. Becky remembers that Mom tried to come up with activities, and we sat around the stove and played who-what-where, each of us writing down a noun, passing the paper on, and adding verbs and adverbs, and then laughing crazily at the resulting sentences.

The baking project, as I recall, was our idea. Becky and I flipped through Mom's collection of magazine recipes and chose Prune Loaf, which probably tells a lot about our food supply, but which turned out surprisingly good: the stewed prunes wrapped in sugary pieces of dough and baked in a loaf pan.

My husband staved off blizzard syndrome at our house by playing games with the kids whenever they came inside to warm up. They played a Monopoly game from start to finish, and I joined them for a three-hour Phase-10 marathon, whirring fruit smoothies in the blender for everyone between turns. "Just think of all the memories we're making!" 17-year-old Emily gushed. "Dad's home all day. How often does that happen? And making smoothies, and playing games, and those huge snowmen. And all our good arguments—we'll always remember this!"

Who but a Smucker would consider our silly arguments good memories? Emily insisted, for instance, that rain was better than snow, and more romantic besides. "Wouldn't it be romantic to be proposed to in the rain?"

"With water dripping off your nose?" I snapped. "No. Romantic would be to be proposed to in the twilight, in the gently falling snow."

"Oh, Mom!"

A large machine rumbled by outside. "Hey, the snowplow just went!" Ben said.

"Snowplow?" Paul said. "That was the road grader. Snowplows are trucks with blades on the front and a load of sand in the back."

"What?" I said. "Snowplows are big yellow machines. How on Earth would a truck have made it through those big drifts after our blizzard? Even the snowplow had to back off

461

and then rev up to get through those drifts, and the snow at the side was piled as high as the top of the school bus when we finally went back to school," I went on, as usual adding more details than anyone wanted to hear.

Our children missed only one day of school and then went back on Tuesday, after most of the snow had melted off the roads.

What will Oregon be like by the time my children have children? I wonder. I imagine Emily, at a sunny mid-February picnic, reminiscing: "Did I ever tell you about the big snow of 2008? We all stayed home from church, and Ben and Steven made these big snowmen, and..."

"Yes, Mom, we know," her kids will say, rolling their eyes. "You all played Phase 10 at the kitchen table and argued about snowplows."

Or maybe, in the middle of the Willamette Valley's Blizzard of the 21st Century, Ben's children will say: "Remember how Dad always thought it was so cool that he survived that 5-inch snow back in 2008?"

And gathered around the stove, they will all laugh, warm and safe inside as the cold wind howls and the drifts pile thickly against the house.

Going On and Giving Back

Tailored Sensibilities

I have a house to decorate, and I am drowning in adjectives and advice.

At Jerry's Home Improvement Center, below hundreds of little square paint samples, I found a quiz to help me discover my "color personality." Since I would like my living room to feel "relaxed and inviting," I am told that my personality is "casual," which can be subdivided into "romantic," "charming," and "cozy," with a separate booklet of paint swatches for each.

I also have a touch of "timeless," the quiz tells me. "Shadowy green and burnished gold fit your tailored sensibilities."

For 95 years, our kitchen and living room were two separate rooms connected by a narrow doorway. They were designed by my husband Paul's great-grandfather, who had simple, straightforward tastes rather than tailored sensibilities. I can imagine him quickly sketching a square in a notebook, drawing a line down the middle from top to bottom, crossing it with another going left and right, repeating it for the upstairs, and there he was. A good Mennonite house for a family of 12. No need to be fancy. His wife, I am guessing, persuaded him to add the few extra touches: a bay window and bead-board wainscoting. The bay window remains intact but the wainscoting was covered with Sheetrock some 20 years ago by my husband's dad, who was as practical and un-fancy as his grandfather.

Despite the boxy rooms and annoying layout, I am fond of this house, preferring history and personality to convenience and artistic design. Soon after we moved in six years ago, we hung garage-sale wallpaper in the living room and put down a linoleum remnant in the kitchen. Our furniture tastes featured a comfortable selection of classified-ad finds and Early Salvation Army.

A few weeks ago, Paul took out half of the wall between the kitchen and living room, and suddenly the downstairs seemed twice as spacious and bright. Then he tore up the carpet, put down laminate wood-look flooring in both rooms, and restored the bead-board wainscoting. The result was a large cohesive room that begged for a whole new look. It was time for serious redecorating.

I had saved up for this, and I knew what I wanted: Something authentic yet up-to-date; something harmonious and simple; not makeshift, not elaborate, but with understated good taste.

Unfortunately, I had no idea how to get from here to there.

Among my daughters and friends I am known for being hopelessly behind the times, wearing my skirts firmly cinched at the waist, rather than two inches below, and using orange and avocado green Tupperware long after the rest of the world has moved to blush, seafoam, or crimson. To leap from years of out-of-fashion decorating to the surreal world of Ralph Lauren paint and Broyhill furniture is to encounter an unimaginable number of choices that collectively freeze, rather than free, the imagination.

At Home Depot, I wandered through sample kitchens and was handed catalogs with stunning combinations of Corian countertops, slide-out spice shelves, and hardwood wine racks. Instead of envy or desire, all I could think of was, "No one ever filled bummer-lamb bottles in that kitchen."

Later, I stepped into the posh atmosphere of a furniture store the size of a Boeing hangar and as dim and hushed as a funeral parlor. There I found a couch and loveseat I liked— for $2,200. With three boys who drape and flop and perch but seldom actually sit, I would be insane to come home with $2,200 furniture.

"I think if you find stuff you think is pretty and put it together, it'll look nice," said my 15-year-old daughter, Emily. "Not everything has to match and stuff, you know."

"Easy for you to say," I sniffed, and went to a secondhand store and bought a stack of magazines with such names as *Cottage Living* and *Farmhouse Decorating* to guide me in my quest of getting it right.

That's when the trickle of adjectives and advice became a river.

"Earthy colors look dark and cavelike," one designer said. Another insisted I need a "lush floral motif" with "maximized romance." But not a "saccharine" or "fussy" living room, I was warned. I could achieve a "zesty atmosphere" with "turquoise cushions" and "airy window treatments."

Two pages later, the floral motif was out and character was in. I must have "soothing" blue and green stripes, "prim panels" and "cultured curtains."

By this time, a little warning light was flashing in my head. Something about all this seemed wrong, but I wasn't sure what it was. Then, a "before" picture showed a bedroom that, among many other faults, had a "nasty mauve carpet." "Hey!" I said, not quite out loud. "I like mauve!" It wasn't that long ago when *Cottage Living* featured mauve and country blue as authentic and charming, indispensible to the country/farmhouse look. And now mauve was suddenly nasty? Who changed the rules while I wasn't looking?

Somebody, I suspected, was having too much fun at my expense. Perhaps there was no science or right and wrong to this, after all, only people stating their opinions as though they were law and trying to get me to spend a lot of money redecorating every few years.

I began to read the magazines with a skeptical eye. A set of dreadful vases was described as gorgeous and elegant. I visualized three young magazine people around a table, working on an assignment. "OK," one says, "let's get a bunch of these ugly vases from my grandma, ceramic with gold trim and big pink flowers stuck on the side."

"Yeah," says another, "and let's arrange them on these shelves where, if this were a real house, everyone coming through the door would knock them down. Then let's call them, oh, how about 'cute'?" (She flips through her thesaurus.) "No no, 'gorgeous.'"

"And elegant," says the third. "We haven't used 'elegant' on this page yet."

"Oh yeah, and I found this creepy green paint for the walls. We'll call it restful and classic."

"Really, Mom," Emily insisted, "if you put stuff together that's pretty to you, it'll look nice. You don't have to worry about what anyone else thinks. Have you seen my bookshelves?"

I had. They contained her collection of old hardcover fairy tales accented with a pink straw hat, a black elephant carving from Kenya, a modern-art sculpture from my welder brother, and a purple-and-black set of nesting "Russian" dolls from Poland. The whole effect was, as the magazines would say, quirky, original, and harmonious.

Now that I have been a mom for 20 years, the advice I most often give to younger mothers is to trust their instincts, the heart-sense that tells them what's right. Strangely, in this area, it was my daughter teaching me the same thing. Perhaps, like her, I should start with what I already had and loved, such as the seascape in oils that I picked up for $5. I could pull a shade of blue from it to paint the wainscoting and a second shade for the trim.

How liberating to assign my own adjectives and write my own advice. If the right color turns out to be an out-of-style "country" blue, so what? I have tailored sensibilities, after all, and if I decide to call it soothing and cultured, that's precisely what it will be.

Once Upon a Writing Class

The books say I should start with a main character who has a problem to solve.

All right, then, I am the main character: Mrs. Smucker, a much-too-busy, forgetful, 40-something mom. And I have a problem to solve: I am supposed to teach eight teenagers how to write fiction, and I don't know anything about writing fiction.

My husband, Paul, as principal, made a new drive this year to get the students' parents to volunteer at our church school. So Rachel and Rita teach an art class, Bonnie and Sharon listen to children read, and Regina helps with cleaning.

And I am supposed to teach the older students how to write.

We have four weeks of classes in the fall and begin with blog posts, an easy choice: I know how to write them, and blogs are relevant to teenagers. "yo my sweet peeps im gonna hang out at jessica's" is not communication, I tell them. "Write a post that actually says something." They dutifully crank out thoughtful essays that will most likely never be equalled on any actual blogs in the teenage universe.

After a two-month recess, it is time to write fiction. I would rather eat a piece of cheesecake, creamy and rich, with a hint of sour cream and raspberries, than figure out how to make it myself. How many eggs? How do I keep the crumbs from getting soggy? Similarly, I would rather curl up in a chair and read a good story than figure out how the author made it work. The *No. 1 Ladies Detective Agency* series, for example, a recently discovered literary treasure. How does the author create suspense? What words make the personality of Precious Ramotswe come alive? Why is this episode inserted here and not three chapters later? What makes me keep reading?

I gather books with hopeful and ambitious titles: *Any Child Can Write; What's Your Story?* and *Writing Smarts—A Girl's Guide to Writing Great Poetry, Stories, School Reports, and More!*

A story begins with a character; the books all agree on this. He or she has specific characteristics such as red hair, stubbornness, and a fear of heights. The character wants something badly or has a problem to solve. He can't solve his problems too easily, or it's not a good story.

I may be the main character in my story, but there are eight secondary characters with a wide range of skills and passions. Two of my children represent opposite ends of the writing spectrum. Emily, who is 16, has so many ideas flying by that all she has to do is reach out and grab the nearest one. She journals prolifically and owns 70 notebooks. Her prize possession is an old green Royal typewriter from her grandparents. At the other end is Ben, age 13, who fills his head with basketball and math. He multiplies multi-digit numbers in his head, but the smallest writing assignment in history or English makes him flop backward on the couch and writhe and grimace as though dying of appendicitis.

"But it doesn't make any sense!" he wails. "I don't know what to write."

In addition to characters, the books say, every story needs a setting. Ours is a bit dull but functional—on chairs around the Sunday school table in the church fellowship hall, two afternoons a week, the thermostat turned down too low, little first-graders peeking in the windows during their break.

I am determined to make the class enjoyable for everyone, writers and nonwriters alike. But, lest this story resolve itself too easily, the first session sets an unexpected bump in my path: Justin and Preston simply won't be quiet. Their murmured asides and choked giggles continue despite my hints and glares. I ding the little teacher's bell in front of me, even though each ding reduces their three allotted good-behavior Hershey Kisses by one.

Later, at home, Paul offers to step in and rescue me, but main characters need to solve their own problems, the books say.

At the next class, I seat Justin on my right and Preston to my left. I also hand out copies of The Rules: "When Mrs. Smucker is talking, no one else talks. When something is funny, we share it with the whole class." It works. From then on, all is well and everyone takes his turn to talk.

We begin by creating characters. Kayla forms "Alaiya," who is 22 years old, wears sweatshirts, and dislikes loud kids. Alaiya wants her students to learn, but they won't listen to her.

Hmmm, I think. I wonder where Kayla got this idea.

The boys' characters are all sports-related. Justin concocts "Travis" who wants to play basketball at UCLA but isn't good enough. The kids' characters are OK but bland, lacking what the books call "juicy details" and "a little zip."

So we head down a side road to learn description. I hand out a list of words and we expand them into sentences that "pop."

Drennan turns "dog" and "cat" into "The huge, fierce-looking, short-haired dog growled at the ugly, flea-bitten stray cat."

We are going places, I'm sure of it.

Finally, it's time to write some actual stories. On a computer, if possible, I say. And about 400 words. I suggest an optional opening line: "Mrs. Finkelstein's dentures were missing."

"Do we have to count every single word?" they wonder.

"Does this have to be something that could really happen?"

"What shall I do cuz I'm staying at my grandma's house and she doesn't have a computer?"

"Just write a story," I say.

And they do.

When I get up at 6:30 one morning, Ben is at the computer, happily typing without a single moan or complaint. As I read over his shoulder, he chuckles and adds another twist in the plot—Mrs. Finkelstein finally finds her dentures on the nightstand, but in her excitement she falls out of bed and breaks her hip.

We read and review the stories in class, and I am thrilled. Stephanie's is full of realistic dialogue and a perfect ending. Preston's story is about football and full of action. "'Let's run a counter right,' Cam said. The play was not a success, and they got stuffed at the line of scrimmage."

Emily begins, "Mrs. Finkelstein's dentures were missing. All 72 pairs were gone."

I take the papers home and grade them, muttering "Yes!" "Wow, look at this." "Amazing."

Then I tuck the papers in a folder and smile.

The end.

Stepping Between Two Worlds

I operate in two completely different worlds, living in one and visiting the other.

The first is my world as a wife and mom in the middle of summer's grass fields and busyness. I never know what waits for me when I get up in the morning. It might be our enormous dog, Hansie, lying on his bed and chewing on pink and blue birthday candles. With detective skills from 22 years of mothering, I deduce that this was the combined work of my two teenage boys and, of course, the dog, each of whom weigh about 150 pounds and have big feet, bigger appetites, and a streak of mischief.

Ben, I recall, had accidentally dumped the bin of party supplies in the back pantry the day before and then assured me he picked them all up. Then Steven took the pop cans out the back door to the car, and didn't latch the door behind him, an error that Hansie always catches, and which has previously resulted in the disappearance of a large container of homemade chocolate chip cookies and an 8-pound beef roast.

So, I gather, Ben didn't pick up the bags of candles and little pastel candleholders, Steven left the door unlatched, and Hansie found something new and incongruous to chew on. A typical beginning to a typical day in my everyday universe.

This world is full of people this summer—my husband and me, six children, and a seed-sacking teenage nephew named Zack. I feel like I live at the Portland airport: Flight 63 exiting by the back door with a jug of ice water, Flight 144 coming in hot and dusty at the front, Flight 26 strapping on his bike helmet and preparing for takeoff.

Harvest brings an increase in activity, dirt, and appetites. Steven grills 20 hamburgers for lunch and they all disappear by 3 p.m. Ryegrass seeds spill out of pockets and lie scattered on the bathroom floor after showers, to sprout from under the baseboards next winter.

I don't always feel appreciated here. My daughters giggle at my memory lapses and say, "Wow, Mom, you're getting a lot of gray hair!" The boys seem to perceive me as an invisible motor that keeps things fed and cleaned but doesn't require much attention. I try to say profound motherly things at the supper table and no one hears me.

Then suddenly, in the middle of laundry or dishes or weeding flower beds, I know it's time. I kick off the muddy garden shoes and head for the shower. Then I slip into shoes with heels that click and a coordinated outfit with no spaghetti-sauce stains on the front or flower-bed dirt on the knees. A quick fluff in my hair and a spritz of hairspray, hollered last-minute instructions to bake the lasagna for an hour and gather the eggs, and I roll my tote of books through the kitchen and am off to visit my other universe.

My Kia Optima is a golden chariot, transporting me to distant galaxies, transforming me from hassled mom to cool, Professional Author. I set the seat and the temperature exactly where I like them, turn off the K-Love station, pop in a CD of melodious a capella gospel songs by the Nathan Good Family, and head down Powerline Road and into the sunshine, singing along if the mood strikes me.

These venues vary from library fundraisers to Lions Club meetings to Bible studies at YaPoAh Terrace. Invariably, an eager woman is waiting at the door. "Oh, I'm so glad to meet you!" she says. "Can I help you with your bag? Here, let me take that." Other equally eager people greet me inside. They are glad to see me, they have read my writings, they bought my book to send to a daughter in Michigan. I am settled into the best chair in the house. Would I like coffee? Or perhaps a cup of tea? Cream or sugar? Would I like a special sort of pen for signing books?

I sip my drink and look around. Everyone in the room is polite and quiet and civilized, the outfits are clean and well-coordinated, there isn't a speck of warehouse dust in sight. People chat about things that belong in this universe— a new tea shop downtown, the latest politics, the symphony on Tuesday night.

"I bought a pint of organic blueberries," I hear a woman say, and I wonder what it would be like to get a pint of fruit instead of multiple gallons.

Soon it's time for my talk, and for the first time in weeks I actually have the attention of everyone in the room. I get to say exactly what I want, and except for the inevitable white-haired gentleman who falls asleep, everyone listens with such full attention that I begin to think I might actually be saying something worthwhile. No one interrupts, no one hollers across the table, no one argues with my conclusions. And at the end they all applaud. People begin to mill around as I sit down to sign books. One by one, they stop by to thank me or buy books or tell me that they had an Amish great-uncle-by-marriage in Ohio by the name of Smucker or Schmucker and, oh what was it, John, or Jake? At least two women tell me I look far too young to have six children. I start conversations and finish them. Everyone is nice.

And then, like the final bite of pumpkin pie with whipped cream at Thanksgiving dinner, I am suddenly utterly satisfied and I know one more sugary bite would mean illness. Everything has been compliments, delight, and affirmation. And it's enough. Time to go.

I tuck my things in the backpack and roll it out to the Kia. Too tired mentally even for music, I drive home in silence, pondering, leaving that universe behind, rolling through a galaxy or two to return to the other. The boys are shooting baskets when I drive in, and a stray shot bounces off the car with a clang. Hansie nudges my hand and drools happily on my lovely skirt as I get out of the car. I click through the kitchen, noting empty ice cube trays scattered on the island, newspapers on the table, enormous sandals tossed by the front door.

"Mom! You're supposed to call Grandma!" a voice shouts from upstairs. "Mom, I'm hungry!" "Hey, has anyone seen today's mail?" "Mom, did you mend my warehouse pants?" "Mom, can I buy a .22?" "Oh, Mom, I forgot to tell you—Coffeys need someone to feed the chickens tomorrow."

A homemade arrow flies past me and hits my desk. I turn to see Jenny showing off her new bow made of a stick and string. The back door slams, the phone rings, and there's a terrible crash upstairs.

I change into comfortable denim, steer one boy toward the empty ice cube trays and the other toward the pile of shoes by the door, send Jenny and her arrows outside, tell Amy to pack a lunch for Zack the nephew, call upstairs to ask Emily if she gathered the laundry, kiss the dusty husband coming in the door, and grab the phone to call Grandma.

The gentle sweetness of my other universe seems far away. I roll up my sleeves and smile. I'm ready for this again, back in my everyday world, back where life is wild and noisy and challenging, back where I'm needed, back with the ones I love, back where I love to be.

What Love Looks Like

*M*y husband, Paul, and I sit in our office chairs, temporarily distracted from his bookkeeping and my computer, and talk about all the things a minister/grass-seed-guy and his wife need to discuss—church schedules, teenagers, employees. Pigga the cat wanders in and hops on Paul's lap. Seemingly unaware of her, he keeps talking, but slowly begins to smooth her fluffy gray fur and gently stroke her back.

Watching, I think: This is what love looks like; this is what it does.

With Valentine's Day coming soon, every store from WinCo to Goodwill to—who knows, maybe even Les Schwab Tire Center—has a prominent aisle exploding in a red-and-white celebration of romance. In contrast, the latest *National Geographic* magazine features a scientific study of love, reducing it to biochemistry—serotonin levels and the "surge and pulse of dopamine." Falling out of love is as inevitable as falling in, we are told, coldly.

Love is an elusive thing, defying description—part emotion, part decision, part something that can't be reduced to candy hearts or chemicals. I prefer to define it, as the Bible does, in action terms: it suffers long, it is kind, it does not seek its own way.

For me, love is best illustrated by the story of two cats and my husband.

Paul has never been an animal guy, one to talk to dogs and scratch cats between the ears. He wasn't the sort of man who kicked cats, or I would never have married him; he was simply indifferent to them. When a black-and-white cat showed up at our doorstep five years ago, Paul said he didn't mind if she stayed, as long as we kept her outside where he could ignore her at will. We named her Katzie, and for years she was queen—lying on the porch in the sun, getting fat, and catching mice only when she felt like it.

Then an enormous German shepherd-mix named Hansie joined our family last November, and Katzie's life changed completely. Instead of living in peace and plumpness, she was on the run, flying headlong around the corner of the house and scampering up a tree with Hansie behind her taking the corner on two wheels and woofing ferociously.

Any cat, it seems, could have known that this place was no longer hospitable. But on a cold, rainy day early in December, the children found a tiny, wet, stray kitten wedged under the heating-oil tank beside the house. Fifteen-year-old Emily knelt in the mud, worked her arm under the tank, and pulled it out. She shampooed and blow-dried the pathetic, oily kitten in the bathroom sink, transforming it into a round gray fluff with stubby legs.

Emily named it Pigga, not because it was shaped like a piggy bank but because it was found under the oil tank. "See, I always thought that tank looked like a big pig, and when I was little I used to say 'pigga' instead of 'pig.'"

Pigga needed to stay indoors a few days to recover, and Paul, who is tough at times but not heartless, saw the sense in this. But we soon realized sending Pigga outside would turn her into instant catburger. Whenever Hansie looked in the patio doors and saw the kitten run across the floor, he crashed into the glass and burst into a frenzy of angry barking.

"German shepherds are death on cats," warned my friend, Rachel. "Ours killed the cat two minutes after we let her outside."

So Pigga stayed inside, leaping at skirt hems and dangling backpack straps, scratching the furniture and clawing the children. Paul grumbled quietly, but sometimes he egged her on under his breath, hoping I would soon tire of her behavior and find her another home.

Meanwhile, Katzie was still outside, spending most of her time in the pine tree or on the porch roof. Instead of nibbling whenever she was hungry, she ventured to her food dish only when Hansie was penned up, early in the morning and late at night. If Hansie had eaten all her food and no one remembered to replace it, she went hungry.

I was feeling worse and worse about this but didn't know what to do. The final stroke came one evening when I went out late to feed her and saw that she had already been there and left. A line of timid, disappointed, wet pawprints led across the porch to her cat dish and back to the steps.

The next morning, she was gone.

Tortured by regrets, I felt that we had betrayed her trust and she was out there starving in the rain. Paul said cynically that I must be desperate for something to feel guilty about if I felt this bad about a cat.

Even though Paul thought one house cat was far too many, I announced that if Katzie ever showed up again she was going to stay indoors until we could train Hansie to stop chasing her.

Paul was sure she was fine. "She came of her own free will, didn't she? And now she's decided to move on. It has nothing to do with you. She can take care of herself."

I disagreed. She was out there hunting in vain for mice in a soggy ryegrass field, and it was all my fault.

The children and I prayed for Katzie, acknowledging that in the grand scheme of things this cat was not like children dying of malaria and starvation around the world, but still, she was our cat and we were worried. Paul did not join in our prayers but neither, to my knowledge, did he pray that Katzie would stay away.

Then one day when I had despaired of ever seeing her again, Paul called me from his truck. "I'm on my way to Kropf Feed," he said, "and I just thought you might like to know that Katzie is beside the road between us and Coffeys."

"Alive?" I shrieked.

"Alive and licking herself." I could tell he was grinning.

Inside his stern exterior, that man is a softie.

I hurried down the road and there she was, sitting on a piece of wood down in the ditch, skinny and wet but still dignified and beautiful.

Both cats live in the laundry room now but pop into the house whenever the door is open. We take Hansie to dog school every Thursday, where we hope to teach him to respect cats.

Love, as I said, is hard to define, harder still to practice in daily reality. While the red teddy bears sparkle at Big Lots and *National Geographic* analyzes, three couples we know parted ways in the past few weeks.

There is, however, a love that lasts: the kind that puts others' interests and needs ahead of its own preferences.

And this is what it looks like: a tall blond man talking about sermons and orchard grass while absently stroking a fluffy, contented kitten on his lap.

The Rich Recipe of Friendship

My sister-in-law, Bonnie, who is famous for many things but especially her baking, tried out a new cheesecake recipe on us: a rapturous mocha concoction, heavy and brown.

"I'm afraid it's a bit strong on the coffee," she worried. The rest of us thought it was perfect, indulging in a narrow slice to fortify us for shopping, another for walking on the beach, and yet another for a late-night Dutch Blitz game around the table.

Like eggs and cream cheese in cheesecake, the weekend had the basic ingredients that every coast trip ought to have—good food, walks on the beach, shopping and falling asleep to the sound of waves rolling in. But the mocha twist in those few days was this: Instead of a normal family getaway with a van full of sandy shoes and inside-out sweatshirts, this was a dozen Mennonite moms and grandmas luxuriating in a rare break from responsibilities and expectations.

By day, we slept late, shopped at the outlet malls in Lincoln City, and sank into deep leather couches for times of worship and discussion. Outside the sun shone through the wall of windows and the spray blew off the rolling waves in a majestic production that seemed to be specifically for our enjoyment. At night we put on our pajamas and let our hair down, both literally and figuratively. We nibbled on fresh fruit, drank hot chocolate, and broke off just-one-more bites of chocolate-peanut bars. We talked for hours of trivial things—the pros and cons of Curves, the kinds of books our husbands like to read. We also covered many mysterious subjects that women discuss among themselves but never divulge to anyone, especially not their children, who can never quite comprehend that their colorless, one-dimensional mothers have a life and history beyond the four walls of their home.

But mostly, we women laughed—the refreshing, contagious kind of laughter that bubbled up from the depths and rang off the walls, washing over us in a healing wave that left us exhausted yet refreshed, with tears on our cheeks. Ours was a warm and easy laughter, not the shrieks of girls at a slumber party or the brittle laugh of those hardened by life. It was the laughter of traditional, industrious women who grab at a chance to let off steam as eagerly as old-time farmers savored a glass of lemonade in the shade on a hot day.

Curled up in a chair at the end of the table and wiping tears with my flannel-pajama sleeves, I marveled, as I do every year, at how fortunate I was to have these women as friends. They vary as much as the food they brought with them and spread across the counter—grapes, layered chip-dip, bars, and mocha cheesecake. Talkative, quiet, solid, daring, organized, scatterbrained, young, old, and in-between, they all bring something nourishing to my life. Some have mentored me, most have taught me something, all have blessed me.

Rachel shepherded me through our adoption after adopting two daughters of her own.

Bonnie gives me menu ideas when I have no idea what to cook for a family reunion. I know I can call her in a crisis, especially when I find a mouse in my kitchen and need sympathy.

Arlene, like me, is a news junkie, eager to discuss Darfur or trapped coal miners. And, plagued with the same sensitivities as I am, she commiserates when I take a chance remark too personally.

Sharon is determined to pull me into the 21st century. "No, no, no! That's way too old-lady-ish!" she hisses in my ear as I finger a prim, teal, woven-polyester skirt at a Koret store. She wants to sign me up at Curves. It would do me a world of good, she insists, refusing to take no for an answer.

I also have many friends who did not attend our retreat. Rita, for instance, is the one I call when I need someone to pray for me. Judy and I have a habit of what we call, irreverently, "throwing up in each other's laps": in other words, giving much-too-detailed answers when one of us asks, "How are you really doing?" Anita refreshes my soul with elegant servings of tea. Geneva calls me and somehow puts all my problems back in the right perspective.

Back when I was young and choosy, I wanted friends who could join me in what I called "deep discussions," in which we pondered theology, philosophy, and the meaning of life and love. This changed when I had small children and I bonded with other young mothers, connecting instantly with any woman who had a baby on her hip.

Living on a First Nations reserve in Canada and desperate to converse in English, I bonded best with anyone who spoke my language. Thus, I developed friendships with women I would never have gotten to know in a normal setting— teenage Ojibway girls, wild-living nurses, and Shannon, the policeman's wife, who was 10 years younger than me.

Today, it seems that I can find something in common with almost anyone. No one person is all things to me, but each one contributes something unique – advice, mentoring, information, empathy, and support. But most of all, at this stage of my life, I appreciate humor. Through the stresses of parenting, the demands of church work, and the realities of life past 40, laughing with my friends has been a healing thread that keeps me connected to sanity and wholeness.

Sharon and Rachel, for example, think it's their duty to keep me humble. After a Sunday morning church service, when I am trying hard to have a proper-minister's-wife conversation with someone, they stand 10 feet away and whisper to each other, glancing my way like conspirators, and hissing my name just loudly enough for me to hear. It destroys all my concentration and most of my dignity, which is exactly what they want. And we laugh.

Then there is Pauline, whose blunt and precise comments on the world in general and husbands in particular keep me in stitches. And Aunt Susie, who has kept her sense of humor through surgeries on both wrists and knees. Chuckling through her pain, she inspires me.

Susie inspired me again that night at the coast, joining in the fun at an hour when most women her age would have been in bed. Back home, the rest of us also would have been decorously asleep. Instead, on this once-a-year vacation, we lounged around the table, a dozen women swept up in stories and laughter until two in the morning. The low roar of waves in the background contrasted with our voices ringing off the high ceiling and the dark wall of windows. As the night wore on, we talked and teased and giggled, we nibbled on chips and mocha cheesecake, and most of all we savored each bite of the rich concoction of friendship.

Wealth Isn't About the Crayons

Even now, I am not quite sure why I bought it. I was at Costco a few weeks ago, scanning the office supplies, and there it was, a thick box of 64 Crayola crayons, with the familiar green and yellow lines slanting down the front.

Perhaps I was simply falling for a clever marketing ploy, but those crayons called to me from 35 years ago, when to own such a box would have meant that God was smiling on me, life was saying "Yes!" and all the doors were opening at last.

So I bought it, and it sits on my desk. The top bends back to reveal tiers of pointed crayons in four neat sections. Wild strawberry, turquoise blue, cerulean, chestnut, and carnation pink. I check and yes, they still make crayons in both green-yellow and yellow-green. It even has that cool little sharpener tucked in the back to keep the crayons perpetually new.

I never had a box of 64 crayons when I was a child. Twelve or 24, maybe, but never a glorious box of 64 like Rachel and Lydia, the two whiny sisters at our little Amish school who did their best to make life miserable for my sister and me. Rachel and Lydia formed "secret" clubs that we were not allowed to join. They hid straight pins in the restroom towels and waited for us to poke our hands. Worse, Rachel and Lydia were rich. They actually got new shoes in the middle of the school year. I, on the other hand, wore holes in my shoes and socks until I sometimes went to school with my big toes exposed. They had pretty notebooks and freely scribbled on a paper, tore it out, and then threw it away—an unthinkable waste.

And they had those big boxes of crayons, a luxury that explained their mysterious power over us, their ability to make us do whatever they wanted even though we resented and even hated them—though we would never have admitted it.

While the Amish are applauded for their sense of community, in some ways they are fiercely independent. To be known as a "poor manager" or to be unable to take care of your family is considered shameful and embarrassing. So my dad, undeniably a "poor manager," taught school for a tiny salary and tried to farm in his spare time, and we were quietly poor. More a scholar than a farmer, Dad bought old, cheap machinery that he didn't know how to fix and farmed with noble but pathetically outdated methods.

Poverty defined our status in the community, our value, and our outlook on life. A black cloud called "The Debt" hung over us, bringing a vague fear of disaster and making us feel that no opportunity would ever knock at our door. Mom filled us up with rice and gravy, vegetables from the garden, chickens that we raised and butchered, and homemade bread. I wore hand-me-down clothes and never had a new coat from a store until I was 19 and on my own.

Much later, I came to realize that poverty and wealth have as much to do with attitudes, comparisons, skills, resources, and a sense of control over one's life as they do with actual dollars or an arbitrary federal poverty level. "Not having money," my brother, Fred, tells me, "is a symptom of being poor. To be poor is to be caught in a cycle of futility, like going the wrong way on the moving walkway at the airport. Everything works against you, interest on loans piles up, you always choose the wrong things to invest in. To not be poor is to go with the walkway. Even if you sit on your suitcase, you're still moving forward."

To Dad's dismay, my sister and I fantasized about marrying rich men, such as Prince Charles. I did not marry a rich man, and Paul and I refer to the first 13 years of our marriage as our "Poor Days." But it was a much different sort of poverty than I had known as a child. Paul had a head for business, and his clearly defined budget of our meager monthly income gave me security and a sense of control. Life could say "yes" even if we were poor, he insisted. When I needed a serger sewing machine, he figured out how to save a little bit each month until we could afford it.

When we lived in Canada on a voluntary-worker stipend, we ate moose meat and rice rather than convenience foods or fresh fruit, and celebrated the children's birthdays with homemade cake and huge soap bubbles made with bent hangers. When Matt was in the bandage-every-bump stage, his only gift for his fifth birthday was a box of Band-Aids. I still think he had more fun taping Band-Aids all over himself than he would have had with a $30 remote-control car. We could never buy much, but with our housing provided and with Canada's national health plan, we were spared a sense of impending disaster.

The hardest of our poor days was when we came back to the United States after eight years in Canada. Instead of living among equally poor missionaries or the Ojibway, we were surrounded by an intimidatingly high standard of living. Our children were invited to birthday parties and we couldn't afford gifts. A church-dinner organizer would hand me a dessert recipe and ask me to make and bring it. Rather than admit I couldn't afford it, I blew the grocery budget on Cool Whip, Oreos, and fudge sauce.

One of the few things I miss about those days is the thrill of finding a great bargain, but mostly, I am not nostalgic about poverty. Grocery shopping was an agony of decisions, coupons, and calculations. Twice, medical emergencies swallowed all of our savings.

Sometimes, however, I talk to struggling single mothers and realize how wealthy I was in other ways. Thanks to my mom, I had the skills to use cloth diapers, grow and freeze vegetables, and make clothes and food virtually from nothing. Thanks to my constantly employed husband, I had the time.

Our fortunes began to change when we bought a grass seed warehouse business from Paul's dad. Today, if I need to, I can walk into PayLess Shoe Source and buy new shoes for the children. However, since habits from poor days die hard, I bought all their school shoes secondhand this year. Since we remember what it was like, we try to share with others in need.

In spite of our struggles, we have one shining success from our poor days: Our children say they didn't feel poor. When they reminisce about those years, it is not about deprivation and garage-sale gifts but about going on walks, playing by the lake in Canada, and hunting for tadpoles in ditches here in Oregon. Life, they say, felt full of opportunity.

There is one exception to this: Emily, 16, says she will someday bring up in therapy how badly she wanted an American Girl doll and we never bought her one. I imagine her therapist will tell her that now that she is successful and wealthy, she should simply go buy one to heal the wounds of the past.

And Emily will find that it wasn't about dolls at all, just as I found out it wasn't about having 64 crayons. It's about accepting what happened to you, being grateful for the skills and lessons you would not have learned otherwise, and sharing with others. Mostly, it's about forgiving yourself for ever letting Rachel, Lydia, and a box of crayons determine who you were and what you were worth.

About the Author

Dorcas Smucker lives in a century-old farmhouse in Oregon's Willamette Valley, where she and her husband, Paul, raised six children and ran the family's grass-seed business. For the past seventeen years, she has written a family-life column in the Eugene, Oregon, *Register-Guard* newspaper. She blogs at *Life in the Shoe* (www.dorcassmucker.blogspot.com). She enjoys reading, sewing, and traveling and spends a lot of time listening to people over cups of tea.